P9-CPZ-675

...ed in violence. Much of the resulting interview ...terial is quoted verbatim, and the reader acquires ...rofound "feel" for the atmosphere of violence.

...author approaches violence as a form of social ...duct. He assumes that a violent act is a charac- ...tic personal reaction which is invoked by cer- ...people consistently, and that such an act is ...or symptom that, if properly interpreted, can ...see the central motives and concerns of Violent ...He feels that violence must be examined in ...context where it occurs and he focuses on the ...in of interactions between aggressor and victim.

...fessor Toch focuses on the "violent incident" ...the key unit for study. He examines assaults on ...ice and hostile encounters between police of- ...rs and civilians. With emphasis on the Watts ..., collective violence is considered with a discus- ...n of etiology. From the available data, the author ...ates syndromes of psychological characteristics ...ociated with violence-prone people. From this, he ...ws implications for therapy, training, penology, ...social action as applied to the regeneration of ...ont Men, and he delineates areas for further ...earch.

...t emerges from this book is a portrait of the ...ent Man—a basically immature person who has ...ned to use force as a compensatory tool and ...can be assessed, understood, and, in time, re- ...erated. Violent Men is important reading for ...hologists, sociologists, criminologists, penol- ...ts, and those concerned with the problem of ...nce in America today.

ABOUT THE AUTHOR

Hans H. Toch received his Ph.D. from Princeton University and has since taught at Michigan State University and the State University of New York at Albany, where he is now Professor of Psychology in the School of Criminal Justice. He has been a visiting lecturer at Harvard University and was Project Co-Director of the Institute for the Study of Crime and Delinquency at Sacramento, Cali- fornia. He is the author of many articles for the professional literature as well as several books in- cluding Legal and Criminal Psychology (editor and contributor); The Social Psychology of Social Move- ments; and Social Perception: The Development of Inter-Personal Impressions (edited with H. C. Smith).

James Douglas Grant was Chief of the Research Division of the California State Department of Cor- rection. He is now a government consultant

VIOLENT MEN

VIOLENT MEN

AN INQUIRY INTO THE PSYCHOLOGY OF VIOLENCE

HANS TOCH
School of Criminal Justice
State University of New York at Albany

ALDINE PUBLISHING COMPANY
Chicago

Copyright © 1969 by Hans Toch

All rights reserved. No part of this publication may be reproduced
or transmitted in any form or by any means, electronic or mechanical,
including photocopy, recording, or any information storage and re-
trieval system, without permission in writing from the publisher.

First published 1969 by Aldine Publishing Company
529 South Wabash Avenue, Chicago, Illinois 60605

Library of Congress Catalog Card Number 69–17706

Designed by Chestnut House

Printed in the United States of America

Preface

This book marks the climax of a group effort, to which various people contributed in various ways. Mine is the reporting role. It is my task to summarize the thinking, to narrate the activity, and to discuss the results.

Times have changed since the inception of our project. When we started work, "violence" was a trade term. The word referred to difficulties faced by members of regenerative professions: police officers, teachers, and prison wardens. Theirs was the problem, and it was a circumscribed one, despite its tragic impact on individual victims.

Some of our objectives responded to the spirit of those simple days. We felt that correctional agencies could use help in dealing with troublesome clients. We hoped that we could supply diagnostic information that would ultimately lead to better management and more effective treatment. And we hoped to furnish one or two general highlights on violence—the type of insight lacking, and badly missed, among practitioners.

Our project was initiated by Douglas Grant, then Director of Research in California's Department of Corrections. His was a pioneering role, transcending that of correctional nose-counter and cost accountant. He shaped our study to include many methodological innovations. He made it possible for us to gather new types of information in new ways, and to answer questions that had not been asked before. Grant's contribution makes the results of our inquiry relevant at a time of infinitely expanded concern, when violence is no longer the stepchild of penologists and the bane of therapists.

In his Foreword, Grant spells out a few of the implications

of our research strategy. He has made explicit the link between our methods and their premises, and between these premises and their consequences. He has shown that research and social action can be combined, with profit to everyone concerned.

Ours was an unusual inquiry, not only in form but in content. Unlike previous students, we did not approach violence as personal disorder, nor did we relate it to hypothetical antecedents and correlates. We did not center on rage or aggression, nor on the ability to control it. We did not catalogue styles of destructiveness, and convert them into classifications. We did not link violence to conventional instruments or labels. Such approaches are currently useful, but our study was designed with the hope of furnishing new or expanded options.

Our approach to violence was in several ways more comprehensive than previous efforts. For one, we saw violence as a form of social conduct comparable to other forms of social conduct. We assumed that physical force is a characteristic personal reaction, and that it is invoked by some people with the same consistency that persuasion, or retreat, or self-insulation, or humor, or defiance, is employed by others. We felt that violence is linked to human personality in such a way that the study of one can teach us about the other. We viewed the exercise of violence as a clue, a symptom, a calling card, which, if properly read, could expose the central motives and concerns of violent men.

We also felt that the study of violence could tell us much about society. Violence, after all, is a *social* response. It occurs among people, and it responds to problems posed by individuals, groups, and institutions. It should follow that violence can be understood in terms of its social incentives. This fact is of practical importance. It suggests remedies in the shape of social reform, as well as of individual rehabilitation.

Violence, in our view, must not be circumscribed by legal or socioeconomic classifications. It must be viewed in the context of taverns and school rooms, in prison cells and living rooms; it encompasses felons and police officers, inmates and guards; it covers brawls and killings, riots and revolts. Our statements must be both general and specific. They must link the contexts in which violence occurs; they must also isolate their distinguishing properties.

One of the universals that is probably of most importance today is the link between police and ghetto violence. Colin McGlashan of the *London Observer* has recently written that

> The black kids and the white cops—their pride, their fear, their isolation, their need to prove themselves, above all their demand for respect—are strangely alike: victims both, prisoners of an escalating conflict they didn't make and can't control.

We have examined some aspects of this problem in the following pages. In doing so, we have attended not only to commonalities but also to differences. For we feel that in some important respects the warring parties in the ghetto live in different worlds. While they are "prisoners" of the same dilemma, they would have to be freed differently. The same holds for inmates and guards, discordant spouses, and for felonious assaulters and their victims.

But in essential respects the focus of this book is on common denominators in violence. Our research deals with Violent Men. It seeks them out in many contexts, and it examines them from several perspectives. It tries to understand them as individuals, and to sort them into groups. It tries to link them to the rest of humanity, while separating them for their violent acts. This is our most crucial aim. If the reader emerges from our discussion sensing the humanity of Violent Men, as well as their uniqueness, we will have accomplished our mission.

H. T.

Foreword

The study reported in this book has implications that go beyond its stated goal, the understanding of violence; it is an excellent demonstration of a general strategy that allows our culture to respond to the demands placed upon it for social change. In addition to these demands, we face tremendous pressure to work out ways for people to participate in the struggles and opportunities offered by our increasing rate of technological development.

There is growing evidence—and this book is a beautiful piece of the evidence—that our technology can be used to enhance individual participation rather than to obliterate it. Five implications of this study and its basic strategy warrant careful attention, not only by scholars but by social agency personnel, politicians, and the voting public. In brief, this study helps to demonstrate that:

—The scientific method can provide a participation strategy for social change;

—New frames new of reference and methodology are available for approaching many of the inaccessible problems of our time;

—Participation in systematic study is a powerful behavior modifier;

—Self-participation is a necessary component of effective diagnosis;

—There is a promising alternative to both the clinical treatment of sick personalities and the brainwashing attempts to change culture values.

Social Change, Science, and the Participation Principle

The need for a strategy of change is certainly not unique to our culture, nor to our time. But the need is rapidly becoming more pressing. For the first time in the history of man it is apparent that the world, the technology, and the values of a parent will not be the same as his child's world, technology, and values. It has never been true that values and the cultural organization were absolutes. It has, though, been an effective assumption that, because the rate of change was slow enough, a culture could survive, the "truths" of one generation being passed on to the next. Our current rate of accumulation of knowledge and technological development, however, demand a frame of reference that can cope with change, uncertainties, and ambiguities. The scientific method provides such a base. It requires decisions not in terms of absolutes but in competing probabilities based upon alternative theories that are continually seeking and being modified by new information.

Thus far this frame of reference has been available to a limited segment of our population, those few who make their living as scientists. Many who are involved with science operate more from a legalistic approach to knowledge than from the probability base of the scientific method. They collect "briefs" to document the "truth" rather than seek testable alternatives based upon defined positions.

But science, though rigorous, is not all that difficult. This study demonstrates that not only some scientists but some members of our confined and poorly educated subcultures can make valuable contributions using the scientific method. Instead of science being the province of an elite and highly educated segment of our culture, with most of the population receiving the discoveries of science as if by magic, it is becoming plausible that all of us can participate in our culture's development through systematic study—that is, through the use of the scientific method. All of us can share a frame of reference that optimizes our ability to cope with ambiguities, uncertainties, and a changing world.

It is not inconceivable that every individual, from the preschool child through the senior citizen, could be engaged in the total function of scholarship, spending part of his time discovering knowledge, part of his time accumulating knowledge, and part of his time applying knowledge. It has been demonstrated that young school children can participate in social research, and course curricula have actually been developed for the teaching of social science in the early elementary grades. Current experiments make it plausible that such opportunities and pursuits could be extended into the preschool years. With such an education base, the role taken by offenders and police in this study of their own violent behavior could be generalized to the staff and clients of other social agencies—teachers and students, health care workers and patients, rehabilitation counselors and the handicapped. Now our population is the passive recipient of science; it can move to participating actively in scientific approaches to our culture's problems and development.

The Frame of Reference and its Inherent Methodology

Along with the cultural advantages of our total population's participation in social science, we automatically obtain vitally needed extra investigating power through the use of subjects themselves as co-investigators. Hans Toch shows that using violent offenders as research colleagues we are able to get at the phenomenon of violence in a way that would not be possible were it studied only from the outside. It is as if the physicist could enlist electrons and protons as conversing colleagues in his study of atomic behavior.

The subject-researcher approach has immediate application to such hard-to-understand phenomena as the youth revolt—the hippies, the student activists, the black power advocates—the political stance and actions of senior citizens, the resistance of agency staff to change, and the communication between peoples across cultures.

BEHAVIOR MODIFICATION

Schwitzgebel in *Streetcorner Research* [1] suggested that delinquents modify their delinquent behavior as they become participants in the study of their own delinquency. Hans Toch gives us further support for the behavior-modifying component of a subject-researcher strategy. It appears that the principle of rehabilitating one offender through his participation in efforts to rehabilitate another is an important specific of a general participation principle. [2] If people who are the products of a social problem are given dignity, purpose, and responsibility in efforts to cope with that problem, they can shift to becoming responsible team members in society's game of attacking the problem.

In a parallel study to the one reported in this book, seventeen out of eighteen offenders with felony convictions were transformed from public liabilities to contributing tax-paying citizens through participation in a self-study training program. [3] Their jobs now include positions as project directors, staff members, and consultants in antipoverty programs, senior staff positions in federal agencies, and university appointments. A small but comparable control group shows the expected high recidivism and sporadic employment history. Studies such as these, and experience with self-help movements such as Alcoholics Anonymous and Synanon, make a strong case for creating meaningful participants as opposed to recipient roles for persons whose behavior we hope to change.

SUBJECT-PARTICIPATION IN DIAGNOSIS

Much was discovered about violent men in this study by having the men themselves work with their peers on the problems of

---

[1] Schwitzgebel, R. *Streetcorner Research: An Experimental Approach to Juvenile Delinquency* (Cambridge: Harvard University Press, 1954).

[2] Cressey, D. R. Changing criminals: the application of the theory of differential association. *American Journal of Sociology* (1955), *61*, 116-120.

[3] Grant, J. D., and Joan Grant. *New Careers Development Project: Final Report* (Mimeographed) (Sacramento: Institute for the Study of Crime and Delinquency, August 1967).

diagnosis and behavior classification. This participation role should not be taken lightly. The classification system outlined here would be meaningless if used now as a set of categories which one attempted to apply to another group of violence-prone men without the participation of the men themselves. The information for appropriate diagnosis cannot be obtained without a procedure which fosters self-study. Further, the hope for behavior modification is contingent upon the participation of the violence-prone. This participation needs to start with the formulation of the problem behavior as a first step in a strategy to modify the problem behavior.

Subject-participation in diagnosis is finding increasing use in personnel practices generally. There are two arguments for its wider application. First, persons concerned with civil liberties are arguing that we have neither the legal nor the moral right to obtain private information to classify people without their consent. Second, and more important, the crucial discriminating information cannot be obtained without the active participation of the person being classified. Subject-participation is essential if effective programs are to be built upon obtained classifications. If you want to change the behavior of a policeman, an offender, a teacher, or a student, enlist his participation in the systematic study of his own behavior, allowing him self-requested feedback on his behavior and its consequences.

AN ALTERNATIVE TO CLINICAL TREATMENT AND BRAINWASHING

Wolfgang and Ferracuti, as discussed by Toch, argue: "Before one set of values can replace another, before the subculture of violence can be substituted by the establishment of nonviolence, the former must be disrupted, dispersed, disorganized. The resocialization, relearning process best takes place when the old socialization and old learning are forgotten or denied their validity." [4] Unfortunately, this technique, at its most extreme, is brainwashing. We have heard accounts of its use in prison camps. We hear sociologists theorizing on the dynamics of culture

[4] Wolfgang, M., and F. Ferracuti. *The Subculture of Violence: Toward an Integrated Theory of Criminology* (London: Tavistock, 1967), p. 300.

value change in ways that come uncomfortably close to forcible conversion. The assumption is that a given culture value system must be eliminated before a new set of values can be integrated by an individual or a group. Psychoanalytic treatment and its derivatives have a similar base. They assume that one must work through the neurotic disturbances of the past in order to minimize their derivatives in adult life. It is only after the reduction of these sick systems that the person is free to develop a healthy new system.

The present study shows that people can transfer their knowledge and awareness of violence to the enterprise of researching. Toch has helped offenders move from the stage of the prison yard to the arena of the scholar. He has allowed and encouraged offenders to use old skills in becoming effective in new roles.

The behavior modification framework in which one moves from one role to another allows utilizing the strengths of the past rather than demanding a display of weakness in negating the past. Behavior is changed not because it is bad or wrong but because it is ineffective. New values are acquired not because they are inherently better values but because the new role demands them. One way to state the behavior modification principle implied by this study is that the aim is to create a climate in which the person uses his prior games as the field upon which he participates in your games rather than using your games as the field upon which he continues to play his own games. The latter is typified by our correctional approach to violent behavior, which, this study would suggest, accounts for the significant lack of behavior modification occurring in our current confinement programs.

Here, we have the outline of a model for behavior change which has implications far broader than violence and the modification of violent behavior. This model offers another frame of reference than clinical treatment or culture value change for approaching the problems of education, of mental health, of communication between generations and across cultures. It is much easier to formulate new games and to learn how to play them than to deny one's past as sickness or as error.

J. DOUGLAS GRANT

Contents

1
Violence in Perspective

Few categories of conduct evoke more concern than the subject of this book. Social critics equate violence with decay, statesmen deplore its prevalence, and unprecedented resources are marshaled to combat it. Everyone agrees that we are a violent people. The mass media are presumed suffused with cruelty, and they in turn claim that the masses have a propensity for gore. We are told that violence lurks within us, that we dote on it, wallow in it, and that we must exert enormous effort to suppress it.

During the crises that follow assassinations and riots, the speculation about violence reaches feverish proportions. Violence becomes the monomania of the press, the core substance of politics, the mainstay of the cocktail party, and the obsession of the public. Violence is promiscuously viewed, and it is seen everywhere. Historically, it becomes the theme of evolution; psychologically, the corollary of human nature; educationally, the enemy of learning; socially, the wrong road to change.

Violence, ironically, creates harmony among otherwise warring elements. Left and right agree that the status quo breeds violence; rival theorists assign key roles to violence and merely differ on the cause they attach to it. The rest of us are joined through psychological benefits derived from violence. We thrill to the threat of violent acts, and we tingle with self-assigned blame for them. Violence, we discover, has the attractiveness of the devil, or of a vicious enemy.

Unfortunately, the concern with violence is directed at a myth. It demands an ocean where there are islands; it constructs a monolith in place of diversity; it calls for formulas to cover complexity; and it presumes cure-alls where we have no diagnosis.

Real-life violence has not the glamour, nor the simplicity, nor the unambiguity of the violence of editorials and public speeches. Reality suffers at the hands of our concern.

To be sure, there has been a demand for "facts" about violence. Science has been enjoined to provide insights and to furnish tools to combat aggression. The response to this injunction has been unimpressive—one reason being that the scientist is not ready to press the panic button. Scientific data show, for instance, that the increase in violence is modest compared to the rates for other crime. Laboratory researches indicate that television cruelty may be imitated, but it is far from mind-molding. Diverse persons under scientific observation show no propensity toward bloody preoccupation or destructive conduct. And whereas publically observable conflict—such as politics and war —does exist, we know that violence in these arenas is not disproportionate in our day. Collective destructiveness, as in urban riots, is indisputable and obvious, but social scientists are reassured by the knowledge that the key causes of such violence are remediable through constructive reform.

A less flattering reason why science has failed to enlighten anyone lies in the restricted nature of its concerns. Science has a history of its own, with continuity and sequence, and with preoccupations that are inbred. Scientists deal primarily with other scientists. This insures quality control, but it frequently keeps their product off the market.

Such has been the case with psychology and violence. Violence has not been ignored by psychologists, but neither has it been addressed in ways that are obviously practical. Much attention has been paid in university laboratories to the relationship between "frustration" and "aggression." This is viewed as an invariant law, according to which the mind translates failure into revenge. It is solidly established that when any person is subjected to unexpected, unreasonable, and arbitrary attack, he tends to react with violence.[1]

[1] The basic relationship between frustration and aggression was postulated in John Dollard *et al., Frustration and Aggression* (New Haven: Yale University Press, 1939). Since the publication of this classic, the psychological literature has been filled with experimental reports and discussions relating to the role of frustration in instigating aggression.

This observation, and others like it, are arrived at in ways that appear remote and tangential to a nonpsychologist. In the typical laboratory study, college students are "frustrated" by being informed that they have failed a test, or by being chided for having bungled a trivial task; "aggression," typically, consists of unfavorable checks on a rating form, or sanguine interpretations of an inkblot.

Although experiments such as these are not concerned with violence on the street, they provide relevant information. They tell us, for instance, that the intensity of a person's violence varies with the extent to which his integrity has been compromised. And they tell us that the object of the attack differs with the situation. If a man finds it difficult to retaliate, he may seek substitute victims. This fact is of practical importance. It relates to such phenomena as scapegoating and discrimination. It helps in understanding compounded interactions. For instance, Offended Person A may damage Innocent Bystander B, who then retaliates, making A even more violent. Or B (if he cannot identify A, or if he cannot reach him) may attack Remote Bystander C, who then explodes. Such chains or cycles can convert private encounters into incidents of serious magnitude.

Other psychological scientists—of a more clinical bent—have viewed violence as the product of unfettered aggressive impulses. Violent people, they have argued, are persons more hostile than other people and less able to keep their hostility in check. In reviewing the histories of such people, clinicians have found their early years suffused with pain, childhoods marked by neglect and disappointment, and lives framed by sterile, loveless surroundings. In these contexts, clinicians assume that reservoirs of bitterness are fed and self-regard and self-control are inhibited. Individuals can thus be formed who are touchy and explosive, and who are unable to curb their own rage.[2]

---

[2] Psychiatric writings consist mainly of case studies of patients. Among relevant book-length discussions, see D. Abrahamson, *The Psychology of Crime* (New York: Columbia University Press, 1960) and M. Guttmacher, *The Mind of the Murderer* (New York: Farrar, Straus and Cudahy, 1960).

THE SHAPE OF VIOLENCE

Patterns of Violence

Clinical science assumes that all men are reservoirs of bloody destructiveness. It maintains that civilization equips most people with the means of discharging their hatreds judiciously and selectively—although there are instances in which this effort fails. Some persons are presumed to remain unchecked in their aggressiveness, so that they become promiscuously violent upon slight provocation.

This picture seems plausible, but even a cursory review of violent conduct suggests that violence is not blind and random. We know, for instance, that members of fighting gangs are frequently nonviolent when separated from their companions; that many extremely dangerous people seem to specialize in certain categories of victims—women or business competitors; that individuals recurrently violent in the street may be model prisoners when incarcerated (or vice versa), and that there is sometimes a relationship between being violent and being socially inept.

Violence takes place predominantly in certain circles, in certain settings, and on certain occasions.[3] If we want to witness a stabbing, we can best do so by locating a family squabble in a slum late on a Friday or Saturday evening. We might also frequent taverns in the same neighborhood, or the street corners inhabited by local teenage gangs. If violence is really blind and random, it is hard to understand why we should find so much of it in specific types of situations. Is the "localization" of violent acts a result of opportunity or climate? Does a man assault his wife rather than someone else simply because she happens to be available? Are bars simply fashionable locations for brawls?

It appears as if violence cannot be equated with angry explosiveness. There is shape and form to violence. Patterns of destructiveness show consistency, and they vary reliably from

    [3] R. C. Bensing and O. Schroder. *Homicide in an Urban Community* (Springfield, Ill.: Charles C Thomas, 1960) ; M. E. Wolfgang, *Patterns in Criminal Homicide* (Philadelphia: University of Pennsylvania Press, 1958) .

person to person. For each of us, violence seems tied to a restricted range of life situations. It seems to reflect purpose, and
it implies the presence of hidden (if perverted) meanings. What
needs does violence satisfy? How is it provoked? What values and
dispositions does it reflect? How do violent people function? We
must have the answers to such questions if we are to face the
problem of coping with violence.

The World of Violent Men

The remainder of this book reports on the results of an effort
to search the minds of Violent Men for whatever sense and purpose they contain. Violence is both the focus of inquiry and the
object of explanation. Our assumption is that if we want to explain why men are driven to acts of destruction, we must examine these acts, and we must understand the contexts in which
they occur. We must know how destructive acts are initiated
and developed, how they are conceived and perceived, and how
they fit into the lives of their perpetrators.

We must also assume that we cannot make sense of violent
acts by viewing them as outsiders. Ultimately, violence arises
because some person feels that he must resort to a physical act,
that a problem he faces calls for a destructive solution. The
problem a violent person perceives is rarely the situation as we
see it, but rather some dilemma he feels he finds himself in. In
order to understand a violent person's motives for violence,
we must thus step into his shoes, and we must reconstruct his
unique perspective, no matter how odd or strange it may be.
We must recreate the world of the Violent Man, with all its
fears and apprehensions, with its hopes and ambitions, with
its strains and stresses.

Another safe assumption is that violence is at least a two-man
game. Even where the victim does no more than appear at the
wrong time and place, his contribution is essential for the con-
summation of his destruction. And usually more than mere physical presence is involved. Common sense and law are attracted
to the image of passive victims mauled by spontaneously malev-

olent aggressors. In the world of violence, however, the situation is rarely that simple. As Von Hentig [4] has eloquently pointed out:

> the relationships between perpetrator and victim are much more intricate than the rough distinctions of criminal law. Here are two human beings. As soon as they draw near to one another, male or female, young or old, rich or poor, ugly or attractive, a wide range of interactions, repulsions as well as attractions, is set in motion. What the law does is to watch the one who acts and the one who is acted upon. By this external criterion a subject and object, a perpetrator and a victim are distinguished. In sociological and psychological quality the situation may be completely different. It may happen that the two distinct categories merge. There are cases in which they are reversed and in the long chain of causative forces the victim assumes the role of a determinant.

To understand violence it is necessary to focus on the chain of interactions between aggressor and victim, on the sequence that begins when two people encounter each other—and which ends when one harms, or even destroys, the other.

Violent acts, and violent interactions, do not make sense when viewed in isolation. The dilemmas people encounter are continuing, their personalities are constant, and their ways of relating to others reflect established habits and dispositions. Some violent conduct is no less lawful than other human conduct. If we examine different violent acts committed by the same person, we expect these acts to carry consistent meanings; we expect these acts to serve common needs; we expect them to result from pressures that operate persistently over time. We also expect that consistencies in a person's approach to others can produce situations in which violence always results—sometimes without the person being aware of the fact that he is the instigator of destructive (or self-destructive) games. And finally, some institutions in our society contain features that reliably encourage, provoke, or elicit violent conduct. These forces, also, contribute

[4] H. Von Hentig, *The Criminal and His Victim* (New York: Anchor Books, 1967), pp. 382–83.

to shape the patterns of violence, and we must isolate and describe them.

What are the data best studied if we wish to understand violence, and if we wish to prevent it? It seems of limited value to concentrate on accidentally or situationally produced violence, unless the circumstances involved are recurrent and modifiable. It also seems of limited value to concentrate on once-in-a-lifetime violent persons, unless the sequences that lead to their violence are uniform and predictable. It seems most productive to study those people who become recurrently involved in acts of violence. These violence-prone men can be expected best to reflect and personify the individual and social forces that produce violence. And these men constitute the bulk of our problem. For, statistically, few people in our society are violence-prone; the rest of us lead lives relatively free of major physical strife.[5] The problem of violence thus primarily revolves around the identity and conduct of Violent Men.

Toward a Typology of Violence

What follows are the results of a research project conducted in California under a federal grant.[6] This project combined two studies of violent acts, one of violence-prone interactions, and one of violent men. It explored situations fraught with violence, delved into institutions plagued with threats of violence, and involved—as subjects—some of the most dangerous offenders in the state.

The study was not sparked by racial disturbances, nor was it inspired by the senseless murder of public figures. It originated

[5] Wolfgang, ch. 9 (pp. 168 ff.) ; K. G. Bromage and H. V. Bell, "A Study of Juvenile 'Battery' Cases" *Alpha Kappa Deltan* (Spring, 1958) 18–24; R. A. Peterson, D. J. Pittman, and P. O'Neal: Stabilities in Deviance: A study of assaultive and non-assaultive offenders. *Journal of Criminal Law, Criminology and Police Science* (1962) , *53*: 44–48.

[6] This research was carried out under a grant from the National Institute of Mental Health (Project MH-08970) to the Institute for the Study of Crime and Delinquency, Sacramento, California. J. Douglas Grant was Director of this study; Hans Toch was Co-Director.

in an isolated meadow along an obscure dirt road, with the murder of a helplessly tied police officer by a pair of escaped felons. This incident, the second of its kind in a week, produced a memorandum from Governor Brown requesting a crash research program dealing with violence. Our project, which dates from this memorandum, was also shaped by subsequent demands. One of these originated in a concern with violence behind prison walls; the other was occasioned by an increase in assaults upon the police in two West Coast cities. These practical considerations dictated our areas of work and our areas of emphasis, and they did so because they coincided with our desire to study violence in settings in which it occurred frequently but took a restricted range of forms. We were thus able to concentrate on real-life circumstances without sacrificing the requirement for a systematic and restricted sample of test situations.

THE INVESTIGATION

Our research effort was both pure and applied. Through our investigation we hoped to discover facts (and to arrive at conclusions) that might facilitate the task of changing violent men. We were also concerned with understanding violence as a form of human conduct: we hoped to improve our knowledge of psychology (and more specifically of social psychology) through our study of violence. Finally, we hoped to explore new avenues of investigation; in this sense our study was partly intended as an exercise in methodology.

The Peer Interview

Probably the really unique feature of our study was the fact that our researchers also qualified as subjects: convicted offenders produced and administered our prison interview schedule; paroled inmates negotiated with the parolees in our sample; police professionals conducted our police study. As a result, every one of our respondents was questioned by someone whom he could reliably identify as a peer.

The uniqueness of this procedure becomes obvious when we review transcriptions of interviews. The following excerpt is typical. It involves the aftermath of a prison gambling incident:

Q: Was it the next day that you were going through the kitchen line and that he approached you and said he was coming down and wanted his stuff, and you better be there with it?

A: He said he was coming to get me, and I better be ready. The inference was—Was I going to be ready?

Q: So you went back to the kitchen and got a shank and then went to your pad. Now this dude who was doing the talking to you now, this is the one who you were playing coon can with? The next morning one of the dudes approached you?

A: The next morning. The same dude. When I came out of my cell in the wing this guy approached me. He lived in the wing.

Q: What is his message?

A: His message is just a play, and they were playing a pat hand. It wasn't anything different from the day before. I told him . . .

The questions being asked here derive from a prescribed system of inquiry, but the wording takes forms familiar to the respondent. Any listener would gain the impression that he is overhearing a snatch of conversation between two friends discussing a subject of mutual interest, using the most natural language possible. No constraints are introduced; the interviewee feels no need to translate or to explain; no information is lost; every nuance of the responses is understood and explored.

In some instances, this sort of communication becomes almost private; it explores events familiar only to those who have lived in the world of the yard or in the jungle of the streets. The interview refers to actions that can be reviewed only by those who have experienced the pressures that produce them. The next excerpt, relating to an incident in which a rumor has been spread, conveys the flavor of this kind of communication:

I: So you were just tripping something about you're knocking him. Do you know how this got back to the guy?

S: Yeah. A lot of guys knew him. He knew all the guys that I knew. It just happened that we knew one another. He was mad and he was bad, too . . . He whipped my ass. But I didn't mind that.

I: He said he could stand anything but to be called a trick, eh?

S: Yeah. Being burnt is part of the game. "You been telling all my friends that I'm a trick." He was a prize fighter, really. The guy was an ex-pro. He was a heavyweight. We started arguing and I thought I better end this now, with a minimum amount of damage. There were a few blows thrown and I told him I was sorry. And I really was sorry that I had said that.

I: Well, he sort of told you what his standards were, and you said, "let your conscience be your guide"?

S: Yeah. He knocked the shit out of me. I wasn't expecting it, really.

I: Was there any way you could have gotten out of it?

S: No. I think that the best thing happened. When I saw him come in, I knew I was going to have trouble. We were pretty good friends. He's good people. I was in the wrong in that situation.

Peer interviews contain evidence of their own reliability. Often they demonstrate the extent to which responses are understood by the interviewer, and bear witness to the degree to which understanding is acknowledged by the respondent. The feedback is instantaneous, and the subject can feel that there is no question of misinterpretation of his answer. The following conversation shows the interviewer clarifying (to himself and to the subject) some steps in a relatively complex sequence leading to an act of violence:

ı: You knew the assignment clerk, and so you went to him to get him to move them both in the same housing unit?

s: Right.

ı: Now where does this other dude come in at?

s: Well, he liked the broad and wanted her for a cell partner after she moved into the ward.

ı: So actually there is three people involved. The old man, the broad and this dude who walks into the action?

s: Right.

ı: Okay. So he said something to her and she said, "don't fuck with me. If you do, I'll get S"?

s: Right.

ı: So S came and talked to you, and you went to talk with the dude. He said, "this ain't none of your business. Get your stuff"?

s: Right.

ı: So you got your stuff, thinking all the time that this dude means business.

s: He did mean business.

Nonprofessional research workers have been used in studies other than our own.[7] In our case, use of peer interviewers has been intensive and systematic, because our objectives made such a procedure especially appropriate and necessary. We intended

[7] Joan Grant, "The Industry of Discovery: New Roles for the Nonprofessional"; ch. 6 in A. Pearl and F. Riessman (Eds.), New Careers for the Poor (New York: Free Press of Glencoe, 1965), pp. 92–124; R. Schwitzgebel, Streetcorner Research: An Experimental Approach to Juvenile Delinquency (Cambridge: Harvard University Press, 1954); L. N. Robins and N. W. Braroe, The lay interviewer in research. Journal of Nervous and Mental Disease (1964), 138:70–78.

to interview people who had been reliably identified as participants in violent acts. This participation is in many circles defined as undesirable; our subjects would be especially aware of this fact, since we would have to locate them through institutions in which they had been (or were being) subjected to sanction. Thus, unless we somehow succeeded in convincing respondents that our research would not intensify their difficulties, our chances of securing cooperation were obviously slim. Interviewers would almost have to be persons known to be least likely to cast a critical eye on the data being generated.

Second, we felt it important that our interviews explore the meaning of violence for the person who had engaged in it. This emphasis on the phenomenology of violence presupposes that the interviewee feel free to discuss his feelings, attitudes, and perceptions in the most natural manner possible, using the language most appropriate to the subject matter and recreating the frame of reference within which he operated at the time of the incidents. He would have to presuppose that his interlocutor could share his assumptions and could understand his vocabulary sufficiently to make communication possible. He would have to presuppose, further, that his interviewer's interest focused on the "relevant" aspects of the situation as he himself saw them.

The use of peer interviews made it possible to gain access to information we could not otherwise obtain. Another aspect of the use of nonprofessional research aides relates to a less tangible and more general advantage. Most social researchers sense some difficulty in the initial approach to subject populations of vastly different backgrounds from their own. Some react at this juncture with an elaborate process of ingratiation or "gaining of rapport," in which the researcher, and the research, are presented in the (presumably) best light. This posturing is often transparently insincere and always wasteful. Worse, it usually achieves merely a wary and delicate stalemate, during which only a hit-and-run raid for data is possible before the subjects discover what has happened to them.

During rare moments of honesty, we may admit that even when we induce subjects to cooperate, our dealings with them are seldom the exciting adventure we tell our students about.

And the main problem here may not be one of communication and social distance at all—it may have nothing to do with habits of dress or the use of colloquial language. It may be that our subjects understand us only too well, knowing that what we ask is unreasonable and unfair. After all, we are supplicants and, at worst, invaders demanding booty of captive audiences. In return for vague promises or a modest remuneration we expect a person to bare his soul or to make controversial and potentially incriminating statements. The "communication" is one way: the researcher maintains his position as a recipient of nonreciprocated information.

We also make our informant aware that we are interested in him not as a man but as a "subject"—a representative of a type, or a case, or an item in a sample. He knows this because he knows who he is and who we are. He knows that he is being approached because he is the inhabitant of a ghetto or a prison, because he is a "consumer," or because he acts as an informer. And he knows that his aims are being subordinated to our own. How can he share our objectives, after all, if he cannot even see the results of the efforts in which he has participated?

The use of peer interviewers circumvents ethical problems in social science research, because it confronts research subjects with research workers who approach them as equals, and who can brief them in terms that make sense to them. For these confrontations to occur honestly, the nonprofessional must feel himself a partner of the enterprise. He can do this if he has been involved in the conceptualization and design of the research.

It is useful to have available the expertise of nonprofessionals at the design stage of a study. It is also helpful to gain the benefit of their perspective in the analysis of data. A well-chosen lay researcher can often be in a position to correct naive inferences by less experienced professionals. For example, one of our own research partners, Inmate Hallinan of San Quentin, once chided me (in writing) for drawing a hasty and incorrect conclusion from an interview we had conducted. The interviewee was an Indian leader, and I had made much of the presumed impact of his ethnic background. Luckily, my colleague Hallinan was there to point out that Indian heritage was unimportant, and that our man was impelled by the "need to establish a personal reputation as a prison tough guy." Hallinan's documentation of this interpretation follows:

> The first incident that the subject becomes involved in is the rat-packing of an Indian child molester in order to ostracise and punish the molester, and also to solidify his position among the low-riders. So, rather than being a leader of these Indians, he is using his Indian blood to further his own ends. He wants to be a tough con, someone to be feared and respected. "The new guys that come in, no one knows about them." "Once you get a reputation you have to protect it." The above statements, and others similar in nature, were made by the subject during the course of the interview . . .
>
> How does the subject go about building a reputation? As he says, fighting for home boys, and interceding for other Indians? No. Of the ten incidents—actually nine, because No. 1 and No. 9 are the same—in No. 6 no violence occurred; No. 2 involved helping a friend, although the details were vague; No. 7 was a fight of his own making; in No. 9 he was attacked; and No. 10 was the rat-packing incident. The remaining four involved custody. He was proudest of No. 8. In regards to this incident the following dialogue occurred:

Q: Do you think this incident helped your reputation?

A: It sure as hell did. I knocked down the Captain.

Q: How did you feel just before you knocked him down?

A: Like a big man.

Q: During?

A: I sure am doing it right this time . . .

> The word circulates that he has fought with the "bulls," implying that he will jump on a convict with little provocation. The facts are never pursued, but accepted prima facie, because those who pass on these rumors and exaggerations are the very ones who are most impressed by them. The rumor re-

turns and the subject begins to believe his own yard reputation . . .

Our subject has completed the building of his reputation,
petty though it is, and now he and his low-rider friends can
observe and honor it. Not that the cons on the yard do, but
the subject feels that they do, and this is all that really matters. If anything he is tolerated, not respected and feared as
he would like.

It is obvious that Inmate Hallinan is not only furnishing me
with a lesson in perspective, but is also demonstrating that he
can compete with professionals in his methodological acumen
and his ability vividly to summarize and communicate research
conclusions. And although this analysis is unusually literate,
because Inmate Hallinan invested lots of prison time in creative
writing courses, much can be learned even from our most un-
lettered collaborators.

Sources of Data

Our information was obtained with the cooperation of officials
and agencies in the California Department of Corrections and
in two metropolitan police departments.

Samples of violent incidents were garnered from the central
files of the Department of Corrections and from more detailed
folders maintained in institutions and in county parole offices.
They were also abstracted from arrest reports in the record
units of the San Francisco and Oakland Police Departments. Our
study of police records was confined to assaults on police officers,
and our investigation of institutionalized offenders emphasized
incidents of violence within prison walls.

The following groups of persons were individually interviewed: (a) 32 officers on the force of the Oakland Police Department who had suffered assaults—in most cases, on several
occasions; (b) 19 men who had assaulted police officers—in
most instances, on several occasions (in all but one case, the as-

saulted officers were among those we interviewed); (c) 44 prison inmates (15 in the California Medical Facility of Vacaville, and 29 residents at San Quentin); (d) 33 parolees with violent records (12 from Sacramento County, and 21 living in Oakland).[8]

The policemen we interviewed were selected on the basis of their experience with assaults. Half of them (14) had been attacked by persons in our assaulter sample, but almost to a man these officers had encountered difficulties with other civilians; the remainder of the officers were chosen because they had been attacked on at least three recent occasions and had accumulated the most substantial records of such experiences in the memory of the department's Bureau of Internal Affairs.

Our police assaulter study concentrated on men with previous histories of assault. Although such a history was not a criterion for the selection of these men, it developed that most of them had assaulted more than one officer.

Our parolees were persons classified as chronic serious assaulters in a scale developed by the Research Division of the California Department of Corrections.[9] The sample is somewhat self-selected, in that the interviewees had to be located (which in some instances proved difficult) and had to volunteer for the

[8] Our police research was made possible through the cooperation of officials in the Oakland and San Francisco police departments. We are indebted; in Oakland, to Chief Gain, Chief Preston, Chief Toothman, Captains Guidici and Connelli of the Record Division, and Sergeant Lucas of the Bureau of Internal Affairs. We are grateful to Chief Cahill of the San Francisco Police Department for permitting access to records. Our inmate studies were made possible through assistance from Dr. Keating, former superintendent of the California Medical Facility, and Warden Wilson of San Quentin Prison. Our survey of parolees could not have been conducted without the help of various staff members of the Oakland and Sacramento County parole offices. The Department of Corrections of California issued directives providing cooperation and facilities at every level. Our study of institutional violence was initiated in consultation with a California Task Force created June 7, 1965. For the research recommendations of this group, See P. C. Mueller, H. Toch, and M. Molof: *Report to the Task Force to Study Violence in Prison* (Sacramento: California Department of Corrections, Research Division, Aug. 1965), mimeographed.

[9] Carol Spencer: *A Typology of Violent Offenders* (Sacramento: California Department of Corrections, Research Division: Research Report No. 23, Sept. 1966.

interview. In each case, the man was approached with the cooperation of his parole agent and was compensated for the time he invested.

We chose the bulk of our inmate sample on the basis of the fact that the men (a) had been aggressors in some incident of prison violence within one calendar year of our study, and (b) had several violent encounters on their record. Several other inmates were added to this original sample because they were known to our inmate researchers as having a reputation for violence. Our inmate interviewees were also compensated, on the basis of pay scales authorized in the institution.[10]

The institutions we selected for our inmate survey were those most accessible to us. In the case of the California Medical Facility, we already had access to a group of prisoners being trained in research methodology; we created another such group (whose training was confined to the objectives of the study) at San Quentin Prison.[11] In both places, inmate interviewers operated in collaboration with professional personnel.

Continuity in staff from the prison to the parolee sample was assured because several of our interviewers were placed on parole during our study. In conjunction with the professional research staff, they conducted the parolee and police assaulter interviews.[12]

[10] It must be emphasized that although our interviewers were drawn from systematically selected pools, the samples themselves are not random. Police were interviewed as their shifts made them available; parolees and police assaulters had to make themselves available. Only prison samples are exhaustive, and they are confined to two institutions. Since each contains a special kind of population, this sample is even more biased than the others. Any possible unrepresentativeness of the sample is not critical, however, since the study aims at a qualitative typological analysis, rather than at extrapolations to special populations.

[11] Our researchers in San Quentin worked under the guidance of Magoroh Maruyama. The group was composed of inmates R. Wilkerson, C. Smith, Fontes, Nacho, and Chaco. Our work at the California Medical Facility was conducted under the auspices of the New Careers Development Project, directed by J. Douglas Grant. The principal participants in our research were inmates Rodriguez, Lester, and C. Jackson.

[12] Rodriguez participated in our work as an inmate and parolee. Other parolees working with our project were J. Preston, K. Jackson, and W. Hunnicutt.

Our study of assaults on police officers was initiated at the invitation of the Oakland Police Department. We were happy to accept the invitation, because it made available to us a pool of violent incidents generated in a relatively homogeneous institutional context.

We secured authorization to analyze an equivalent incident sample in the San Francisco Police Department, to test the generalizability of our findings and to secure a large enough pool of incidents for more detailed analysis.

Our interviews with police officers took place in the Oakland Police Department. They were conducted by a professor of police administration and a graduate assistant, who both had been active members of metropolitan police departments and had intensive experience with research on police–community relations.[13]

Our interviews varied in length from somewhat less than an hour to several days. They were tape-recorded in their entirety. The same interview schedule was used for all interviews, although questions were added to secure supplementary information, as dictated by the characteristics of the sample and the context of the interview. In all instances, the same information about each incident was secured. In the case of inmate and parolee interviews, the analysis procedure was uniform in all essential respects.

The Interview Schedule

Our interviews were designed to provide a full picture of the violent encounters of our respondents. Each person was requested to list "incidents or fights" he had been involved in over the years. In relation to each such event, we inquired into the sequence of acts leading up to it, the contribution of various participants, and the feelings and attitudes of protagonists. We also tried to place each such encounter in the broader context of the person's relationship to others. All our questions were

---

[13] The interviews were for the most part conducted by Prof. Raymond Galvin of the School of Police Administration of Michigan State University, assisted by Robert Wasserman.

posed in as systematic a fashion as possible, without sacrificing the natural flow of informal communication.

The content of our interview was structured, with a standard series of queries directed at each incident mentioned by the respondent. Question-wording was left flexible, however, and interviewers were permitted to vary question order, as long as they maintained the step-by-step exploration of violence-prone sequences.

The introduction to the interview stressed its general information-gathering function. The interviewees were told that the purpose of our research was "to get some help with the problem of preventing fights or assaults." They were requested to provide "your side of the story of some of the fights you have experienced." Subjects in the police study were apprised of our concern with violence between police officers and civilians. All respondents were assured of complete anonymity, and were told that they could monitor the interview tape.

Each interview consisted of discrete examinations of individual incidents. Every respondent was asked to describe violent situations in his own words, including as much detail as he could. He was then taken through each incident again step by step. He was asked about his contact with the other party and about the beginning of the chain of events culminating in violence. He was asked to relate (or confirm) each successive step in the interaction. The interviewee was also called upon to describe his feelings before, during, and after each violent incident. Offhand, it might seem offensive to question experienced police officers or long-term convicts about "feelings." Surprisingly, however, we experienced no difficulty with this inquiry, which more often than not produced rich introspections and elaborate rationalizations of purpose. The following relatively short response (relating to a gang fight) is typical of the material we obtained:

i: How about during the incident: can you remember how you felt while you were fighting?

s: Yeah. Well, from the beginning of the fight, I felt low, got butterflies in my stomach, you know. But then you always feel that way, more or less, when you getting ready to fight. But after the first blow, you don't feel anything. Because you know either you going to win or you going to lose, and you're trying your best to win.

I: How about afterwards?

s: Afterwards? Well, I just felt, well, "I sure am small to whip that great big dude." This made me feel confidence in myself.

I: Kinda good?

s: Yeah. It makes you feel kinda good to know that you won. But actually it was senseless really. You know this.

I: Looking back on it now, how do you feel about it?

s: Well, looking back on it now, I feel that it was just one of those incidents while I was growing up. I feel that now maybe more or less if the situation would occur again I probably would, I'm not going to say that I would, walk away from it; it depends on how much he pushes, how much was said, and went on. But looking back on it, I don't think I would go through those chances again.

Another set of questions touched on the contribution of persons other than the main contenders. We asked about outside efforts, if any, to encourage violence, or to try to prevent it. We inquired into the impact of spectators and friends, and into the role of community pressures. The following excerpt (relating to the same gang fight) exemplifies these questions and the sort of answers they obtained:

I: Did anybody else beside yourself encourage the fight?

s: Yes. This friend of mine, he told me, he say, "You know we with you, baby. Go ahead and dust him."

I: The guy that you jumped on, did he sort of challenge you? Did he encourage the fight too?

s: Yeah. Well, actually he encouraged it due to the fact that I hadn't said anything to him outside the party. So when he came out, he laughed, you know, he laughed. This righteously did make me angry cause he's more or less trying to floor show for the young ladies he's with. That is the whole thing.

i: During the fight, did anybody try to prevent it from going on?

s: No. Back towards this period of time, everybody was struggling for a reputation, recognition. You get a reputation, you go where you want, nobody messes with you, you get your understanding. This was more or less during that period of time; this was what it was for.

i: You think things would have been different if just you and him would have been by yourselves somewhere? Or do you think the fight would have come down anyway?

s: More or less. I think that if the situation had been different, it probably never would have transpired, due to the fact that I wouldn't have said anything to him, he wouldn't have said anything to me. But like I said, due to the fact that there were a lot of people around; this young man, his brother was supposed to have been semi-bad anyway and he felt that he had power. He was more or less going to whip me cause I was smaller than he was.

In relation to the violence itself, we inquired into the extent of the damage our subject had intended. We asked whether the harm corresponded to the intent, and we explored changes in the respondent's destructive objectives. In the case of fatal incidents, we asked whether the victim's death had been desired. In the following example, the answer is affirmative:

i: Now, when you were going down to get it on, did you have the intention of dusting him? Or get him off your back, or what?

s: Yeah, I was going to dust him, there's no doubt about that. Yeah, there was no doubt in my mind about dusting the dude.

If he hadn't have come back there, then I would have assumed that the night before was just a play on his part to see how far he could push me; maybe he would not even have stabbed me. But when they pulled his bar, why, I was down at the end in a position that I could see along the tier, and instead of him coming on down the front stairs, and going like he should have with everybody else, he come out of his cell, kind of looked around a little bit, and walked toward the back stairs. Well, the moment he started heading toward the back stairs, I think in that moment, that was the time that I said, you know, "one of us has got to get dusted, man, and it's better him than me. So, let's not talk around or something when he comes down, let's get him. Let him say whatever he wants to say, and the first time he blinks his eyes for just a second, he's mine." On my part, the talking was done as soon as he started down the back stairs. I assumed then that he's serious. He's got his stuff, I've told him where I am, and he's coming directly to me. So as far as I was concerned it was the final thing, the moment he walked out the door and started toward the back stairs.

Finally, each of our interviewees was asked to assume the role of his opponent and to review the incident from the other's point of view. Empathy was not notable in the responses to this question. Most frequently, our respondents regretted that the victims had not made a more timely inventory of their ways. This type of reply was not invariant, however. Some interviewees went to great pains to reconstruct their opponents' motives, as in the following example:

i: What was your reaction in the clothing room, when the guy said "move those shirts to another stack"?

s: I didn't leave him actually any out. From my point of view, the only out he had was to walk away and leave the shirts the way they were. I didn't give him any out. I believe that if I had given him an out—any kind of an out—that he may have taken it. I was just blunt and told him that this was what was going to happen. And it was a challenge more or less, you know.

I: But you would have moved the shirts had you been in his position?

S: I believe I would.

I: How about in the library?

S: Okay, as a matter of fact, I heard that some guy had just ripped off a book of his, a reference book, and had told him to go fuck himself. He was hot about that. He told me this later when I talked to him just before we went into the Lieutenant's office. He told me this. Some kind of a special book. He was the reference library clerk. You know where the reference section is? Well, that was his section. He was responsible for it. And someone had just taken a book and told him to fuck himself. He wasn't in a very good frame of mind when I walked in. And I was the next one in. I threatened his authority by denying this paper that he had sent me. I told him this isn't valid. In other words, "you are lying." He wouldn't even take the time to check it out. He didn't want to hear this. "Its not invalid, its perfectly legal, and I did it and there is no question about it." This is the feeling that I got from him, you know. "There's no time for you, I sent you the thing. Now where is the material, and don't give me a lot of bullshit about it being in the filing cabinet because I don't have time." So one thing led to another. I made the mistake of walking behind the partition.

I: When you walked back there, looking at his point of view, do you think that you posed a threat?

S: Yes, I did. Probably I didn't have such a nice look on my face. I was very exasperated—if you will—put out.

At the conclusion of the regular interview, we subjected our respondents to several fairly general questions. We talked with them discursively about violence, and we delved briefly into their personal history. We also tried to involve them in an examination of their own data. We asked each whether he could discern any patterns or similarities in the incidents he had related to us. Some respondents rewarded us with insightful comments, but most of them produced material varying considerably in quality. We thus came to view our procedure of subject self-analysis as promising but as too undeveloped at this stage to permit systematic use of responses.

Analysis of the Interview Data

As previously indicated, the inmate and parolee interviews were subjected to a uniform analytic procedure. As a first step in this procedure, each incident was reduced directly from the tape recording to a diagrammatic form, in which the steps were graphically represented.[14] Relevant feelings and other observations pertaining to each incident were recorded with a checklist. These tasks were undertaken either by the interviewer or by a nonprofessional researcher belonging to his team.

The next step consisted of preparing a summary of the interpersonal pattern of the interviewee's violent involvements. In each case, this analysis was based on all the incidents obtained in the interview. This summary was prepared by a group comprising both professional and nonprofessional researchers. The procedure followed by these groups can be outlined as follows:

1. Read aloud the diagrammed sequence for each incident.
2. Select out (through discussion) any formal similarities in the genesis of the incidents.
3. Select out (through discussion) any similarities in the approach of the interviewee to other participants in the incident.
4. Select out (through discussion) any possible inferences about the interviewee's social orientation, his approach to others, his special or general aims, as they contributed to specific incidents.

[14] We are indebted to Dr. Maruyama for the suggestion of this procedure, and for training personnel in its use.

5. Check the resulting hypotheses against every incident in the interview to assess their applicability.

6. Review and revise as necessary.

The results of these group discussions were then dictated. (The subsequent analysis of the "study group" summaries will be discussed in a later chapter.)

To clarify our procedure, it may help to reproduce two segments from one of our interviews, and to trace their contribution to the analysis produced by the "study group." In this particular illustration, the cards are "stacked" by virtue of the fact that the incidents involved are almost replications of each other. In Chapter 5, which will explore the logic of "patterning" more intensively, several more complex illustrations will be developed.

The Case of "Jack the Lady Killer"

Since Jack had recently served a long prison sentence for the murder of a close female friend, the discussion, in the initial stages of his interview, easily turned to this incident. In the free narrative portion, Jack related the circumstances of his crime as follows:

I: Tell us about the incident in which you finally killed her.

s: Well . . . She'd go to work every day and she'd come in at six or seven or eight o'clock at night, and never would bring no pay. So I told her, I ain't going to leave her anything. So we had a big argument. And I told her, I say, "Well, I'm leaving tomorrow. And I tried to do what was right, but I can see you don't want to accept." So we went and got—I went to the store and got two cans of beer. And set it down on the coffee table and she and I started drinking. So, I wasn't feeling bad when I came back. And I got cleaned up and went to bed. In the meantime, she was nagging—you know how a woman keep nagging and nagging—And I asked her, I said, "What's wrong with you, girl?" I said, "I'm telling you, I'm leaving tomorrow." And she said, "Yeah, tonight is our last night." I said, "Last night of what? What you talking about?" And so, she said, "Well, you'll find out."

So I didn't pay her no mind, you know. And I'm sitting here sipping on a beer. And I started necking with her, and she had a butcher knife on the table. And I'm wrestling, trying to get the butcher knife away from her. And I takes the knife away from her. In the meantime, when I take the knife away from her, I throw it in the kitchen. She jumps up and she runs to the coffee table—we had a coffee table sitting on the end beside the bed. And I reached over there, and she had a little old penknife. I had one, and I gave her one about the same size. Oh, a real little small penknife. And I took the knife, I hit her right here. Hit her one time in the jugular vein or neck. After I'd hit her jugular vein, she kept coming after me with that other knife and I stuck her a few times in the stomach, you know.

There followed an exploration of the interviewee's quasi-marital relations with the victim, after which the interview reverted to details of the final encounter:

i: I wonder if we could just go back to the rundown of that night? How were you feeling that day?

s: I wasn't drunk or nothing . . .

i: Was everything going along pretty good between you and her at the time?

s: Yeah.

i: And she came home that night. And what started the argument?

s: Money. The landlord come in behind her when she came in, about seven-thirty or eight o'clock. The landlord come in behind her, and I had cooked her a good dinner and everything, and she walked in and kissed me on the cheek and tole me, she said, "Honey, I sure do thank you for cooking

for me." She said, "Well, the landlord's here," and I said,
"Well, my hands is dirty." Well, I had a apron on, you know.
And I said, "Reach in my pocket and give him some money."
And she said, "That's all right, I can give him some of mine."
And the thing actually started over money. Because she had
told me, well, he give her a receipt. And she had been working six days a week, you know, and if a person work six days
a week, you know, and if a person don't come home with no
money, something wrong.

i: I don't understand that part. You say that she gave him the
money and he gave her a receipt? Did she pay him some
more money?

s: Yeah. She gave him ten dollars more. But she didn't have no
money after the ten. She didn't have but five dollars and that
was over a three or four week period. Well, she and I started
arguing, and we ate and then I left and went to the store and
bought me a half a pint and two cans of beer. And I came
back to the house and she and I sat up and talked and talked,
and I takes me a shower and I said, "I'm going to bed." But
I had no idea that she was going to have a butcher knife
under her pillow.

i: You said earlier that you said, "I'm leaving in the morning,"
and she said, "This is your last night"?

s: Yeah, she mentioned that. I was laying there and said, "What?"
And she said, "Well, you don't know." I had no idea that she
had planned to hurt me or something. She had something and
I didn't have nothing; I didn't even carry no knife, cause a
penknife, it ain't even of no worth to you.

i: Well, how did you feel when you were going to bed? You
were going to bed with her?

s: Yeah, see, we were together at the time.

i: And that was the last night?

s: Yeah, that's right.

i: How were you feeling at the time?

s: Well, I was disgusted. That's how I was feeling. I was depressed and disgusted. But I'd said over and over that I have tried everything in the world I can think of, and I couldn't make a go of it. So I decided I wanted to give it up.

i: She attack you with a butcher knife?

s: Yeah.

i: How did you feel then?

s: Well, I was scared actually, I was more scared than anything else.

i: Did you get angry?

s: Yeah, I got pretty mad.

i: Did you fight back?

s: No. The only fighting back I did was with my hand to protect myself from that knife. And she reached on the table and got that penknife.

i: Did she cut you?

s: No. I didn't get cut.

i: Was the penknife open?

s: No. Wait a minute, they said it was. I really don't know.

i: Things were happening pretty fast right then, huh?

s: Yeah. Things were pretty hot.

i: Then what happened?

s: Well, I got her in the jugular vein . . .

The interviewee was able to relate six other incidents of involvement in violence. In Incident 6, he returned to his problems with women. The free narrative of this unhappy situation runs as follows:

Let me see, that must have been in 1950—oh, well, I forgot what year. Anyway, I come home one evening from work, and her boy friend was in my bed . . .

I started drinking some whiskey, I never will forget it. She hadn't cooked. And I told her, I said, "Girl," I said, "I finally caught you at last! I'm asking you, do you believe that you can fool around and me not know about it?" I said, "Now, what you got to say for yourself?" So she said, "I don't have nothing to say." "I gave you money so you could cook." She said, "I ain't got no money." So I said, "Okay."

So I went down the street and bought myself a pint of whiskey and came back, and I told the landlady, I said, "I'm moving in the morning." And she said, "Well, you going to pay me?" And I said, "I'm going to pay you nothing," I said, "My rent's paid up till tomorrow noon. I'll be out of here by noon."

And about ten o'clock at night, I took my clothes off and went to bed. And she got up and started walking the floor. I said, "Now, you got to go to bed, girl, cause I'm moving in the morning." And she just kept walking the floor and started cussing, and called me a lot of bad names and things, and I told her, I said, "You going to go to sleep, or I'm going to get up and just beat your butt," you know, just like that. She kept cussing me, and I said, "Well, okay, you just keep walking the floor."

So, I don't know what got into her, but I was mad, and the more she cussed the madder I would get, you know. And I jumped up and went to the dresser, I don't know why. I got there so quick, and I picked up a mirror. When I picked up a mirror she saw the flash from the light of the mirror and, you know, I didn't even get the chance to touch her with it and she jumped out of the upstairs window and hurt herself. And the landlady called the police. And the police got there and after I told them what happened and they said, "Well, that happened before to others," they said. "If we let you go what would you do?" I said, "Let me get away, man." I said, "Can I come back tomorrow and get my clothes?" and he said, "Okay."

i: And that was the end of it?

s: Yeah, but that wasn't the end of it. He let me go. And we got out of the house, and he said, "Well, do you want to go?" And I said, "Yeah, but let me get my coat." And when I was reaching up in my clothes closet to get my coat she told him that I had a pistol. And when I reaches up there to get the pistol, I mean get my coat, he grabbed me.

The detailed exploration of the incident follows:

I: How were you feeling that day in general?

S: Well, I just got in from work. You know how it is coming home from work. And I was happy, and it was payday, and I'd already planned to take her out that night. In other words, I was in high spirits till I got home.

I: Then how were you feeling?

S: Terrible. I started to get angry and everything. When I walked in there and seen them, it's no good feeling for no man to walk in and see his old lady in the rack with someone else.

I: Oh, you saw them actually?

S: Yeah. They was in the room; in my room, in my bed.

I: Did she say anything then?

S: Well, I tried to get in there, but they wouldn't open the door.

I: How long had you known this girl?

S: Oh, let's see, must have been about two years.

I: Had you been living with her that long?

S: No, I started living with her six months.

I: Had you had any other hassles prior to that?

S: No.

I: So you were feeling pretty good that day, and then after you got home you started feeling terrible, angry at what was going on?

S: I was getting angrier and angrier. The more she would talk, the angrier I would get.

I: Just anger, is that all you felt?

s: Yeah.

i: How did you feel afterwards?

s: Well, after that happened, I said, "Well, it's hard to put your faith and hope in a person when they do you like that." And then I stopped thinking, what with people having things happening to them all the time . . .

i: You just felt philosophical about it?

s: Yeah.

The diagrammatic summary for the first incident is fairly long, because the sequence involves a relatively large number of steps. Incident 6, however, is a sequentially modest one, and we have reproduced the entire diagram in Figure 1. This diagram serves to illustrate the type of data available to our "study group." The group also had access to the checklist, which in this particular incident notes, among other things, that the interviewee felt angry throughout the entire sequence:

(1) X comes home, can't get into house because it is locked.

(2) Y has company Z (boyfriend). A (landlady) lets Z out back door. A then comes and lets X in the front door.

(3) X comes in, sees house in mess, also no food, says he is leaving tomorrow. Goes out and buys a pint of whiskey, comes back, drinks and goes to bed.

(4) Y is walking up and down the floor swearing at him (X).

(5) X tells Y to shut up

(6) Y continues to swear at X

(7) X decides to get even, gets up and grabs mirror, the mirror flashes on the ceiling

(8) Y sees light against ceiling and jumps out the window thinking the mirror is a knife or something. Y calls the police. The police arrive and Y tells the police X is reaching for a gun. Police grab X and wrestle.

(9) X wrestles and knocks policeman on bed.

FIGURE 1.1 DIAGRAM OF INCIDENT 6

In assessing the text of the "study group" summary, which follows below, we must recall that the group had seven summarized incidents available to it. The group's task was not easy, because the other five incidents were not simply replications of the two encounters we have reviewed. The contribution of our two involvements to the postulated pattern, however, does emerge in the group's report:

OK-4 is a remarkable gentleman in several ways. For one, we have in him a situation in which there is almost a complete repetition of incidents, one in which even in minor details we have the same action occurring twice in the same way. For instance, we have a set of two situations which start with an announcement one evening to the effect "look woman, I'm going to leave you." Then there follows a feeling of annoyance because the woman to whom this announcement is made becomes angry and nags, disturbing our man's drinking and sleeping. Finally, there is a very violent act which is viewed as self-defense.

We have two traffic situations in which our man thinks of himself as unprovokedly assaulted and where he reacts by pulling a large weapon and assaulting his apparent attacker. And in a few other incidents we find that he mobilizes a considerable amount of opposition. If this opposition is impressive enough he is not above whining, explaining, and trying to organize some kind of undignified retreat. Now, what seems to unify the entire set of incidents is that this man has a habit of placing other people into the most awkward situations without appearing to realize what he's doing—without anticipating the obvious reactions to his tactless opening moves. He isn't aware, for instance, that when you cohabit with a woman you just can't come in one evening and simply announce your imminent departure, and then expect to spend a congenial evening with her. Now, when the other person reacts—the person who is going to be abandoned or who has just been insulted—then we have a second stage in which our friend sees himself as attacked out of the clear blue sky. He can then be quite brutal while viewing all of it blandly as an act of self-defense.

Afterwards, we have an indication, even in this incident, of his real helplessness, as when he proceeds to give himself up to the police. So he has this pattern of provoking people in a rather selfish way, not seeing the consequences. There is a complete blindness to the other person's point of view. Then, if possible, fear and whining if aggression is not possible. And a kind of general demonstration of his weakness and his lack of ability to get along in the situations that he himself engineers.

The summary above may help to illustrate the role of the "study group" in our research. It should show that the group is a "pattern analysis" tool, in the sense that it functions to isolate common denominators in samples. It does so by focusing logic, social science analysis, and practical experience on a group of incidents in an effort to characterize the violent person's contribution to them as far as this may be possible without going beyond the information he has provided. The analytic process involved here is frequently intricate, since our incidents are often superficially heterogeneous and the inferences far from obvious at first reading. Despite this sophistication, however, the "study group" merely finds commonalities. It provides a bridge to the task of fitting patterns of conduct into more general categories, or assigning to them theoretical significance.

The final step in our self-assigned task consisted of evolving a typology of violence-proneness of precisely this kind. The object here was not simply that of grouping violent men in terms of central themes governing their conduct, but of assessing the psychological import of these themes and of estimating their significance for programs of rehabilitation and prevention.

2
The Violent Incident
as a Unit of Study

The psychological study of violence can include situations in which physical objects are the targets of violence. It makes sense, for instance, to examine motives for vandalism or reasons for the demolition of buildings in an urban renewal project. But our interest in violence is more narrowly focused. Our concern is with interpersonal violence. We assume that society is more damaged when one person injures another than when property is destroyed. What we wish to explain is the complex of motives which may lead a person to commit an act resulting in physical harm to a fellow human being.

The act of violence itself cannot serve as our unit of study, because its motives are never self-explanatory. We learn very little when we hear that a woman has been found strangled in her bed or that an inmate lies in the prison yard with a knife in his back. The least information we must have to make sense of violence includes the immediate antecedents of the violent act. We can start to speculate meaningfully when we discover that a forcible rape has taken place in the woman's apartment and that our inmate has been executed for failing to make good on a loan. The psychological unit of study implicit here is the "violent incident"—an interaction which begins when one person approaches another with some purpose in mind and ends in an act of aggression. Our investigation is concerned with what transpires between the two parties at the time, and it would seek to determine how the final step evolves out of the initial approach.

Another way of talking about "incidents" is to talk of "games" or sequences of "moves." In this context, a violent incident would be a sequence beginning when two or more players make their opening move and ending when one player proceeds to hurt another. We are interested in such games because we wish to know why and how they are played—and ultimately, why some people have a propensity to play them.

There are several perspectives from which games can be studied. The one that probably comes to mind most readily is that of "game theory." [1] In this type of approach, each move is seen as the rational response by one player to the play of another. The focus is on logical possibilities left open by preceding moves and on logical implications of each move for successive moves. These possibilities and implications can be conceptualized and quantified. In this type of approach the players are abstractions. A given game, for instance, could be played on a chess board, in the stock market, or on the battlefield; it could be played by computers or spy networks; it could end with a bankruptcy hearing or the destruction of one nation by another. And the "players" in such games are always guided by rational, calculated self-interest.

By contrast, our focus must be on the perceptions and motives and needs of real players in concrete settings.[2] We must study the psychological results of their moves, in the sense of finding out

[1] M. Shubik, *Game Theory and Related Approaches to Social Behavior* (New York: Wiley, 1964); T. C. Schelling, *The Strategy of Conflict* (Cambridge: Harvard University Press, 1963); A. Rapoport, *Fights, Games and Debates* (Ann Arbor: University of Michigan Press, 1960).

[2] The definition of "games" we are using here is closely analogous to that offered by Eric Berne in *Games People Play* (New York: Grove Press, 1964). Berne's analysis—like ours—focuses on the roles played by people in recurrent interpersonal transactions; Berne sees "games" as standardized sequences of moves, just as we do. Where Berne differs with us is in his assumption that game sequences are predetermined and pre-designed. For Berne, games lead to "well-defined, predictable outcomes"; they have "concealed motivation"; they involve "a snare or 'gimmick'." (p. 48) In our view, games spring from personal orientations that produce characteristic opening moves. Thereafter, sequences are cumulatively determined, in the form of actions and reactions by the players. In violence-prone encounters, we find violence built in rather than intended. As we see it, the successive moves of game participants carry increased probabilities of destructive consequences: they carry decreased probabilities of constructive solutions.

how one person's action affects the other person's feelings and perceptions, and how this second person acts as a result. When we can thus describe sequences of actions and reactions that end in violence, we can sensibly proceed to the question of why people permit themselves to participate in such games, or why they feel compelled to do so.

The dissection of violent incidents into types of psychological moves is a difficult one. The task is facilitated if the incidents take place in a relatively uniform setting, and it is made even easier if they are described in relatively standardized fashion. It is for this reason that we elected to focus our study of violent incidents on the assault on police officers.

Assault (or battery) committed on police officers is an increasingly popular violent "game." The Los Angeles Police Department, for instance, reports that it has experienced an almost 400 per cent increase in attacks on its members between 1952 and 1965; [3] other law enforcement agencies have issued similar statistics. The Oakland Police Department saw a 55 per cent increase in this type of encounter in the year preceding our study. [4]

Police assaults are far from chance encounters. The typical assault on a police officer takes place on a slum precinct street, and it is perpetrated by a young Negro who has experienced previous brushes with the law. Who the police officer may be is also important; in a recent memorandum, the Crime Analysis Section of the Oakland Police Department points out that younger, less experienced officers tend to get disproportionately assaulted. The Oakland analysts also note that there are some officers (irrespective of age or experience) who appear to be especially assault-prone. [5]

Our own concern is somewhat independent of who gets assaulted and who does the assaulting, although it ultimately re-

---

[3] Los Angeles Police Department, Administrative Research Unit, Planning and Research Division: *Attacks on Los Angeles Police Officers.* (Mimeographed report, dated April 18, 1966; page 9.

[4] Oakland Police Department Crime Analysis Section, Memorandum related to "Survey of 148–243 P.C. Offenses Against Oakland Police Officers," undated manuscript.

[5] *Ibid.*, appended table (not numbered).

turns to this question. Our problem, first, is how the *typical* police assault usually evolves from the initial contact between a police officer and a civilian. What kinds of actions set off the sequence toward violence? How is the initial occasion for conflict reinforced or mellowed? What stimulates the physical part of the conflict? What sorts of feelings are involved? How does one party perceive the other, and what constitutes the basis of their impression? In sum, how do routine interactions degenerate and how do tensions escalate in the type of game represented by police–civilian contacts?

THE CLASSIFICATION OF MOTIVES FOR POLICE ASSAULTS

As a first step in our analysis, we constructed a code for the categorization of the reactions of police assaulters—of persons involved in incidents in which they assaulted police officers. This code (together with instructions for its use) is included here as an appendix.

The instrument was designed on the basis of incident descriptions relating to assaults on officers, obtained from the Arrest Report files of the Oakland Police Department. The code was then applied to a more systematically drawn sample of Oakland reports —an exhaustive review of the 100 most recent incidents available. The Code was later used, both as a simple classification scheme and in the form of a more sophisticated "sequential" analysis, with a set of 344 incidents obtained from the San Francisco Police Department. The following chapter reports the results of these investigations, together with illustrations covering the salient findings.

Our Police Assaulter Code divides the motives displayed in our incidents into five general categories, each comprising several more specific ones. These categories were applied in two ways: (1) every move present in the incident was recorded and coded; (2) the move leading most directly and immediately to the assault on the officer was separated out as a "primary" cause, and all other moves were relegated to the status of "secondary" causes. The coding was done by a trained graduate student; the operation included a reliability study, which insured identical results in independent codings of subsamples.[6]

Table 2.1 provides information in terms of the general categories into which we classified causes of assaults in our code. We see that violence against police officers comes about in parallel fashion in the two communities we surveyed. If we examine the last columns first, for instance, we note that the two categories that are more important than others in accounting for assaults in both Oakland and San Francisco are (1) reactions against some perceived tampering with the person in the shape of physical or verbal contact by the officer, and (2) reactions following some indication of hostility directed at the officer, such as threats or expressions of contempt. Such threats or warnings diminish somewhat in importance when we consider immediate or primary causes only, as summarized in the first two columns of the table. Here we note that in both Oakland and San Francisco, the second-most-important immediate motivation to assault an officer is the desire to rescue or defend a person receiving the officer's attention. This cause appears almost exclusively at the end of causal sequences leading to assault. Another immediate cause of violence appears to be the desire to escape from the officer. This desire, however, may also appear at earlier stages of the procedings.

The two main differences between Oakland and San Francisco are the greater predominance of rescue efforts in Oakland and the relative frequency of efforts to escape arrest in San Francisco. These differences may be related to the ethnic composition of Oakland and the arrest procedure in San Francisco, respectively. The latter is a risky assumption, but we can conjecture that the lesser use of paddy wagons in San Francisco makes of the arrest more a one-stage process, whereas in Oakland some of the tension following arrest is reserved for the arrival of the wagon officers.

The information we have presented here is of somewhat limited interest. It does not enable us to visualize how the typical officer finds himself typically assaulted, because we have extracted slices out of live sequences. It is now incumbent on us to show

---

[6] I am indebted to S. Sherman for his assistance in this part of the study.

Table 2.1. Gross Categories of Interpersonal Causes of Violence Against Police Officers in Oakland (N=100) and San Francisco (N=344)

IN RANK ORDER OF FREQUENCY *(As per Oakland Sample)*	AS PRIMARY CAUSES		AS CONTRIBUTORY CAUSES		TOTAL	
	Oakland	*San Francisco*	Oakland	*San Francisco*	Oakland	*San Francisco*
sault in Defense of Personal Autonomy (Touching, Orders, etc.)	24	108	32	214	56	322
sault as Expression of Contempt (Retaliation, etc.)	14	56	39	191	54	247
sault in Effort to Escape	19	72	22	68	41	140
sault to Prevent Being Moved	13	55	21	50	34	105
sault to Protest Captivity	14	43	20	46	34	89
sault as Extension of Other Violence	13	17	19	75	32	105
sault in Defense of Others	23	91	5	12	28	103

how these items generally group themselves in real life. To achieve this aim, we return to the incident descriptions and record *in series* the steps leading to each assault. We then group these series. In doing this, we start with the opening move and take all the sequences in which the same first move leads to a similar second move; we then combine all two-move series that are followed by the same third move, etc.

For instance, we may start with all the episodes in which, to begin with, a suspect objects to being arrested; some of the episodes will end right here, with the officer being subjected to violence because of the suspect's bitterness at being detained; in other instances, the subject may next try to escape, and we then have a two-step series, "objection to arrest, followed by struggle to get away." If violence does not result at this juncture, it might occur when the suspect is recaptured and an effort is made to transport him to jail. This would give us "objection to arrest followed by struggle to escape, followed by refusal to be transported, resulting in violence." We continue grouping in this fashion until we have no cases left over.

Such sequences are lists of the "moves" in the "games" that produce assaults. They represent preliminary or preparatory reactions by the assaulter to the approaches and actions of the officer. As such, they are steps or junctures at which violence becomes increasingly probable and less avoidable.

The method of analysis outlined here was applied to 344 arrest reports secured from the files of the San Francisco Police Department. The incidents were recorded in three blocks of several months each between 1962 and 1965. (Each of these samples was complete, and we have no reason to assume a systematic bias relating to the missing months.) [7]

In the remainder of this chapter, we shall review the principal chains of action and reaction that precede the assaults on the officers. There are two main sequences, and together they account for over two-thirds (255 out of 344) of the incidents. We shall present each sequence in a schematic frequency table and

[7] The reports used covered every month of 1962; September, November and December of 1963, and January through September of 1964.

then illustrate, with excerpts from some of the police reports, the types of interactions involved.

Pressing the Police Button

Figure 2.1 traces the main set of sequences, which starts with a suspect's reaction to a verbal approach by an officer. This group covers fully half our sample. It is the type of sequence where, in the first step, the officer starts an interaction with a civilian by means of an order, a demand, a suggestion, a question, a request, or some other communication. Usually, no serious offense has been committed by the civilian (where there is a formal infraction, the most common is a traffic violation) and the contact is classifiable either as preventive police work or as an effort to cope with a nuisance act. A group of boys is "told to move" or "questioned as to what they are doing"; an errant driver is "told to stop" or "notified" of his violation; a person who is engaged in an altercation is queried as to "what the problem was" or is "instructed to be quiet" or "told to go home." A request for name, address, or identification may also provide the opening spark of the sequence.

The violence may occur as early as immediately after the initial approach but more often does not materialize until one or two further exchanges have taken place. Most typically, the civilian first fails to cooperate with the officer. In three-fifths of all the episodes we studied, the person somehow manifests his displeasure with the officer's approach, and he attacks the officer after the officer has made additional moves. An arrest is often the final precipitant of the attack.

Situations in which violence occurs as soon as the officer has made his opening move provide the fewest clues concerning the motives involved. We know that the civilian is reacting to some highly charged, non-routine interpretation of the officer's act, but we usually do not know precisely what he is reacting to. The officer, who tends to view his own action as harmless, plausible, and routine, tends to make the assumption that some "irra-

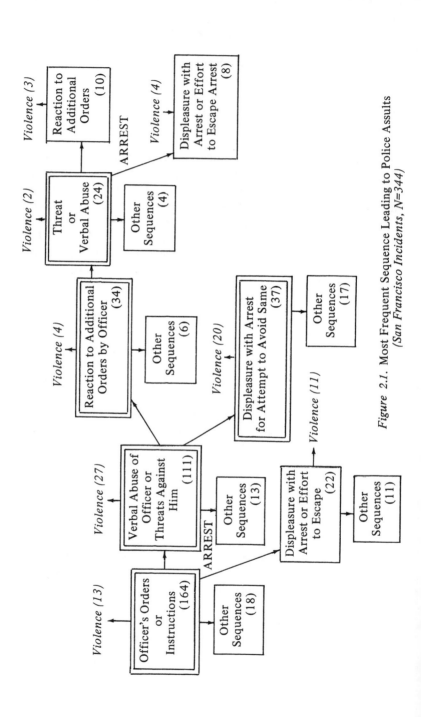

Figure 2.1. Most Frequent Sequence Leading to Police Assaults
(San Francisco Incidents, N=344)

tional" factor within the attacker might be causing him to react precipitantly in the face of no real provocation and discouraging odds. This assumption—and the basis for it—are illustrated in the following incident:

> While on routine patrol, Reporting Officers observed the below suspect standing at the above location for a lengthy period of time. [The officers] questioned suspect and asked for identification. The suspect stated he did not possess any. Suspect's mannerisms and actions were such that [the officers] felt suspect possibly could be under the influence of a drug. Officer G., who was driving, got out of the driver's side of the Radio Car, and [his partner] Officer C., opened the passenger's side of the car to get out; without provocation, suspect struck Officer C. twice in the face, opening a gash over his right eye.

Since we do not know what "mannerisms and action" are being referred to here, it is hard to evaluate the diagnosis. It does appear that when the officers resolved to suddenly descend on the presumed addict, he rather badly panicked. This lends credence to the postulation of a special state of mind—as does the nature of the violence, which started with two slaps administered to one officer and ended with the biting of the other officer's leg.

Much more usual in cases of "one-step" games is police attention to a heavily intoxicated individual, as in the following report:

> While on foot patrol this date, an unknown citizen stated to me that there was a woman in the vicinity of E and T Sts. standing in the street shouting and drinking liquor. At approximately 10:40 P.M., I observed the defendant walking in the middle of E St. drinking from a pint bottle of gin, and shouting lewd language to citizens between swallows. At this time she had bloodshot eyes, strong AB [alcoholic breath], slurred speech, and staggering walk. When I attempted to talk to the defendant she threw the bottle at me and started to kick me. At this time two other officers arrived and it took

force to subdue the defendant and place her under arrest. In the ensuing struggle she kicked the reporting officer on the shinbone of the right leg. The defendant has a long record of drunk arrests in this city.

Here the state of mind of the person, which enhances the probability of violence, is clearly manifest in her actions prior to the arrival of the officer. In this connection it is worth noting that the role of alcohol in assaults on police officers—the incidence is extremely high—no doubt varies from one situation to another. It is probably safest to assume that being drunk simply sharpens whatever psychological reactions occur and that these can take many forms. If a drunk challenges an officer to a duel, for instance, he may be displaying an "I'll fight anyone in the house, regardless of uniform" attitude, a sharpened contempt for sources of sanctions, a relatively casual assessment of possible consequences, a "devil may care" mood, or one of many other violent-prone frames of mind. Moreover, alcohol obviously also becomes a factor in less direct ways, such as causing the individual to violate the law and therefore making him subject to arrest; making the person more conspicuous (as he winds his way through traffic or along the pavement), or producing greater vulnerability if drinking is habitual. The actual impact may therefore be a complex of such factors, such as in the individual driving in an alcoholic stupor with a license suspended (as a result of similar prior activity) who is apprehended speeding the wrong way on a one way street, and who strikes the officer in the face because he knows that his ticket may have serious consequences, or because his judgment is impaired by alcohol, or because he is suffused with the joy of direct action.

Where there is no chemical reason for the hypothetical irrationality of the "short game" police assaulter, we can sometimes draw an analogous inference from the self-selected status of such persons. We assume that some type of special motive is advertised by the fact that the person charges in where others fear to tread—or where others see no cause for action. The police assaulter's response, after all, is a nonroutine or unconventional reaction to a situation where acquiescense is the rule. It is easy

to illustrate this by examining incidents in which one person
out of a group makes a stand. Such occurs, for instance, after
a waitress identifies several unwelcome customers to two officers
called to a restaurant:

> She pointed out several of the patrons and when I asked
> them to leave all left but one. I asked him to leave several
> times and when he refused I ordered him to leave and he
> turned, striking me in the right eye.

In a second incident, inhabitants of the City Prison Misdemeanor Tank are escorted back to their cell by an officer:

> On the above-mentioned date at 1:15 P.M. while moving the
> 2:00 P.M. court return prisoners to Toper Tank #2 for their
> noon meal I instructed the prisoners to enter the cell; all did
> except the above-mentioned suspect. I instructed him to enter
> the cell like the other prisoners but he refused and told me,
> "Don't tell me what to do." He began to curse. I told him
> I would place him in isolation if he didn't enter the cell. At
> this time he swung with his fists at me hitting me on the left
> arm and inflicting scratches on the Reporting Officer's left
> arm. He was very belligerent. I then placed the suspect in
> isolation cell #4 with the assistance of several officers. He
> stated that he would "make a big case out of this."

In both instances, the officers have been served notice that
they are dealing with an individual who is not amenable to a
standard approach. In such instances, it seems as if police routine
calls for the invocation of additional power. The officer escalates
verbally from a request to an order or from an order to a threat.
No doubt such show of authority or use of fear often motivates
compliance. In the case of very resentful individuals, however,
it can initiate the transition from truculence to violence.

This sequence—a change from passive to violent in the face
of a standard sequence of police approaches—sometimes occurs
with more extended interactions. The following incident, for
instance, represents a three-step version of such an encounter:

Officer M. investigated and found that there was no reason for D. to be stopping autos, and told him to go to the sidewalk, and D. refused to go to the sidewalk. Officer M. asked the Suspect D. to show some identification and D. refused, and started to leave the area. Officer M. called to D. to come back and to show some identification, and he again refused, and he then struck Officer M. about the face and body.

Here the person's strategy of not responding, and finally of physically withdrawing from the scene, faces the officer with a situation where he must almost embarassingly chase him. In turn, the suppressed resentment revealed by the person's refusal to respond bursts forth as he feels himself increasingly "crowded" and helpless in the face of orders and injunctions. The following incident, involving a pedestrian and an officer directing downtown traffic, reveals this sequence more dramatically:

The subject was told to stop at the island and wait for the vehicular traffic to clear the intersection. The subject continued across the street and as she passed the officer, pushed his outstretched arm down and then proceeded North on P. Officer Z. overtook the subject and tapped her on the shoulder to gain her attention in order to reprimand her. The subject turned around and struck the officer in the face; he then attempted to detain her, but she began struggling and trying to get away, and the above officer found it necessary to place the subject in handcuffs.

This example is of special interest, not only because it provides a fairly clear picture of the officer's dilemma but also because it contains evidence of the fact that the last steps of the sequence cannot be interpreted unless they are viewed in the context of preceding steps. The report notes:

Numerous persons were present at the scene who felt that the above officer had mishandled the situation; a Mr. M. L. was the only subject who wished to give us his name as a witness. He, as well as most of the other parties present, admitted that they had only witnessed the officer placing the subject in handcuffs.

The following is a somewhat different version of the same sequence. It features a civilian who retains control of the situation and of himself, and who tries to stay "cool" even at the juncture of physical contact. The civilian warns the officer of the fact that he intends to resist if the action is escalated. The officer must face the showdown, however, because his only perceived alternative would be to admit defeat:

> As auto boosting is a constant problem in the park, I approached suspect, identified myself and asked him what he was doing around auto. He said that he was looking at it. Suspect was carrying motorcycle-type helmet and I asked him if motorcycle parked nearby was his ('63 Yamaha registered to suspect). He replied that it was. I then asked suspect for some identification and he stated that he would show me nothing. He then walked over to the motorcycle and removed a knapsack from it and walked away. I followed suspect and again showed my identification; he said that he understood that I was a policeman but would refuse to talk to me. As suspect was walking rapidly away, I attempted to block his line of departure. Suspect then pushed me aside and stated, "If you touch me, I'll hurt you." I attempted to physically restrain suspect and we both fell to the ground. Suspect continued his threats of bodily harm and upon arising attempted to pull me to the ground. I then pursuaded suspect to peacefully accompany me to the police stables.

Warnings and challenges are often issued by persons who view their encounters with police officers as "man-to-man" confrontations, a premise which officers find it impossible to grant by virtue of their role as representatives of law and authority. The challenging individual may finally resort to violence as a last-ditch effort to establish his premise, in the face of a conclusive demonstration of its invalidity:

> Stopping to investigate, these officers made identification and

asked subject to do likewise, and then asked what he was attempting to do. Subject refused to make any identification, or to answer questions as to his intentions, but replied to the initial question, "Who gives a fuck who you are." He then continued to use profanity, directing his statements to these officers, still refusing to answer any questions. Upon being searched for weapons, just after placing subject under arrest, he stated, "You better not give me a chance, because if you do, I'll drop both of you." . . . He repeated this threat two other times, stating he was going to strike these officers whenever he had the opportunity. The patrol wagon had been summoned and before it's arrival the subject turned quickly and struck out at these officers with his closed fists, and kicked Officer H. in the left leg.

Another type of incident begins with an officer subjecting an individual to a sanction that the latter wishes to avoid. When the man indicates his unwillingness to comply, the officer ignores his protests, and thereby converts the situation (as the person sees it) into a confrontation between two hostile parties. The officer responds by placing the individual under arrest, thereby demonstrating his own authority and power. The person now feels his powerlessness and thus reacts by requesting that the officer encounter him on a "man-to-man" basis. This type of incident is an almost inevitable consequence of the exercise of police authority in a context where its legitimacy is not granted:

Reporting Officer on routine patrol this date at 4:25 P.M. was in the process of writing a traffic citation for a Viol. 22514 —fire hydrant CVC [Civic Vehicle Code] to an auto, when a NMA [Negro Male] came running out and jumped into the car. I asked him to wait until I finished the citation. He said, "You ain't giving me a tag," started his auto, and moved it to another spot. I finished the citation and tried to hand it to him as he came back [and] he stated, "I ain't takin' no tag." Reporting Officer walked over to his auto, placed the citation on his windshield. He ran over, grabbed the citation from the windshield and stated to me, "You white mother

f——". I asked him to repeat what he said. He replied, "S——
you, you Mother F——". I told him he was under arrest. He
then placed his hands on my shoulder attempting to shove me
out of his way, using profanities all the time. At this time,
Reporting Officer pinned him to his car. He was struggling to
get away, when another NMA came over and asked what was
going on. The suspect at that time stated to me, "Take off your
badge and gun and fight." I wrestled the suspect to my bike in
an attempt to get assistance. The suspect broke away and ran.
Reporting Officer pursued him and was attempting to bring
him back . . . when the suspect repeated his statement about
taking my gun and badge off and fighting him.

In the following incident, the person establishes at the outset
that he views the officer's interest in him as illegitimate, but he
collaborates to the extent of permitting himself to be arrested
and booked. When the officer, however, takes one step further
(by asking him to move), the man apparently decides he must
take a stand. In an incident such as this, we seem to see three
factors intersect. First, there is the assumption that police are
acting unfairly. Second, the person concludes that police unfairness has reached a point where it cannot be further tolerated,
or where the officer, in a manner of speaking, has divested himself of his badge by going too far. Third, the person must feel a
sufficient sense of potency (or disregard of consequence) to initiate violence. In the following report, the last sentence illustrates the operation of this premise:

The suspect was staggering and stepped into a doorway.
When I asked him what he was doing, he replied, "None of
your business, Daddy." The suspect had a heavy alcoholic
breath and was staggering. The speech was slurred and he
dropped his wallet on the sidewalk. I placed him under arrest
for violation of 647F PC and transported him to Co. "I" via
"I-4." After the suspect was booked, I placed him in the #3
cell at Co."I". The lock on the cell door would not work so I
asked the suspect to move to Cell #1. The suspect replied,
"You move me, Mother." When I entered the cell, the suspect

struck me in the stomach with his right hand and attempted to knee me in the groin. I was forced to use my night stick in an effort to subdue the suspect. During the struggle, the suspect attempted to pull my service revolver from my holster. The suspect was subdued and placed in Cell ♯1 . . . . At the hospital the suspect stated to reporting officers that he has killed before and won't rest until he has killed five policemen.

"Tackling" a police officer is an act that can serve a variety of purposes. Some of these relate to the perceived role of the police, while others are somewhat more general, having to do with the person's self-image and with his appraisal of his social role. Among police-related incentives is the assumption (prevalent in black ghetto areas) that law enforcement is a tool or symbol of oppression. The following incident is one that on the surface does not appear to fall into this group. On first impression, it represents an explosive reaction by an intoxicated individual to what he sees as an act of personal harassment:

The driver was approached by the Reporting Officers and asked why his auto was in such a position. He replied "What the Hell is the difference—this is a drive-in". He was then asked for his driver's license. He replied, "What the hell are you bastards bothering me for—leave me alone." The subject was observed to have a strong odor of alcohol on his breath and appeared to be in a state of excitement. The subject was placed under arrest and the officers attempted to escort him to the police vehicle. At this time the subject turned and struck the reporting officer in the face. He was thrown to the ground by the reporting officer and an attempt was made to handcuff him.

The incident, however, acquires different connotations as we continue to review the report:

During the struggle with the subject approximately fifteen Negroes from the drive-in and occupants of the subject's vehicle gathered about the reporting officers threatening violence towards the police. A statement was yelled at the officers, "This isn't Mississippi, you bastards. We are sick of the police bothering the black people." There were several agitators who consistently shouted jeers and abusive statements towards the police. The reporting officers had been forced to call for assistance over the police radio due to the immediate situation which closely resembled a near riot. After the subject had been transferred to the station for booking the reporting officer questioned the subject's wife as to the possible reason for his actions. She stated that "he had been drinking and that he was angry because he was unable to find a job, etc., and that he was generally angry at all white people, because of this."

Here the police are perceived as an illegitimate and hostile "outside" force, and (in at least the case of the main contender) conflict with the police is welcomed as a form of social protest.

A related motive stems from the assumption that police act as invading forces when they transact business in one's turf, neighborhood, city block or vicinity, and that any officer is an aggressing enemy if he engages in a conflict with one's neighbor. The following incident shows the operation of these assumptions:

While on patrol, Reporting Officers stopped to cite an auto for parking on the sidewalk. Below Suspect #1 stated, "keep movin', you got no business here." Reporting Officers advised Suspect 1 that his auto was parked on the sidewalk and if it wasn't moved, it would be cited. Suspect 1 at this time became very loud and profane stating, "You f—— cops can't tell me what to do." Reporting Officers began writing a citation for the suspect. He continued his loud and profane harangue . . . . Reporting Officers advised him to cease using that type of language on the street and in the presence of others and suspect stated, "Just write the ticket and get your ass out of here." At this point Reporting Officers stated to suspect that he was under arrest, whereupon suspect ran through the doorway and up the stairs with Reporting Officers in pursuit. Our entrance to the

doorway was blocked by Suspects 2, 3, 4 and two or three un-
knowns. Reporting Officers forced their way past these persons
and entered the flat and cornered Suspect 1 in the bathroom,
where he continued to resist our efforts to place handcuffs on
him. As Reporting Officers were attempting to restrain him,
Suspects 2, 3, 4 set upon Reporting Officers, grabbing Officer D.
by the throat, coat lapel and necktie and Suspect 2 stating,
"You're not going to take him out of here." It became necessary
for Off. D. to use force in an effort to get Suspects 2, 3, and 4 to
relinquish their holds. Off. W. while attempting to restrain
Suspect 1 was kneed in the leg several times by Suspect 1. Off.
W. then ran downstairs to the patrol car in an effort to get
assistance and suspects tried to stop him from going down the
stairs. Suspect 4 stated, "Let's get him, he's going for help."
Suspect 1 then ran out the rear door and as officer attempted
to pursue Suspect 1, Suspects 2, 3 and 4 continued grabbing
Officer D. and pulled his tie from his collar. By the time Off.
D. freed himself from 2, 3 and 4, Suspect 1 escaped over a
fence from the rear.

In another type of incident similar factors operate, except that
the officer is not a mere victim of connotations assigned to him.
In this example, the officer initiates the encounter by making a
relatively petty demand of one person and by arbitrarily requesting identification of another. The officer thus becomes an
involuntary participant in a somewhat lighthearted game, which
he ultimately puts an end to by physically restraining one of
the players on a transparently flimsy pretense—thus revealing
a complete loss of self-control. The only citizen who intervenes
on behalf of the officer in this incident is later identified as an
off-duty fireman:

While on patrol at approx. 6:20 P.M., this date, Reporting
Officer observed Suspect #2 standing in front of ———,
throw a magazine on the street. When asked to pick same up
he did so after some argument. (Aforementioned location has
been a problem area in this district for several months, i.e.,

juveniles congregating and abusing merchants and pedestrians verbally and physically). I then asked Suspect #1, who was sitting on a motorcycle at the same location, for ID and registration, and when he produced his driver's license, he had no registration for the mtr/cycle. He took a card, business card type or something similar, and threw it on the street. After telling him to pick same up, he did and then proceeded to tear the card into small pieces and threw same on the street. When I told him to pick up the pieces, he replied, I'M SICK AND TIRED OF YOU F———G COPS TELLING ME WHAT TO DO." I then took Suspect #1 by the arms, telling him he was under arrest for littering, and started to take him to the radio car. Suspect #1 pulled away and told me I was taking him nowhere and a scuffle ensued, during which I suffered a sprained right thumb and several superficial scratches on the right hand. At one point during the scuffle a private citizen, name unknown, attempted to help me, but was knocked to the ground by Suspect #2, and according to reportee, was also kicked by Suspect #2 while he was on the ground. While I was attempting to subdue Suspect #1 further, Suspect #3, who had been standing by while the scuffle was occurring, approached the private citizen and stated that he had better stay out of the fight if he knew what was good for him, threatening him with bodily harm.

Undoubtedly, a disproportionate number of attacks on police officers originate with men whose self-image includes being a champion or a defender, taking on overwhelming forces, or demonstrating toughness in pitched battles with lawmen. The following incident, for example, has a distinctly "Wild West" flavor, with the gunman advising womenfolk to leave the scene as he prepares to charge into devastating opposition with his bare fists:

While on patrol this date, reporting officers observed the below described suspect accompanied by the below arrested juvenile parked on the crest of B Heights in a pick-up truck. Upon questioning both subjects the suspect pushed the juvenile and told her to run and proceeded to attack both officers. Off. S. suffered a possible fractured finger during the scuffle. Upon subduing the suspect, Off. S went in pursuit of the juvenile, while reporting officer stayed with suspect.

Suspect then attacked this officer, pushing me off a small cliff after a brief struggle in which this officer suffered a laceration of the neck and sprained middle finger and hand.

The young man in this incident makes his escape and is arrested at home ten days later. The next afternoon, in the corridors of the city prison, another officer becomes the proving ground for his self-perceived toughness and manhood:

At approx. 3:20 P.M. this date, the below described prisoner was observed walking in the corridor of the Misdemeanor Wing, City Prison, by reporting officer. Due to his unusual demeanor, I questioned subject as to why he was wandering about, and at this juncture, he said "You ——— cops, are all the same, etc., I'm going to get you". Subject then lunged at me in a vicious manner in a vain try to commit violence upon me. Reporting officer was then forced to use reasonable restraint measures in order to contain said subject.

Police officers sometimes unwittingly cooperate with self-defined champions by letting them play their role and crowding them into a duel. In the following incident, for instance, an arrest is made (as it very often is) for uncooperativeness and refusal to comply. This type of act confirms and reinforces the individual's role as a defender of principle and a champion of his kind. He can then in good conscience fight the officers on behalf of his role:

In response to a call, Reporting Officers observed a very large group of juveniles in the playground. They were standing in a circle, within which a fight was in progress. As we tried to disperse the crowd and break up the fight, the below arrested juvenile refused to move. After telling him twice, he finally moved with a large group of WMJ's [white male juveniles] and NMJ's of which he appeared to be the leader. At the corner the gang stopped and refused to move. Reporting Officers again told the arrested to move on and he refused. At this time he was told that he was under arrest, whereupon he called the Reporting Officers "Mother ———" several times. As we tried to place him in the radio car, he started fighting, striking Officer R. with his fist and kicking Officer L. in the chest.

Even a relatively innocent inquiry by a polite officer can prompt a violent response from a person who views his manhood as challenged or his reputation as at stake. An individual contacted in public, for instance, may use the occasion to give a "benefit performance" to his potential admirers:

This date while Reporting Officer was on routine patrol, I observed the below arrested suspect walking. Reporting Officer had not seen the below arrested in some time and rolled the window of the radio car down and said to suspect, "May I talk to you a minute Mr. S." With this the below arrested suspect with a large number of people around said in a very loud voice, "Kiss my a—— you mother f——." Reporting Officer got out of the radio car and told the suspect he was under arrest; at this point suspect repeated the above phrase twice in a loud shouting voice as to attract a large number of people. At this point Reporting Officer grabbed suspect by the arm and told him he had been placed under arrest and attempted to get him to the radio car, so as to radio for patrol wagon. At this point suspect raised his right hand and struck Reporting Officer in the right shoulder, and had to be physically restrained.

Subsequently in this incident, the person's challenge to the police and its relationship to his self-image are made explicit in conversation with the officers:

Suspect stated at this point and also at a later point in the Patrol Wagon to Reporting Officer that "I am too smart and foxy to be caught by you police. I've made thousands of dollars on 6th Street rolling drunks and you haven't caught me yet. You never will." Reporting Officer asked suspect if he always managed to be released and he stated, "Yes. I had a jury trial once and got off because of a hung jury, I'm too smart to be caught. I even bragged about it to an inspector in the Robbery Detail and told him I had committed strong arms in the Southern District, but that I always picked on drunks and people who could not identify me or who refused to get involved at a later point." Suspect was then asked if he always got rid of incriminating evidence and he stated, "Sure, I'm not stupid. I'm too foxy to be caught."

None of the above is intended to imply that police always function as passive stimuli to assaults on themselves. Our premise is that an assault grows out of an interpersonal sequence in which both parties participate to some measure. We assume that each assault is the product of a unique transaction between the assaulter and the victim and that it could not occur in the same way if either party acted differently in his relation to the other. We would further assume that even where the assaulter contributes most of the motivation (as in the above incidents) the officer somehow makes the nature of the contribution possible. He does so, at minimum, by acting in accord with the assaulter's expectations; more seriously, he may unknowingly play an assigned role in the other person's "game."

Interestingly enough, even in an analysis of police records one finds incidents which seem to result primarily from actions by the officer (with the other person's motives playing a subsidiary role.) The assault described below, for instance, seems to arise out of the officer's effort to cope with his hurt self-esteem:

While on duty this date the arresting officer saw Suspect #2 throw a bottle at a passing auto, barely missing the window. When told to pick the bottle up from the street he became belligerent and refused to comply. At this time the #1 Suspect intervened, saying, "Go pick the m—— f—— bottle up. You don't want to go to jail. That m—— f—— caused me to get in trouble when I had just come out of the pen." I asked him if he were aware that it was a violation of the Police Code to use profanity in public, but he ignored me and continued to make obscene remarks. When it became evident that he had no intention of stopping I told him that he was under arrest, but he continued to walk away. I grabbed his arm, but he jerked away so I grasped his coat lapels and tried to talk to him but he began struggling to free himself. The #2 Suspect grabbed my arm and attempted to break my hold upon B's coat, saying, "That's my brother. You're not going to take him to jail." I told him to take his hands off me and stop interfering or he would go to jail also. While I was attempting to cuff B, M (#2 Suspect) removed his coat and grabbed me from behind. I released B., threw M against an auto, and used my club on him, and when B. advanced on me from behind I struck him also. He ran from the scene and I caught him a block away with the assistance of a Special Officer who came to my assistance. Several other Specials from the dance also stood by because of the menacing crowd until the wagon and a park radio car arrived.

Here the officer seems to go out of his way to assert his authority and attempt to control others. He translates refusals to comply with his wishes into law violations and ends up attacking a person who technically is making his job easier. The officer is also resorting to considerable force, so that a sequence which starts with a petty provocation ends with a lacerated skull. There is also some indication that the officer almost succeeded in promoting a riot.

In another incident, an officer undertakes fairly insistent questioning of a drunk whom he finds waiting for a cab.

While on foot patrol, Reporting Officer observed defendant R. L. standing in the S. corner of C. street. F. was leaning against a pole. I approached him, asked why and what his business was at this hour in this vicinity. He stated that he was waiting for a cab. Asked where he made the phone call, he stated that it was made from the R. Bar and that he was told

by the operator to wait on the corner. Subject was very uncooperative in answering questions, such as, "Where do you
live? What is your address? How long have you been waiting
here?" F. would not give his home address. When he refused
to answer any questions, I placed him under arrest for 152
MPC. When told that he was under arrest F. remarked "F——
you, cop." When I placed him against the side of a building
to search him, he began to move about and began to move
his arms and hands, pushing me aside, using his arms and
hands in a swing manner. I had to strike the defendant once
in the abdomen to restrain him from becoming violent and
until the radio car arrived to transport him to the Richmond
Station. The defendant used the four letter word several
times.

The officer arrests the man because he cannot extricate himself
from the dilemma of having arbitrary questions inadequately
answered. Moreover, it is the officer who commits the violent
act in this situation, and attacks a person who is virtually de-
fenseless. Here, again, one infers excessive irritability in the
officer from his use of serious force against an individual who
seems neither disposed nor able to offer real problems. And the
notation "the defendant used the four letter word several times,"
which is offered in justification, seems more of a reflection of the
officer's sensitivity than a logical explanation.

When one indicates, as we did at the outset, that most assaults on police officers start with an officer verbally approaching a civilian, one leaves open the question of what kind of
officer approaches what sort of civilian, how he approaches him,
and under what circumstances. Our illustrations suggest that violence does not result from just any police approach selected at
random. Rather, the degeneration of an interaction can usually
be traced to psychological dispositions and motives that pre-date
the incident. These motives endow an otherwise innocuous opening move with explosive connotations, which either may be
revealed at once or may emerge cumulatively as the interaction
between the parties unfolds.

The Extension of Violence

The second most frequent group of sequences leading to police assaults (schematically represented in Figure 2.2) is of a somewhat different order, in that violence exists to begin with. Half of these sequences tend to be relatively short, ending in an assault within two steps of their inception. Here the officer intervenes in a conflict among civilians, and his purpose is to identify the aggressor (if any) and to deal with him. The assault generally takes place in response to the officer's effort to cope with the suspected aggressor.

The reason why civilian violence transfers to the police, and the manner in which it does so, vary from one incident to another. The common denominator in most incidents is (1) that violence is already accepted as a means to cope with problems, and (2) that the officer may be perceived as a new problem.

The only type of situation to which this analysis does not apply is one in which the violence has no interpersonal connotations at all. We occasionally encounter an individual blindly bent on a rampage of destruction, and to him a police officer can be merely another object to be indiscriminately destroyed:

> At approximately 4:10 A.M. this date Sgt. A. and me were called by the above complainants, who stated to us that the below arrested person came into the hot dog stand, picked up the push broom and struck the counter causing considerable damage to said counter. The below arrested then ran into W. Do-Nut Shop and deliberately pushed over a large tray of doughnuts. Upon seeing reporting officers enter, he ran to the extreme rear of premises, whereupon he picked a ladder and attempted to strike officers, and he then threw ladder at Sgt. A.'s head. Considerable force was necessary in properly restraining him and during which time both officers were repeatedly kicked and struck with fists. In removing him from this rear room he deliberately kicked over a large rack containing snails and doughnuts. He then kicked over a metal

container with approximately ½ gallon of jelly. Upon taking
him to the sidewalk area he attempted to kick the plate glass
window of the adjoining premises and during which time
both officers were kicked again.

A different type of incident is one in which the aggressor is
a person who habitually reacts to disappointment and discomfort
with rage and destruction. Such a person may attack several
police officers after smashing his furniture or his children, but
he will not do so simply because the officers are present and
available. The police, rather, are subject to attack because they
act as another source of frustration. To the person, the connotation of the police becomes comparable to that of the divorcing
wife or incriminating witness or crying child who precede the
officer as victims:

> Victim stated that at approximately 1:35 A.M. this date, he
> heard a loud noise, whereupon he looked out his front apart-
> ment door and observed that the adjoining apartment be-
> longing to the reportee had its front door torn from its hinges
> and lying on the ground, and that loud noises were being
> emitted from the apartment. The reportee and her cousin P.
> came running out of their apartment and took refuge in the
> victim's apartment, stating that the suspect had kicked down
> the front door, entered the apartment, torn the victim's Im-
> migration Registration Card, threatened her life, and was
> now overturning the furniture. Victim's wife summoned the
> police whereupon the suspect fled the building, only to im-
> mediately return and re-enter the victim's apartment and
> strike at him with a beer can opener, missing the victim with
> the can opener, but striking him on the nose with his knuckles,
> causing victim to defend himself. Victim displayed a slight
> swelling of the nose, but declined medical treatment. Reportee
> stated that her divorce from the suspect became final in De-
> cember, and she displayed a restraining order. When respond-
> ing officers attempted to place the suspect under arrest, he
> resisted by striking and kicking out at the officers, compelling
> them to use force necessary to effect the arrest. A Bureau of

Identification check revealed that the suspect has a past record of 148 PC (corporeal injury to wife and children) .

There are various ways in which an officer who intervenes in a conflict situation can be perceived by participants as a source of annoyance or as an objectionable development. In some incidents, for example, the officer is defined as illegitimately interfering in what the person views as his private affairs:

Reportee stated that her husband, the suspect, had arrived home shortly before, and had broken the window next to the door, entering the premises. The suspect was asked by the Reporting Officers what had occurred, and he stated he had broken the window and did not like our presence in his apartment. When told we were requested to come up by his wife, he became very belligerent and stated that we'd never come through his doors without a warrant. He was advised that we were merely attempting to ascertain what had occurred in the interests of preserving the peace and in the interests of his wife's safety in that she was emotionally distraught and literally shaking in what was assumed to be fear. The suspect became very bellicose, and ordered us from the "f——g house." At this time he took a swing at Officer N. In the course of the next few minutes it took considerable effort to restrain his onslaught of fists and feet, Officer N. incurring a severe laceration of the index finger of his left hand. Once handcuffed, the suspect attempted to further carry on with his violence to the point that it was necessary to handcuff his ankles together.

Sometimes the frustration experienced by the aggressor is a by-product of the officer's routine. For instance, it is accepted police procedure in cases of domestic dispute for investigators to interview the victim, and then to listen to the aggressor's side of the story. Although this procedure is fair, it is also risky. An angry and excited man may be instructed to be silent and may be forced to listen to unfriendly characterizations of himself. Not infrequently, he uses the time to work himself up into another rage. When he begins to give vent to this anger, the next step usually involves ordering him to be calm, which may serve to annoy him further. When as a result he explodes, and has to be physically immobilized, his impotence and humiliation become a source of extreme frustration to him. It is probably partly because of such procedures that violence generated by violence does not easily abate over time:

> Reporting Officers attempted to arbitrate and abate the disturbance; however, the below arrested person continued arguing and shouting in a loud voice, waving his arms about and it was necessary to leave him in one room while Reporting Officers conversed with the other two subjects in an adjoining room. The subject was advised to refrain from interrupting the conversation several times and in spite of Reporting Officers' admonitions continued to shout and finally entered the room where Reporting Officers were attempting to converse with the reportee, and when asked to leave again, turned to Officer H. and swung with his right hand, striking the officer on the shoulder; Officer H. stepped back out of the room, the defendant followed him and grappled with him, attempting to throw him over the railing into the stairwell. The stairwell is approximately 20 to 25 feet in depth, this being a third floor flat. The defendant was subdued by Reporting Officers and handcuffed. However, he did continue to struggle and it was necessary to physically carry him down the stairwell where he was transported to Co. D. At Co. D in removing the handcuffs from the suspect he again attempted to attack Reporting Officers and again was physically restrained.

The following incident shows the sequence from initial resentment through frustration cumulating over the interviewing process:

> The suspect who was obviously the aggressor started yelling at this citizen and attempted to strike him for no apparent reason. Reporting Officers decided to investigate further and entered the apartment house. As we came into the hallway, we heard screams for help and we ran up to the second floor in

time to observe the suspect hitting at a woman who we learned was suspect's wife. The suspect ran into the apartment and closed the door. Reporting Officers entered the apartment and found the suspect sitting in the living room, and upon our asking what the trouble was the suspect belligerently demanded that we get out of the house before he put us out. Reporting Officers calmed the suspect momentarily and interviewed his wife, who stated that her husband, the suspect, "Was trying to throw me down the stairs." Witnesses to the suspect trying to throw the victim down the stairs were the victim's parents . . . During the interview of the victim the suspect became more excited and belligerent and, upon the arrival of additional officers, H., R. and S., the suspect grabbed Officer S. and attempted to forcibly eject him from the apartment. After a struggle the suspect was subdued and Officer S. broke the upper plate in his mouth when he bumped his chin on the suspect's elbow.

It is easy for an officer trying to curb aggression to be seen by the aggressor as a partisan, a contender, or an enemy siding with the other party. Violence directed at the police can be viewed as another phase of a continuing battle. It may be assumed, moreover, that while the fight with the other civilian was fair (even if the other civilian was a frail woman in the process of being choked or beaten to death) the officer's intervention represents an illegitimate, unfair intrusion by an obvious bully. Ironically enough, this view may be shared by the losing contender, even after the latter has been rescued through police action. We thus often witness the strange spectacle of the officer being clawed by the victim while trying to subdue the assailant. The following scene (in which the officer is ultimately reduced to despair and almost pulls his gun on a group of women) depicts this kind of sequence:

We were met by the reportee who ran up to the radio car with torn shirt in his hand and stated the below named suspect was beating up some people at a party, and he asked Reporting Officer's assistance. We went into the house with him and suspect had a woman by the throat against the wall in a bedroom of the house. I told him to release her but he refused to answer. I told him a second time and took hold of his wrist to remove his hand from the area of the woman's throat. I pulled his hand away and told him to come with us. He then swore at me and swung at me. I knocked him down on the bed, and he came up with both fists, kicking. In the ensuing struggle a large number of females who had come from different rooms in the house attacked my partner and I as we were struggling with the suspect. There were at least 15 women fighting and clawing and striking at us while we were attempting to subdue the suspect. We were finally able to place handcuffs on the suspect, and my partner held him down while I went to call for assistance. Two of the women who had started the fight and had refused to back up when I told them to, struck both Reporting Officers several times and were arrested with suspect. My partner, Officer F., incurred a laceration of the hand by one of the suspects. It is unknown which one. His wristwatch disappeared completely and his tie was torn from his shirt. Officer Q. sustained the loss of the button from the front of his shirt and also damage to his hat during the struggle. At least one of the women who was striking me was holding a baby in her arms, and it was very difficult to subdue her without injuring the child. I finally threatened in a loud voice to pull my gun if they (the women) didn't back up. At this time they backed up but continued to yell and scream and harass the officers and antagonize the male suspect.

An officer dealing with a conflict is especially apt to be viewed as a contending party by participants who feel a need to demonstrate their toughness or manhood. The following incident is one which seems to combine both of these motives:

While on routine patrol, Reporting Officers observed a number of juveniles involved in a fight at the above location. When Reporting Officers attempted to stop the fight, Suspect #1 swung his fist at Officer H. in an effort to strike him.

Officer S. and Sgt. L. then tried to grab Suspect #1 but were struck about the face by him. Suspect #1 broke away and ran through the service station to a corner where there were large containers of garden rakes and hoes. Suspect #1 removed a rake from the container and swung it at the pursuing officers, narrowly missing same. Suspect #1 was forced to drop the rake, at gun point, but considerable force was necessary to arrest and handcuff Suspect #1 . . . . Suspect #1 was taken to the [hospital] for treatment, where he shouted obscene verbal abuse toward all persons he came in contact with . . . , and stated that "some white man would pay for what had been done to him." Suspect verbally repeated all the badge numbers of the policemen around him, and stated he would remember these when he got a gun . . . Suspect #1 also stated that he was a member of a boxing group being coached by Officer S, and that the only reason he was participating in the activity was to get the opportunity to beat some police-man.

Some persons see the appearance of police in a conflict as always a partisan act because of strong feelings about the police or about their own role vis-à-vis the police. In other instances, violence may be extended to police officers simply because of the excitement or amusement this expanded activity might seem to promise. This sort of game is played in a fairly lighthearted fashion by its originators, but it tends to be taken very seriously by some officers involuntarily involved in it:

This date at approximately 2:00 A.M. Reporting Officers observed the below suspects come out of the S. Club. Once the suspects were on the street we further observed Suspect H. jump on the back of Suspect T. and begin lewd physical gestures (humping). After this act both parties fell to the street and on regaining their stance both parties began swinging at each other. Reporting Officers got out of the radio car and when we attempted to separate the parties, they turned on us and began striking officers with their closed fists and attempted to kick officers. A reasonable amount of force was used to subdue the parties and they were handcuffed. On arrival of the park wagon and as Suspect T. was entering into the wagon he again attempted to kick officers in the area of the groin.

Finally, there are occasions in which officers appear to attach sinister connotations to minor physical involvement, or seem to make insufficient allowance for the agitated condition of persons encountered in post-conflict situations. Such incidents lie on the border between the need to protect police integrity and the requiring of unreasonably rigid standards of conduct:

> Reporting Officer approached the below arrested and asked what the trouble was. Suspect stated to officer that he was just in a fight with one J.R. The suspect was highly excited and was dramatizing his story by repeatedly poking Reporting Officer in the chest with his finger. Officer advised the suspect to cease poking him with his finger. The suspect disregarded this advice and at this point placed his hand on officer's arm in an offensive manner, at this point officer pushed the suspect away and place him under arrest on the below charges.

Here we see the other side of the coin. It is the officer in this case who plays the more violence-prone role; it is he who reacts angrily to the excited gestures of the other; and it is he whose motives thus shape the unscheduled outcome of the incident.

From Incident, to Person, and Back

If we can summarize our course of action in the analysis of police assaulter incidents, it has been a process of finding general categories such that the unique incident acquires more depth. We have proceeded from simple classifications to chronological accounts in order to locate feelings and perceptions that enter into these short-term-motivated moves. We have found that once we reduce incidents to standard game form, it becomes possible to inquire into the various ways in which different participants play these games. Our main benefit here is not simply the achieving of order, but the fact that when we come to view grouped incidents as similar games differently played, we become more aware of the unique personal contributions of players. And we have seen that these personal contributions occur in the shape of violence-prone premises and their behavioral consequences.

To be sure, we have thus far accomplished little. The picture we have presented is confusing and chaotic. It comprises a large number—and an imposing variety—of discrete incidents. And our observations about these incidents are admittedly impressionistic and disjointed. But we have taken a necessary first step in the achievement of psychological ordering. We can next inquire into the place of the incident in the person's life and into the role the same incident plays in the lives of others.

Once we have come to understand the incident as an interpersonal product, we shall focus on our main concern, which is that of trying to achieve some understanding of the protagonists of violent games, and of their central motives.

3
The Violent Incident
in Its Personal Context

Our analysis of police assaults, as summarized above, has suggested that incidents such as those we have described are largely precipitated by the feelings of one or another of the parties involved. In the case studies that follow, we shall examine this relationship in some depth. We shall try to show that the various occasions of violence in the life of a person can be symptoms or manifestations of his personality. We shall draw on three interviews: one, with a chronic police assaulter, one with an officer who has been often assaulted, and one with a troublesome prison inmate. In each case, we shall record incidents of violence, trace the motives behind them, and examine these motives.

We shall confine ourselves in this chapter to the involvement of one person (our subject) in each incident. The next chapter will deal with the relative contribution of two violence-prone people involved in the same incident.

1. JIMMY, THE PRECARIOUS TEASER

We interviewed Jimmy in prison, where he had recently been returned on a charge of statutory rape. Jimmy was 23 years old, with a work record consisting of a successful career as a minor league pimp. Jimmy's "rap sheet" included many and diverse offenses, such as forcible rape, crime against children, kidnapping, intoxication, grand theft, petty theft, and disturbing the peace. Most revealing, there were several instances of battery and assaults with deadly weapons, and two attacks on police officers. The police incident that Jimmy chose to discuss with us is not included on this record because it took place while he was in his pre-teens.

As the scene opens, Jimmy is being turned away from a school dance by a police officer, who is aware of Jimmy's record of delinquent involvements, and who apparently wishes to preserve peace and decorum in the ballroom. Jimmy is smarting at the rejection, and is embued with resentment against the police in general and against the officer in particular. He therefore reacts by throwing a can at the officer's feet and by making a disparaging remark. A lengthy sequence follows, and it can probably be best captured by reproducing the interview excerpt relating to it:

i: So you wanted to show him that you didn't like him; so you put this can down. And is that when you started singing?

s: Yes.

i: Can you give us a little demonstration of how you were singing?

s: Well, it wasn't nothing, you know, that I could . . . . I remember all the words, you know . . . . . . but I was . . .

i: What were the lines about?

s: No . . . I'll tell it . . . you know, this song about his son, you know. A song . . . "f——" and all that, you know. "Got jumped on . . . his daddy's a police," you know. His daddy's a punk," all that, you know. But he couldn't hear . . . he could hear me singing, but he couldn't hear the words.

i: Could he hear it now and then, like "son" and "police" and "punk" and key words like that?

s: He could probably hear something like "police" possibly . . . I say it out loud. "Police are sissies."

i: So he did have some indication that this song you were singing might have something to do with him, huh?

s: Yeah. He might have, you know. It was . . . it was against the police department, you know. So, well, I guess since he's a part of the police department, he gotta you know . . . so I told him, "It ain't nothing, anyhow."

i: But so far, you think this is all pretty amusing?

s: Yeah. I knew it was irritating him. That's why . . . . that was my purpose of doing it.

i: How did he show that he was irritated?

s: Well, when he hit me, you know, it showed me that he was irritated. I hadn't provoked him to hit me by . . . . I mean, I didn't swing at him, and I didn't say nothing to him directly that would provoke him like that, but you know . . . What I was saying, I guess, that could have provoked him, when I kept on singing and "shining" him on, knowing that he was walking aside of me, and he kept on telling me to shut up and I wouldn't shut up, cause I was off the school grounds. He had no . . . . I mean freedom of speech, you know.

i: Let's get this game a little bit in detail. You start singing and he was showing that he doesn't like this singing?

s: Yeah.

i: And he's showing this by what? By telling you to stop?

s: Yeah.

i: In a tone of voice that kinda gave you the feeling that . . .

s: He didn't like it.

i: Did your volume increase or decrease?

s: Increase as soon as I'd passed those gates.

i: Your volume increased as soon as you'd passed through the gates, and he kept on telling you to stop? Then what? He didn't hit you right away . . . he told you not to walk?

s: He told me to shut up.

I: He told you to shut up . . . and certainly you weren't doing that?

S: No, I wouldn't shut up.

I: So then, what was his next move?

S: He said, "Come here," and I said, "Man, well, I'm going home." You know, like that. And he said, "What are . . . ?" He said something funny, he said, "Well, this'll teach you to shut up." Or something like that. And that's when he hit me, you know. It just glanced off and you know, and tears started coming down my eyes.

This sequence is highly revealing, because it suggests a pattern of deliberate teasing, with intention to irritate. Jimmy appears to be gaining satisfaction from the fact that he is producing considerable irritation to the officer, while he himself is retaining both equanimity and control over the transaction. The officer's pain and annoyance grows, however, to the point where he feels that it is necessary to resort to violence, and at this juncture the entire situation changes for Jimmy. He now loses his "cool," and feels terribly hurt. He concludes that retaliation is in order and proceeds to secure his shotgun:

I: What was on your mind when you went to get the shotgun?

S: Shooting him if I can . . . you know, . . . I wanted . . . I wanted to hurt him, you know.

I: You wanted to hurt him. So you must have been awfully mad?

S: Yeah, I was pretty mad. You know, that was the first time, you know, I was ever hit in my face at all, you know. In my face, and left a scar on my body, first time any blood was ever drawn on my face.

His feeling, at this juncture, is that the officer has committed an unjust act. He views his own actions as relatively harmless, and, although he recognizes their provocative character, he sees the reaction as out of proportion. In other words, although the game has the inevitable consequence of producing a violent reaction, its aims are short-term and therefore the result is seen as arbitrary, capricious, and unjust. Jimmy now perceives himself faced with an act of unprovoked brutality:

s: And, see, I hadn't did nothing for him to hit me for, you know.

i: You knew you had been annoying him. But you thought . . .

s: In my own way, I was annoying him, but it wasn't enough to provoke him to use his billy club on me.

i: I got you. So it was at the point when he hit you with this billy club that things stopped being funny and started . . .

s: Getting stiff.

Jimmy is next apprehended and is immobilized by being handcuffed to a pole in the vicinity of the school, pending transportation to the police station. This is a terrible hurtful and humiliating experience for Jimmy because it is potentially damaging to his prized self-image and his reputation. He feels that the tables are turned and that the officer is now in control and showing him contempt—a situation he finds utterly intolerable:

i: You mentioned that he had taken you over there to show you off?

s: Yeah. You know, parade me like I was some kind of a freak or a clown or something.

i: This is how you felt? At the time they are taking you, you are awfully mad? Now you are standing out there, handcuffed to the door of the school. Now the feeling on top of your mind is that of being mad at this guy and being awfully upset about the fact that here you're being exposed as a kind of show?

s: Yeah. I was kinda feeling embarrassed by being exposed like I was a freak.

I: That was on top of your mind now?

S: Yeah. That was on top, but you know, it is being moved out, you know, 'cause all my animosity was building up toward J., you know. He was my prime subject at the moment.

I: So every once in awhile this anger that you felt towards this man was still peeking through?

S: Yeah. Every time I see his face, you know. He would leave me and go into the dance. Like, well, "this punk ain't going nowhere." You know, something like that. Well, he knowed I couldn't go nowhere, so . . .

I: So you felt that he was showing you contempt by not watching you even?

S: Yeah.

Although Jimmy is reluctant to discuss other incidents in which he has been involved in physical conflict with police officers, he is fairly voluble about verbal conflicts he claims to have engaged in with various officers:

I: Have you had a lot of arguments with them?

S: The police? I cussed them out practically every time they arrest me.

I: About how many times is that? That you can remember.

S: About a thousand.

I: Really, you have been arrested a thousand times?

S: I don't know, I . . . I . . . just off and on, you know. They pick me up for something like . . . they don't actually put me in jail, but they stop me. I say, "Punk, why the hell don't you leave me alone? Don't know what the hell you do but fuck with me all day long, anyhow."

I: Just about every time you get stopped or arrested, or they have any communication with you?

s: Yeah. Any time I have communications with the police, I . . . I get violent.

i: And that has happened quite often?

s: Quite often.

In exploring the details of such conflicts as Jimmy sees them, the following account is obtained:

i: Yeah. Now I'm wondering about one thing here: Here are the officers coming up to you, and then they get all this stuff back, and yet, you know, somehow, you don't go to jail. You don't get hit over the head with a nightstick. You don't have to hit anybody. How do you get out of this? You know, what happens that makes it possible for you . . . one of you to go one way and the other, the other way?

s: I don't know.

i: Well, what happens usually? Here I am, and I'm an officer, and I come up to you and I say, "Look fellow, may I see your I.D.?" And you say, "Naw, I don't have to show you nothing. I didn't do nothing. Look here punk," and all that. Then what? What's the next step?

s: Well, you says, "Get in the car." and I say, "I'm not getting in the car or nothing like that," you know.

i: Yeah. Then what?

s: "Well, we just want to find out who you are," you know. "If you got any warrants." "Well, I ain't got any warrants out for me. You can take my word for it." You know, like that.

i: Yeah.

s: Then I walks away. That's when he usually grabs me and . . .

i: He usually grabs you, and then you go to the police station?

s: Sometimes they don't even take you down there when they call in. 'Cause he can't arrest me for nothing, you know.

I: You mean he can grab you and put you in the car and you won't hit him?

S: Uh huh.

I: So you are just sitting . . .

S: I won't . . . I won't . . . I won't be the one to provoke anything. If he hits me first, I might hit him. I'm not for sure.

I: But isn't this usually what happens? So they put you in the car and you just sit there, and they call the police station and they let you go, telling you, "don't do it again," or something like that?

S: Yeah. He says, "You'd better . . ."

I: Change your attitude. Is that usually how it ends? They tell you to change your attitude, then you go away and . . .

S: And I tell 'em, "Well, my attitude is better than yours, sucker!" You know, I just walk on.

I: Oh, and that's it? That usually ends it?

S: As far as my conversation goes with the police.

I: Do you usually have the last word or do you find something said as you walk away?

S: Most of the time I have the last word, but quite a few times I be so far away that they can't do nothing about it, you see.

I: Well, how do you feel about these sorts of conversations? You know, now that you're sitting there looking back at it, what do you think of it, if anything?

S: I mean, it's still a joke to me.

According to this characterization, Jimmy successfully defies hundreds of police officers and leaves them irritated and impotent while he walks away unscathed. He views himself as coolly manipulating the feelings of the officers, with no consequences to himself. Unfortunately, the situation as he described it does not accurately summarize all his encounters. A 1965 police arrest report, for instance, described the terminal sequence of one of Jimmy's less successful interactions with the police:

> We approached suspect to assume custody. Complainants took suspect by the arm to escort suspect to our vehicle and suspect refused to go. Complainant and Witness 1 each took one of suspect's arms and began walking him back to the car. Complainant and Witness 1 were able to get handcuffs on suspect, who continued to resist violently, and refused to get in the patrol car. Officers forced suspect into the car and suspect let off a continuous stream of insults toward officers from S. Avenue to the jail. As Reporting Officers pulled into the jail entrance suspect leaned back on seat, raised his feet and kicked at the divider between the seats. When Witness 1 was able to stop suspect [he] made a lunge at Witness through the left door which Witness 1 had opened to take suspect from vehicle. Suspect at this time fell from the vehicle to the ground. Complainant and Witness 1 picked suspect up and carried him from car to the jail. En route, suspect kicked Witness 1 and Complainant several times. Once in the jail, Reporting Officers were attempting to remove handcuffs when suspect kicked Officer D. in the groin. Jailers were finally able to remove handcuffs and suspect during the interim spit directly into Officer D.'s face, saliva also hit Officer M. Suspect was finally put into a padded cell at City Jail.

Again, the picture we obtain is that of an effort to generate irritation in others, which boomerangs because it succeeds. When pawns become the controlling parties because they react violently, our man looses his "cool" completely and lashes out frantically and helplessly. He also becomes aware, at this juncture, of the fantasy world in which his aggressive games have taken place:

s: Well, you know, when I'm actually under arrest, you know, it's a serious matter, you know. It's something . . . it's something . . . I gotta face reality then.

i: When you only have arguments with them, how do you see it?

s: It's nothing, you know.

i: A joke?

s: Yeah.

i: So that's more like this same thing then?

s: Oh, yeah, you know. That's the attitude I always have taken, you know. That seems like the only thing I can irritate them with, you know.

Jimmy's involvement with police officers fits into a pattern that manifests itself in relation to various other persons in his life. For instance, Jimmy tells us about a form of entertainment practiced by a social group to which he belonged as a boy, which consisted of contacting a rival gang, with a view to provoking them into a fight:

s: We know something is going to happen every time a club is there.

i: Oh you do? Did you say you let 'em in to take stock, until you are able to fight?

s: Usually, you know. That's what it all is, is gladiator school.

i: But they don't have to do a thing. When you guys get ready . . .

s: They'll know about it.

i: Yeah. Then they don't have to do anything?

s: Yeah. But they go on . . . they will provoke the fight. Won't provoke, but we will make em fight, you know. We'll say certain things, you know. One of 'em goin' get mad, you know, and soon as he gets mad, all of 'em have to go into it, you know, 'cause if they don't, they're fools.

Jimmy himself, when questioned, sees the similarity between

this game and the incident with the police officer at the school dance:

I: Seems like you were sort of egging (the police officer) on. Do you see yourself doing the same thing when one of these gangs, . . . when you get ready to pick a fight?

s: Oh, yeah.

I: So this usually is there . . . that you know that they are getting more and more annoyed, and that sooner or later they will give you the opportunity to attack?

s: Yeah.

I: Do you see the same thing when you don't fight the police? You know, sort of a fun game, like when you fight these guys?

s: Part of the game.

Jimmy then elaborates on the nature of the game, stressing the pride he feels in the fact that he can retain his equanimity while manipulating the feelings of others. His "coolness" is obviously equated with status and with "reputation" achieved by demonstrating one's superiority over persons who reveal their vulnerability:

s: This is what I do. You see, I . . . I can take things that other persons can't take, and I can accept things that another person can't accept. You know, I can know how far I have to go before I really will get mad, you know. I can see . . . a person can stand here and slap me all day, you know. I won't show a thing. He can talk about anything, you know, and I can accept all this. But I can take another person, and I can say one word and get him mad.

One final—and major—area in which Jimmy plays his violence-producing game is in relation to the women in his life. Jimmy admits to hitting women. He attaches little importance to this activity and even proclaims that the evidence indicates that women like to be beaten. The evidence he adduces is that women will keep saying things to him that are predictably productive of violence. The things they say, it appears, are in the nature of "love-talk" and of hints about marriage. Here it becomes clear that Jimmy himself has led various girls on with promises and hints, and that he then precipitates conflict by proclaiming that he has every intention of retaining his independence:

i: Did you do anything to provoke her into picking up the phone?

s: I told her I wasn't going to marry her, yeah.

i: Could you have told her in such a way that she wouldn't have wanted to pick up the phone?

s: I could have, you know, but it didn't cross my mind. I wanted to make her mad, but I didn't want her to pick up the telephone.

i: Was the same thing happening then . . . that you were trying to provoke her?

s: I wanted to provoke her into saying that she was sorry, and didn't mean it the way it sounded. She knowed she was going to get hit.

i: Because she was pushing you? And you were being pushed.

s: Yeah. I am being threatened with my freedom.

i: Your freedom?

s: The last act.

Jimmy, in other words, provokes violence with police, with rival gang members and with women in his "stable" by deliberately teasing them until they are forced to react. The purpose of this game may have relatively little to do with the victim as such. Rather, it serves the purpose of permitting Jimmy to test his stance as a man of steel and as a person capable of controlling not only his own destiny but also the feelings and reactions of his fellows. Unfortunately, he often fails both of these tests.

2. OFFICER JONES: THE POWER OF PERSUASION

Officer Jones, who has been assaulted more frequently than almost any of his fellow officers, sees himself as a practitioner of applied psychology. In dealing with people, he advises and claims the need for patience, flexibility, and diplomacy wherever possible. He puts the matter this way:

s: Well, I would like to think that I'm a student of people. I've been dealing with people for a good part of my life in the sense that I've spent, you know, almost ten years on the police force. This is a long time. If I told you that you just seemed to know, it might not make sense to you, but it's just maybe 'cause I . . . the guys kid me around here and say that I got the, you know, the old bullshit, but you'd be surprised how this will go. I think if it was a car stop, by the attitude of the driver, the immediate attitude of the driver; how he takes his license out, if he does—what he says to you. The man who says, "What are you stopping me for? What's going on?" Well, he is not going to . . . you can be nice to him, you can kill him with kindness, or you can be rather abrupt and you can treat him, talk to him the same way. I think you should look at the person and you just decide. I've spent so many years working around whores, narcotics addicts; I had an incident yesterday where this prostitute tried to cash a stolen payroll check. And by being nice to her (I bought her a pack of cigarettes), we talked; the other officer I was with wanted to make a lot of noise. He wouldn't have got to first base. She admitted being a hype; she gave me her kit and some narcotics she had on her person. She also told me where the check came from, and the fact that it involved more than one person. So, you see, again, by being nice and by saying that, you know, "If I can help you, I will; I'll try my damndest to get you to the hospital." 'Cause she was starting to go through withdrawals. This is one way to handle a person.

But Officer Jones also prides himself on his reputation for a consistent willingness to take physical action where appropriate.

His "rep," in other words, depends (as he sees it) on his known readiness to back up his commands and threats with action:

s: . . . Well, now, there's another reason too, and perhaps, you will understand it and other people wouldn't. When you walk a beat and you've been walking it for a long time, it's a little different than a car beat. You know people, and there's a certain reputation that an officer gets, and an officer gets a reputation of being a good cop, what they call a square cop. They call me a square cop. Even guys I have arrested say, "Well, Officer Jones will give you a fair shake, provided you treat him right. But if you're wrong you're going to go to jail." And I'm not adverse to telling them that if I have trouble I will give them lumps if that's what they want, and I'm not afraid of them. So, again, it's a matter of, well, it's not really a false sense of pride, but it's pride in the fact that you know that you can handle your beat, that you can keep it clean, and that you're big enough and man enough to be able to take care of whatever happens to come down the line.

Officer Jones forms quick judgments about civilians, classifying them as candidates for either persuasion or intimidation. In some cases he feels the need to use a direct and aggressive approach consisting of "no-nonsense" injunctions and of physical threats. In the case of one "mean" individual, for instance, Officer Jones reports:

s: I have had occasion over a period of years to have to fight with this man. The last time I had trouble with him . . . now, this again, as long as we're not talking for the courts, this is not what you would call regular police procedure. However, again, I will run my beat the way I see I have to. I told J. he had been involved in a beating of a man and his wallet being taken. The man refused to make a complaint because he's afraid of J. On –th Street, just on the other side of T's Bar, I got hold of J., got him up against the wall, I drew my service revolver and stuck the barrel of my gun up to the cylinder in his mouth, and I told J. that if he pulled any more capers on my beat, that there would be two witnesses to his murder, he and I, and he'd be dead. Now, this is the only type, this is the only thing this man would understand. This man spent time in Leavenworth army stockade for almost beating his commanding officer to death during the Second World War. This is the type of man you're dealing with.

The officer's approach to this particular individual is in the nature of a physical confrontation, a display of power, a challenge, a bluff, an announcement of his readiness to fight if necessary. Officer Jones conveys to the man that "I will use the slightest excuse to engage in a duel with you, and I know I can lick you." He does this in a man-to-man position, without invoking the law or calling upon his brother officers. In one incident, for instance, he has a summons to serve on the same problem person. He proceeds at once to the pool hall where he knows this man to hang out. "He was a pretty tough man," the officer explains. "But then, this is going back a few years; perhaps I was in a bit better shape and wasn't too worried about being able to take him." And as Officer Jones approaches his encounter with the suspect, he does so feeling that he will "take him." He tells us:

s: I had the feeling, knowing him, that it's either going to be a Mexican standoff or a fight. Either he is going to go along with me, only because he's afraid that I'm either going to shoot him or beat him, or he's going to figure that he's got nothing to lose and he's probably got more help than I do, 'cause I'm by myself.

In other words, Officer Jones knows that he is walking into a room full of enemies, but he also knows that he will get his man. He knows this because he has confidence in himself, in his fists, and in his gun. He therefore proceeds to the poolroom, bursts through the door, and the following scene unfolds:

s: I walk in, I said, "J., I got a warrant for your arrest," and

I had it in my left hand. And I said, "You're going to jail with me." And he looked at me, and he knew my name, and he said, "Well, Officer," he said, "I'm not going to go to jail." And I said, "Well, you're going to go to jail." I said "There's only two ways to go; you're either going to walk out of here with me, or you're going to get dragged out." Now, again, I know the man, I've had dealings with him before, and this is the only way that you're going to get across to him. There's no other possible way to do it. So, at this point he picks up a pool ball and throws it at me, which I ducked. He grabs the pool cue and he swings, and I head for him. Now I don't have my gun out, but I go after him and I got hit across the arm, I got my arm fractured, but I didn't know that at the time. Well, we fought and we grappled from the rear of the pool hall where this occurred. Now, this is about four tables back (you know the size of a pool table) so this is about, we'll say, 50 feet from the front. And all these other people in here. Now, up to now nobody's said anything. They're just backed away. Well, the fight ensues. We go all the way to the front of the pool hall, where I knock him through the front of the plate glass window, and I go out after him onto the middle of the street. Finally I get him down and with my hand and my stick, I beat him into a semi-stupor, and at this time, I look up and I see a very, very unhappy crowd of people.

Now, we carry two-way radios now; at this time we didn't. We had to go to the call box. The nearest call box was a block and a half away. At this time someone in the crowd said, "Let's get him," and I drew my service revolver and I said, "The first person that comes close is going to be shot." I said, "This man's in custody; I have a warrant for his arrest, and I'm warning anyone in the crowd, if they come and try to take this prisoner, I'm going to shoot." Well, he starts coming to, and he starts hollering, you know, "Help me, help me," you know, "Don't let them take me away."

Well, a man comes out of a restaurant, and I said to him, "Call the police." And he just shook his head and didn't do anything; he just turned around and walked away. So I know I'm not going to get any help from the crowd. I've got to get

to this call box. I'm hoping that a car, a police car, will come
by, but none does. So, I walk this prisoner, walk and drag
him, and he's fighting; he's not going to go that easy. With my
gun drawn, and I have literally to threaten the crowd that
I'm going to shoot and I have to walk a block and a half to
the call box. I get to the call box, and this guy starts to run
away from me and I have to chase him again. I grab him; I
bring him back to the call box, and then I phone in and ask
for help, right away. Well, as soon as that call went out, I
got help right there. But during this time there must have
been 150 people surrounding me again. They'd followed me
up the street to the call box. And I had to continually turn
around with my gun drawn in order to . . . and I had to keep
saying, "The first one that gets within six feet of me is going
to be shot, and I'm not fooling." And I had pulled the hammer back on the gun, which is usually a sign, if you do this,
that you're going to, you're definitely going to do something.
So then, again, as I say, we got the wagon there and, well,
first a police car came and he was put in the back of the
wagon, and he was transported to the hospital, and then
from the hospital back to the jail. And then I went up for
treatment.

It is obvious that Officer Jones has placed himself, at least
by the time the incident ends, into an extremely dangerous and
explosive situation. At each juncture of the sequence, he has
seen no alternative to a show of force, to an ultimatum, to a
demand for complete surrender. Officer Jones is a man who uses
last resorts as first steps. Obviously, in at least this instance, he
has narrowly escaped the consequences of desperate bluffs.

Officer Jones views himself as a Man, and it is important to
him to preserve his self-image of invulnerability and omnipo-
tence. Even in the face of highly probable danger, he favors a
frontal approach. In one incident, for instance, there is a problem with a large, intoxicated sailor who has been disturbing
patrons in a tavern. As Officer Jones enters, the sailor is quietly
sitting on a bar stool:

s: . . . I tell him, "Get off the stool and come outside." He just sat there, and I told him, I says, "Did you hear what I said? Get off the stool." He just looked at me and very slowly and very, very calculatedly, I mean, this is done for my benefit . . . he's all the time looking at me, and then in order to get behind him, an officer in front of him and me behind him, I took my hand and I put it in the small of his back, so I could move around him. And he told me, "Get your hands off me." And I said, "Just never mind—outside!" And that was the extent of having touched him at this time.

i: All right, now you get outside. He does come slowly, calculatedly.

s: Yes, very slowly . . .

i: You don't consider him to be drunk at this time?

s: No. There's a definite odor of alcohol. You know that the man has been drinking, but he's not drunk. At least he has none of the usual symptoms of a drunk

i: What do you think about this guy at this time?

s: Well, I think that we're going to have trouble with him.
He's giving me one of these hard looks. He's a big kid and he's got a lot of cuts on his face. He's got a lot of scars, he's . . . after being on the police force for ten years, sometimes you can just tell. And he looks like he's going to be trouble.

i: So you think he's going to be trouble?

s: Right.

Again, we note that Officer Jones knows he is facing a duel, but he is not really concerned about evading it. He evaluates his opponent and waits calmly for the encounter. Several minutes later it comes, and the sailor requires 25 blows with the baton to put him out of action. In the first round, oddly enough, Officer Jones' main concern appears to be the fact that the fight may appear unfair to spectators:

s: . . . But our primary thing too is we don't want . . . the image is bad enough. The image is worse when there's three policemen and one guy fighting, although people may not realize that the older you get you're not as swift as you were. Now, here's a twenty-one-year-old sailor in the pink of condition, and he's big, and he's tough. And you're dealing with guys in their thirties and, sure, we're a little bit soft, and maybe not just as quick, and so, consequently, we've got our work cut out for us. And the idea here is too that we know that the three of us can put the guy down. We can do it without risking hurting him. But if it's one to one, somebody's going to get hurt.

i: So, you're grappling with him . . .

s: Right.

i: . . . and he's cussing and fighting, and you're just trying to get him down.

s: . . . down. And then my partner, and then this other officer comes up, and between the two of us, we finally, well, I get a nice shot at his jaw with my right hand, and it stunned him, and we got the wagon door open, down so that we jackknifed him, both arms up, so that we could throw the cuffs on him, and get him in that wagon, and then we said, "Well, let's get out of here, and down to the jail."

i: Is he still cussing?

s: Right, and he's still fighting. So then he starts kicking again, he kicks out, he keeps kicking out, and he gets hit one more time and he's unconscious.

Officer Jones' recounting of the two incidents we have quoted contains several indications of the pleasure he derives from physical conquest. The officer appears to enjoy dealing with a worthy opponent and conquering him after a good fight. His conception of himself is that of a man who dares to take risks and who emerges vindicated; a man who achieves the respect of his enemies, because he faces them squarely, and a man who finds it unnecessary to yield or to compromise. His incidents of violence are thus demonstrations of his manliness, and they arise, at least in part, because he welcomes the opportunity of putting his masculinity to the test.

We have so far provided two contrasting illustrations to show that violent incidents can reflect pervasive personal needs. We have in each case traced a psychological theme—sometimes distinguished by different orchestrations—running through the person's career. This theme appears as a recurrent pattern amid variations occasioned by time, place, and social context.

Themes of violence are not manifest in a person's conduct as ritualistic sets of repeat performances. The life of a violent person, like that of any other, is a flowing, sequential stream, and patterns take shape, evolve, and die over time. To fully understand the consistency amid change, we must review a violent career longitudinally, and trace its evolution through stages. For this sort of picture, we turn to our third interviewee, an inmate with a reputation as an influential problem prisoner.

3. SAM, THE GIANT-KILLER

In tracing his violence, Sam assigns a strong catalytic role to fear. He tells us that his prison problems stemmed from dark expectations, which were shaped by lurid images traced for him by veteran inmates. He refers to a conversation in county jail, where he was awaiting transfer to his first state institution:

> And they talked this shit, you know, "You got to do this, and you got to do this," and man, you think it's just like the movies, I mean you go in there and chug, chug, and you know, beat on you all the time and all—at least this is the impression I got from all these people because they fed me a lot of shit. And by the time I did get to the prison, you know how Vacaville is, with all them doors going like that, man you're just like this, and I was pushed to the point of panic that I possibly would have killed.

Sam tells us how his irrational apprehension caused him to

get into several fights shortly after arrival in prison. The first one, he relates, was:

s: . . . over nothing. . . . We was watching TV. Well, you know, you're all in your whites and you're fish, and all that. And this dude kept walking back and forth, hitting my leg. He hit it about four times.

i: Was he in whites also?

s: No, he was a con who was there, he had a little skull cap on, you know, and he was really one of Those. And I didn't pay any attention to him until about the third time it happened. And then I knew something's going on here because he had plenty of room to get by me. The fourth time he come by, he kicked my foot and he had his spit-shine Romeos on, you know. And then I noticed his partners around me. He had his partners standing there and everything. I seen what he was going to do, so I fired on him before he could do anything and split. That was all there was to that. But it was out of panic, because I was scared to death after I leapt up and seen what was happening to me.

The next fight occurred on the first day of Sam's arrival at his next step on the prison ladder. Sam described himself as feeling "pretty good" because of his reception at this prison:

s: We got there and they let us go eat and everything, and you know, here they are out in the open and, more or less, the feeling of fear left me. And I went on and ate and everything, and later they assigned us to cells. They put me in with one of the penitentiary troublemakers. He was back in medium security doing thirty days for messing up. You just never could get to the guy. He was one of Those that wouldn't conform to anything. I might add he eventually became my best partner after this. He was a big dude; he was about 6′ 2″, and everything, and he was one of Those. I wasn't in the cell 10 minutes.

I: He was a bully?

s: Yeah. I had my stuff laying on his bed. He wasn't there at the time, he was taking a shower. He come back and he threw my things on the floor. I just thought, "Here I go, man, I know, I'm not supposed to let him do this." And he damn near annihilated me. He whipped me down once and I got up then and jumped on his back, again. We fought around there about three different times in one night. I had to get him, you know. And finally it was all right. I couldn't whip the sucker, man, and he knew it. But he was tired of getting bruises too. So then we just let it go and become real partners after that.

I: How did you feel just before the incident? Did you have any of the same feeling? I think you stated that when he threw your stuff on the floor, you thought, "Well, I got to do something."

s: Well, what I think I was feeling was like at Vacaville. I was getting one of these sissy complexes because I look young, anyway, and they tend to come around me, you know. And I was getting one of these complexes about it and this is what dawned on me, is that the fact that I was scared, I was afraid of him personally, but I didn't have the same kind of fear complex that I did with this other thing. I was more afraid of the other guys than I was of him. And this is one of the reasons if he dumps me, man, still he's going to know.

Sam's comments reflect the admixture of fear, awe, and admiration in which he holds "Those," as he calls the prison power figures. Sam feels that the encounter he describes is a test case, and that he must fight in order not to be classified as vulnerable to sexual advances and to exploitation. He reports feeling wonderful after the fight, because he had passed his test: "I felt like now, well, I was putting myself on." He feels accepted not only by the man whom he has tackled, but "by this one fight, I completely lost this complex I was getting." In the next breath, Sam admits that his apprehensions may not have been based on real danger; he ventures the guess that "I was putting it on myself."

Next, we discover that Sam and his imposing cell partner have become best friends, a fact of which Sam is immensely proud, particularly because this places him in a position of reflected power and prestige: "He was 'The Man' there, at Chino, when I was there. He had all the action . . . and me and him were tight, and so this put me right in with him, and I felt that this is the only way I'm going to make it in here."

On the other hand, Sam soon develops the feeling that he might not be sufficiently earning his keep: "I felt I had to do something, 'cause I wasn't doing nothing but going for a big free ride." The "something" he chose to do is to assault a creditor who had been slow in repaying a loan. The intervention is an unsolicited one:

i: Had your partner given you any indication that you had to do something?

s: No.

i: You were doing it because you thought this is the way it's supposed to be played?

s: Yeah.

i: Did you talk this over with your partner at all, that you were going to do this?

s: I just said, "If he don't have the stuff, man, let's just bust him up." Only, I hit him before he did; he would have hit him too.

i: Was he hurt?

s: No. I just put a knot on his head.

This new act of violence gives Sam even more confidence in his ability to survive on his own terms: "After I had done this, I really started relaxing," he says, "because I knew, myself: 'Well, I can handle this in here." Sam adds somewhat nostalgically, "things kind of tapered off for me after that." And Sam feels that he no longer needed "the feeling of protection and easiness" he derived from his powerful partner: "Like I say, after this happened, then I felt I could cope with it by myself—I didn't need anyone."

Despite this talk of independence and of self-assurance Sam's next battle finds him once again embroiled shoulder to shoulder with his powerful friend, and it results in a further feeling of consolidated power. Again, his opponent is one of "Those," "Those" who have to be defeated in order to demonstrate one's worth. The scene opens with a cozy evening by the institutional fireside:

s: Well, they got barracks there like camps. We're living in the barracks at the time, and were all jacked up on beans, and were watching this card game.

i: You were loaded on Benzedrine pills?

s: Yeah, and we were watching these cats play cards, and we were standing behind this colored dude. He was one of these big iron-lifters, you know. About ninety feet wide, you know, he was one of Those. And he turned around and told us, "W., man, don't stand behind me, punk, when I'm playing," you know. And I just looked at my partner and he looked at me, you know, and didn't say nothing, just stood there. 'Cause we were running the barracks anyway. We felt we did.

i: Who was W.?

s: He was my partner. I just looked at him for his reaction, and he looked at me for mine. I just smiled and he smiled and we stood there. We felt like, you know, more or less, what I said was, "Do what you want, I'm with you." And he looked at me like, you know, "You there?" You know, because he wasn't about to whip that big sucker. And he turned around again, and he said, you know, "I told you not to stand behind me." And he said, you know, "Fuck you, man." And the dude got up and we were both on him, man. And we beat him to a pulp. Fixed him up bad, man. And nobody jumped in, you know. Course, we had about six or seven partners in the barracks and at the time there was only about four colored dudes in there. And they didn't get into it; you know how they are, man, about half of them got to have tin with them. So they didn't get in it. So we just, once we got going we just wasted the dude. And that was that. Sent him on down to the hospital. And after that I felt like a king, man. I felt like, you know, "I'm the man. You're not going to mess with me."

Again, Sam feels that he passed the test of reacting to defiance by a prison bully, that he has redeemed himself by loyally supporting his friend, and, above all, that he has solidified his empire further. He gets almost ecstastic in describing his feelings of enhanced worth: "I felt like I could handle the whole bit, you know. I felt like 'The Man,' you know. I felt like everybody looking up to me, and . . ."

Sam informs us that his victim had recently arrived in prison, and had been loudly boasting of his sexual prowess and his wealth on the street. Sam thought he had demonstrated to the man "what a phoney he was," and had incidentally shown everyone else "that this guy is a nothing. He's a loud-mouthed punk."

Sam is not proud of his next fight, nor did he like it at the time. The reason for his reservations have to do with the identity of his opponent, who is relatively small in size.

s: . . . And we were playing handball; we played quite a bit, and we were playing two guys for stuff and we were beating them and I was playing up front cause I was shorter and this little Mexican dude was playing up there with me and I was beating him bad up in front. And he started loud-talking me and I was letting it go and letting it go, 'cause he was nothing, you know, I mean it was just ridiculous, somebody you just don't hit.

i: He posed no threat while he was doing this loud-talking?

s: No. I'd be loud-talking him back, you know, and something like that and laughing at him and all that, telling him, "Well, you can't play, you don't belong on the court," and all that. And so we were battling it out there, man, I guess we had about five or six strokes going right into each other and boom! he missed, and he blew it, man, and I wasn't even looking and he hit me, you know. And he didn't even hit me hard enough to hardly turn my head, and I just grabbed the dude and I said, "Man, hey, you know what; come to yourself," and pushed him back. And, well, he come at me again, you know, swinging like that, so I pushed . . ."

Sam tells us that his restraint in this conflict was in itself somewhat of a demonstration of worth; "I think I was trying to show the people that I wasn't trying to hurt him; I didn't feel I had to prove anything to them."

The next battle occurred in the gymnasium and involved another one of "Those"—a powerfully built Negro who fails to respect Sam's integrity by questioning his jurisdiction over a set of weights. This fight took place in the ring at the request of the coach, which proved convenient to Sam, " 'cause I wanted to see what I could do in the ring." The fight ended in a draw and was followed (like Sam's other prison fights) by a relationship of mutual respect and cordiality.

The next fight involves an effort to teach a lesson to a delinquent narcotics peddler. Once again, the object is to demonstrate "that he couldn't do this to me," rather than to rectify injustice in the world generally:

s: . . . I bought some stuff from this dude and it was a burn. I don't know what it was, some kind of garbage, man. Went up there and plucked it off a spoon and it was, anyway, it wasn't what it was supposed to be. And I come back down and hit on the dude. I was living in the honor unit then. Told him I wanted my stuff back now, man, that this ain't what's happening, you know. "Think I'm some kind of punk or something?" And he tried to give me a big story, man, "I don't want to hear anything about it, I want my stuff now, man." And he told me he ain't got it, man, so I just fired on him. Punched him out, man. Got my stuff back the next day.

I: How long had you known this guy?

S: Oh, I knew him for about two years. Had dealings with him. I didn't, I never did particularly like the guy, 'cause he'd burned some other people before, you know. And this was the first time. He used to score for me all the time and shit like that. It's the first time I ever got anything from him that was a burn. I guess it, more or less, goes back to the old prestige thing. I just dumped it in a spoon and I seen it wasn't stuff and picked it up and put it back in the paper and took it back over.

I: What were you feeling when all this was going on?

S: I thought, "Boy, this sucker's out of sight, man. He can't do this to me." And, threw it back on him.

We encounter Sam now as a civilian, but the change from prison blues to tailored suits does not appear to be accompanied by a striking psychological transformation. The first conflict Sam narrates not only is a replication of his prison encounters, but starts, as Sam sees it, because his opponent reminds him of the type of inmate who used to annoy him in the institution. His enemy is "one of Those" —operationally defined as a large-sized, loud Negro who thinks he can pick on Sam. Sam's companion represents power Sam is buying into (his Boss's son); the fight itself is intended as a dramatic demonstration of Sam's immunity to harassment:

S: . . . I was down there in the Tulip Room . . . And I was with my boss's son and we'd been out drinking wine and hitting all the bars and drinking whiskey too. Pretty juiced. We're in there, you know, and it was packed, and these impressions again, you know. Typical loud-mouthed type. For some reason there, I just can't communicate with them at all. I have no patience with them. And he walked by me and poked me out of the way, walked right up front and I thought, "That's the way it goes," you know. I was mad, and we stood there for about, I guess, about ten minutes or something, and we were going to leave and he was coming back and he poked my boss's son out of the way, and was coming like he was going to do it to me, and I just fired on him and decked him. And that was it. And everybody jumped on us, you know, and I split . . .

i: You were drinking wine?

s: Yeah. Wine's the only thing that'll do that to me. And I think what it was is he pushed me back to what was going on in the penitentiary, you know. This kind of disgusted me.

i: The guy was a bully?

s: Well, that's what he was doing, you know. Pushing people out of the way, growing a little goatee and all that, you know, and looking like something else.

i: Was he pushing other people around?

s: Yeah. He was bumping into everybody, man, you know. And he wasn't loud-talking or nothing, you know, but he—I could

see it in him. And I think it flashed me back to the penitentiary, which was an unpleasant thing. And this brought my anger on more and then, when I seen that he was going to bump into me, I just blew it completely and tried to smash what I seen.

i: You wanted to hurt him?

s: Yeah. I would have really wasted him, but I got jumped on.

Sam's next civilian encounter also involves a large-sized Negro opponent, and takes place in front of a bowling alley. In this instance, Sam is interceding on behalf of his teen-age brother, who he feels is being bullied. The object of the intervention, as Sam sees it, is to teach the large bully about Sam's ability to protect his brother: "I felt like I needed to let him know that this guy [Sam's brother] had something—some protection for him".

Sam tells us next about an earlier encounter, which he thinks may be in large part responsible for his prejudice against Negroes, and against Negro bullies in particular:

s: . . . Yeah. This was back when I was about sixteen, you know, had a hole down there, and we used to go down there and play pool all the time, me and this dude. And we were in the pool hall, that nigger in there, you know, and the dude was shooting next to me and he hit me with his cue, you know, not too accidentally, but, "get out of the way." And I was shooting at the time, you know, and I took the cue, man, and jerked it out of his hand, and threw it on the floor, and we went at it. And, man, they broke it up and made us go outside and so we went out in the alley and I started punching him, man, I started wasting him. And he pulled a blade on me and . . . , I still didn't feel any fear of him cause I was dumping him pretty good. So I jumped back, you know, man, and he got me, got my arm with a knife and then I got around there in back of him and we were wrassling around there and he got loose again and I went at him again, man, and he got me across the head through my hair up here and I panicked and ran. You know, I figured, "You win." That's all there was to that.

i: You were sixteen then, and how old are you now?

s: Twenty-six.

i: How well can you remember how you felt before? What were you doing that day?

s: We were just smoking a little weed and shooting pool, you know, jiving with the rest of them.

i: You were generally feeling good?

s: Yeah.

i: And then, this guy pushed it? Did you feel he was a bully or was he trying to roll over you, or how did you feel?

s: Yeah, and I felt it as a, more or less, black-white thing. I felt that I belonged in there because I knew people in there and we got along real tight, you know.

i: Oh, you were saying it was a colored or a Negro pool hall and he was making as if you didn't belong in there? Any words exchanged?

s: Oh, I guess so, I can't remember, though.

i: Was there anything said before the time you went to shoot and he went to shoot too? Did he look at you, were you looking at him?

s: I don't think so, I can't remember. No, it was just one of these things, he was poking me, and, "Watch it, jitterbug." That kind of thing, you know, and I'm already bent over, set to shoot, you know.

i: He said, "Watch it, jitterbug"?

s: Yeah, something like that.

We see that even in this early fight, the incident starts with someone questioning Sam's right to consider himself "one of Them," and with a slighting, deprecatory allusion. Sam prides himself on the privilege of moving in relatively exclusive circles, and he finds this privilege abruptly challenged. To make matters worse, Sam discovers that he cannot successfully demonstrate his worth and that he must leave the battle scene badly defeated. (He returns later with a knife, but a friend convinces him to forego revenge.) The inability to meet the test of this conflict, and the necessity imposed on him to evacuate an arena in which he had felt accepted, easily lends credibility to his hypothesis that anti-Negro sentiment could have originated in this fight. The incident, since it was unsuccessful, was undoubtedly traumatic.

Our interviewer tries to take Sam further back in time, and Sam recalls the first encounter that he views as memorable.

s: Yeah. The first fight that you could call it, that had any impression on me, was when I was thirteen in junior high school. And I was going to Kit Carson. You know that park they got by there? I always seemed to run with older people than me, for some reason, I don't know why. And I was running with these guys and they had some kind of open house over there at night time or something and everybody, you know, "Meet at the park, man," and we were drinking beer and all that shit. And these dudes from high school were over there with us, and I knew one of them, he lived a couple of doors from me and he was with his partner and they were bullying everybody and all that shit. And he was messing with this one dude, and this other guy that was with him told me to get down behind him, you know, and he was going to push him over, you know. So I got down behind him and he pushed the cat over me. And that was it, you know. The dude wanted to fight but the other dude said, "Leave them alone," you know, and all that. But the next day in school the sucker got me and we used the park at noon and all this, man, and I was panicked, you know, and so I was going to go regardless, you know, got to keep up with things. And I went over there at noon, man, and we fought and he beat the f—— out of me. And that was it, though, you know.

i: What sort of person was he?

s: Well, he was the typical sort of a guy like me, I guess, except older, and trying to be a hoodlum, you know.

Here, again, Sam is associating with powerful persons who might transfer some of their status to him. Again, Sam seeks to behave like a Man, and as a result feels he must pass a test; and he does not feel that his defeat was completely ignominious, because he thinks the test consisted of his willingness to face overwhelming odds, rather than of his victory over them. A parallel with later incidents is the definition of the opponent as a harassing bully, despite the fact that the precipitating action makes the definition dubious.

Sam is asked why he had to go to the park and face inevitable defeat, and his response is revealing: "I'd come up from San Francisco," he says, "and I wanted to be accepted by everybody." Our interviewer prods him with regard to this point:

i: Does that ring a bell? When you got to Vacaville and when you got to Chino, is that the same thing?

s: Yeah, same thing. Acceptance. I felt I needed this acceptance.

Sam claims that the incident in the park left a profound impression on him and that it contributed to shaping his subsequent violent encounters. For one, he continues to be afraid of his opponent and "was probably mad at myself for being afraid." Second, he felt that the incident had turned him "into a hoodlum":

s: . . . I was determined not to ever let that happen again. I felt shame and all that, you know—all the girls watching.

i: And that changed your life, more or less?

s: Yeah. I think right there told me I had to prove something to people. I got to let them know that they can't walk on me. That I'm as good as they are, if not better. I know this was the changing point of my whole life, because I was a real studious person before this, and after this happened I started running with the more wilder crowds. The wilder the better, you know. And that's when my trouble started.

The incident in the park also has a sequel thirteen years later—partly, Sam tells us, as a result of the grudge carefully nurtured throughout the interval. At the time of this second incident, Sam is a member of a "tough" clique that at one time has included his opponent. He describes himself as a key figure in this organization.

i: What was your status with the clique? Were you one of the toughest dudes?

s: Well, if there was trouble someone would have to come and get me too, you know. They know I'd go with them.

i: Usually in a clique there are some dudes that are tougher than others, and if there's a beef, they're going to get him because this dude is a good fighter.

s: I put up a pretty good front with those people I used to know; there was quite a few of them that I knew could take me, but I always had it there. They had doubt. I never fought them. All my friends, we used to run around with, we never fought. I would put this doubt on them all the time, protecting myself.

I: There are two things going. You were using the clique action to mask over the fear, and then you were also bluffing, would you say?

s: Right.

I: Even amongst the clique itself, you were one of the toughest dudes?

s: Right.

I: Did this put any demands on you?

s: Yeah, because when the fight started, I was always the first one in it. And things like that. I would get to a point where a friend of mine would start a hassle and I would get in there with him and hit the guy before he could. Stuff like that, you know. Sure got some broken bones that way.

The return engagement Sam had been looking forward to takes the same, familiar form as his previous and subsequent conflicts. Sam is attached to people of some status; Sam is challenged by a person he can define as a "bully"; Sam redeems himself, consolidates his status, and disposes of his opponent, whom he both fears and hates:

s: He got out of the service, and he was an insulting person. And I treated him nice, I talked to him nice. We'd run around and get drunk, you know, stuff like that, he was one of the clique again. But I never liked him because I knew he beat me and made me look bad when I was young. And one day we were sitting in there in the bar drinking, and he started it with me and threw a drink on me and I jumped on him then and beat the shit out of him. And everybody let me do it, nobody broke it up. And I felt pretty good after that, you know, an old debt paid.

i: What comments led up to his throwing a drink at you?

s: Oh, "Fuck you," and all that, you know. You'd try to talk to him, or something—I was trying to get him to settle down. He was talking that kind of language loud and there was people in the bar and everything. And this was a bar where most everyone knew me, and liked me, and I was really accepted here. Here was a group I was accepted in and wanted to belong to, not for a mask, but I felt I had friends there. Not just somebody to protect me or run with or hide with. And I felt I really had friends here, because if I had a problem I could go in there and talk to them, and all that, and they'd tell me their problems.

i: This guy was insulting a home, then?

s: Right. He was insulting a home, he was insulting me because he was breaking down everything I had built up in here. As far as I was concerned, he was getting out of hand. And I never actually really accepted him since he'd come back, 'cause I never forgot.

The last incident in Sam's interview again involves a "bully," and the scene is a nightclub in which Sam is on intimate terms with the owner. The bully in this incident is "drunk, loud-mouthing and everything," and is being escorted out of the establishment by Sam's patron. The man attacks Sam's influential friend, and Sam intervenes. The bully then turns on Sam and attacks him with a broken pitcher. Sam stabs the bully and leaves the scene.

As Sam reviews his incidents of violence, he sees them as an effort to handle fear by displaying a "mask" of toughness. He sees himself as going out of his way to arrange for tests or demonstrations of his worth and his prowess.

s: . . . It was a way I could prove myself and give myself confidence. Now, I think I would avoid any kind of situation like that. And before, if I seen trouble, I would get near it, not, more or less, into it, but near it, in case it wanted to come my way. Because I felt I could go over here. Test, you know.

i: You would say, now, that that was a similarity in your pattern, that you would set yourself up so you could fight in order to test yourself?

s: Right. I wouldn't go to the point of just getting myself right into it, but I would be close enough, to where if it did come to me, I would be right there.

i: You put yourself in a vulnerable position?

s: Vulnerable positions. Testing myself.

The Mobilization of Violent Predisposition

As we examine Sam's incidents of violence, we see that they relate to each in several different but interlocking ways. First, there is a replication of precipitating stimuli: In almost every instance, Sam sees the other person as someone whose defeat can help achieve or consolidate his status and prestige. There are several sorts of people who can acquire this meaning for Sam. Among others, there are powerful people whose victory over Sam could convert Sam into a satellite or exploitee; there are smaller-status persons whose actions imply that Sam could be taken advantage of in small but symbolically significant ways; there are persons who directly challenge Sam's status, and individuals who claim recognition that could cut into Sam's empire; and there are people who stand in the way of Sam's powerful friends, who are viewed as opportunities to consolidate Sam's standing as a Loyal Supporter.

Every one of these potential enemies must take some action (or must appear to take some action) that Sam can define as an illegitimate claim. People who do not play this role are immune to Sam's violence: powerful persons who permit Sam to be a minor partner, or powerless persons who are willing to remain passive have nothing to fear from Sam. It is only the person who makes a move toward Sam that Sam can define as challenging or encroaching who become stimuli to his violence. And they do so because they can be converted into proving grounds for the consolidation of Sam's worth. In this fashion, almost every opponent can be substituted for every other opponent, and Sam's incidents of violence are repeat performances, with different actors playing essentially the same roles.

Sam's incidents are also, however, related to each other somewhat in the fashion in which rehearsals are related to subsequent performances. In every setting in which Sam demonstrates his worth through violence, he reinforces the premise that the road to self-esteem must be paved with defeated challengers. Curiously enough, this premise is strengthened by both success and failure; success indicates that violence works; failure signifies the need for further violence to achieve redemption; both assumptions are based on (and feed back into) the more fundamental premise that violence commands respect and that respect is the measure of personal worth.

Although fundamental assumptions such as these have their origin in subcultural norms and in personal childhood experiences, they acquire shape through implementation. In the case of Sam, two unhappy first encounters focused his suspicion and dislike on specific people and categories of people as challengers of his worth. On the other hand, it is clear that Sam is mistaken in attributing his violent involvements to such experiences, in view of the fact that all the elements associated with Sam's later incidents are already present in his very first ones.

The relationship among incidents within a violence-prone pattern is thus one in which premises are shared, and in which the documentation is gradually accumulated. The premises relate to the role of other people as impediments or aids to the achievement of one's objectives, and to the way in which these aids and impediments should be handled. The documentation has it that violence does the job.

4
The Intersection of
Perspectives of Violence

Every conflict between two parties is in reality two conflicts: one, the contest which is seen by the aggressor, and the other, the situation perceived by the victim. These different perspectives often represent systematic divergences in the way the world in general is viewed and approached. They tell us as much about the person as they do about the events being described. And in the case of violence, they can often reveal who contributed what to bringing the conflict to culmination.

Games that Go Sour in the Night

As a first illustration, we shall examine an incident that begins with a disgruntled officer who has been ordered to investigate reports of firecracker explosions. The time is dusk, and the sequence is initiated near a school building, where the officer sees what appears to be "the figure of a man" sitting on a bench in the playground. The officer decides to investigate, stops his car, and begins to approach the sitting shadow. The latter happens to be a teen-age Negro boy, of solid middle-class family. The boy relates what happens next:

> So he said, "What are you doing here?"
> I said, "I was just sitting here."
> So he says, "Come around here."
> So the set-up was that there was a long fence, and I was

sitting right in the middle of it . . . So he said, "Come all the way around," and I said, "I was on my way toward home."

So he said he wanted to talk to me. So I said, "Well, I haven't done anything wrong. I'll tell you my name if you tell me what I did wrong."

So he goes to the car and says something about a youth or a man into the radio—such-and-such a street what we were on. And then he comes back, and he says, "Look, I don't want any trouble from you." And I said, "Look, I don't want any trouble either."

So he walked to one end, to the opposite side of the fence; so I started walking in the other direction, up to the end of the bench about ten or fifteen feet. So, he walks up that way and I walk back the other way. So he says, "Listen here, I don't want any trouble from you." I said, "I don't want any trouble either. Just tell me what I did wrong and we can talk. I haven't done anything wrong."

So he gets into his car and he drives up to one end of the fence. And all of a sudden, I'm thinking to myself, you know, "this is a dumb cop". . . So I started running to the other end of the playground and I yelled to him, "You'll never catch me this way."

It is obvious that the policeman is perceived as arbitrary in his demands, and that he mobilizes a stubborn, resentful response in our young friend. The boy brings into play a pattern of aggressive playfulness designed to produce an evening's amusement out of the incident. How does the officer respond to this game? We must turn to the police officer's version for an answer to this question. The officer tells us:

He gets up off the bench and he turns around, and at this point I think he's either under the influence of alcohol or dope or something, cause he's got a goofy, dreamy look about him, and he gives me a little cynical laugh, and backs up on his feet facing me, with the fence between us, and he says, "Come on in and get me." Well, at this point I was ready to go in and get him.

There's two gates. It's a block long, and one's at the west end of the school, and the other at the east end of the school. I'd walk west, he would walk east; I'd walk east, he'd walk west; and we played this little game for about three or four minutes. And I finally walked over to my car with my one eye on him, and I grabbed the horn, and told them that I needed another unit there, I had somebody in the school yard who refused to identify himself or to come out. So I heard them dispatch a unit out there, and I turned to put the mike back, and I saw him walking fast away from me, which would be north across the school yard.

So I get in the car and I blast up to the west end of the yard. I ran through the gate; he saw me and changed his course and he ran out east, through the gate, and slammed it as he was running down the road, and he was laughing like crazy, you know. And I hear him yell something about, "You're going to die," or some stupid thing. Well, I'm out the gate, and he's gone, you know, it's very obvious to me that I'm never going to apprehend him, he was running like a deer.

So, now, my vehicle is a block away, so I run back to my vehicle, get on the radio and I told them that there was a possible 50-50 loose, which is from the Welfare and Institute's code, referring to a person that is mentally unbalanced. He had yelled something that in my opinion was a possible threat to my life, and I think that we should get somebody up there and flush him out before he hurts somebody.

We note that the officer feels that he must persevere after having made his opening move. He copes with the boy's playful response by convincing himself that he is faced with a raving, dangerous, lunatic. He also concludes that his opponent must be speedily curbed. This fact has consequences in the next scene of drama. Here the young man—who could have easily made his escape—instead decides to return to renew his interaction with the officer, which he regards as entertaining. The officer, unfortunately, does not. The following description of his second encounter with the boy reveals the grimness of his view:

. . . I'm walking at him like this, you know, talking to him because I honestly believe at this point that the guy is a nut . . . But, anyway, I told him, "Look, kid, now, I don't want to chase you. Come back." I estimated his age at this time at about 19 years old. He was 16. He says, "Look, man, what do you want me for? I didn't do anything." Well, I says, "Look, if I have to chase you, there's going to be a real problem. You might as well come over here." And he's still backing away, only now he's taking a few bigger steps. And I guess I'm about as close as from here to the cabinet, five or six feet. So, then I come out with, "Now look, I don't want to shoot you." Which was the classic statement. I didn't have my revolver out, and I would never have taken it out 'cause naturally a misdemeanor (refusal to identify, 647E of the Penal Code) is certainly no grounds. But it did shock him enough, so that he stopped and said, "What do you mean, shoot me?" And when he stopped I grabbed him by the right arm. I got sort of a half-nelson on him, and I'm walking him back to the car, and I says, "Look, you get in the car." And then the beef starts. He comes out with, "Get your hands off me, you (obscenity), I'm not getting in no police car." And the beef's on. The kid was big, and I don't mind telling you, he gave me one hell of a hassle; we were all over the street.

We see that the officer has parlayed himself into a state of fear such that he loses control of himself, and even offers to shoot the boy. He then attempts to physically control the dangerous monster he has mentally created, all the while continuing to exaggerate the magnitude of the opposition. This new development presents the boy with a somewhat different type of playmate from the "Dumb Cop" whom he had originally tackled. The dawning of this discovery is traced for us in the boy's version of the return engagement:

. . . Here he comes flying down the hill; he almost hits me; he stops the car; he jumps out, and I back away. He says, "Now, listen here, you nut," or something like that, and he says, "If you run or try to get away again, I'm going to

shoot you." Well, I have a fairly good knowledge of the law,
and I know that you have to have done a felony or he can't
shoot you. And I hadn't done a felony or anything. And he
says, "Come get into the car and we'll talk." So, I knew right
then and there that that was a lie, right there. First of all, he
wants to talk, now he wants to get me into the car. I said,
"No, I'm not going to get into the car unless you tell me what
I did wrong." Then he keeps trying to ask me my name. I
wasn't going to tell him my name or anything, unless I could
get some understanding why he wants me.

So he starts coming toward me, and I can't run 'cause he'll
shoot me, so I just stood there. So he comes up, runs up to
me, and he jumps on me. You know, he doesn't have—you
know, he just overpowers me and gets me into a full-nelson.
Well, right then and there I knew it was hopeless to run or
try to get away; so, you know, naturally your body's going to
tense up when somebody grabs you. So I told him, "Let me
go. I'm going to go over to the car and let's talk." In the
meantime he's really struggling with me and I'm trying to
tell him to let me go, I'm willing to talk. All of a sudden he
gets this attitude that I'm strong. "Strong as a horse" his
exact words. He said, "He's strong as an ox (or horse)."

The tables have turned, and it is now the boy who perceives
the officer as irrational. In fact, later in the interview he refers
to the point of his return engagement as an experience of discovery. He tells us:

> . . . I was feeling pretty good right then cause I figured,
> "This cop, he's dumb. I haven't done anything wrong, I
> should give him trouble; he was giving me trouble, I should
> give him trouble." But, then, after he grabbed me, I says,
> "Oh, no. This can't be, it's all over now. We're through play-
> ing games, I have to talk to him, now. He means business."

At this juncture, both participants are suffused with panic,
and as a result have become unable to transact business with each
other. Whereas the boy feels ready to throw in the sponge, the

officer conceives of himself as engaged in a desperate fight to the death. The lines of communication, such as they were, are now nonexistent. We turn to the officer's description of the final debacle:

> . . . So, then I really start putting the heat on him. And he starts bucking a little bit. All you can hear out of him, "You're choking me." See, but he's starting to slow down a little bit. So I figure, well this is it. Boy, I'm getting tired, I'm either going to have to do him in now, or forget about it. So, I gave it all I had and finally put the kid on the ground . . . As I recall, I had exerted so much strength that my left arm, I couldn't even unfold my hand the muscles were so cramped up. . . . . And this is what it took to get the kid down. And he's put into the car.

So far, we have seen how an officer and a civilian may interact to produce violence, but we have not yet shown that these persons may have reacted typically. In order to illustrate this point, consider the following incident involving the same officer, at a time when the latter was custodian of a police paddy wagon. The officer is recalling an incident involving a prisoner who had been arrested for prowling:

> He didn't give the reporting officer, the arresting officer, any trouble whatsoever, completely cooperative. Quiet, hard-working man, type-thing over-all. Obviously from his hands, you know, the man worked. I opened the door of the patrol car; we got to the wagon, and I says, "All right, step out of the car," I said, "Put your hands up on the back of the wagon." "What for?" "I want to search you." "I haven't got anything on me," and he starts to go into the wagon. I've got one side open and I pulled him back, and I said, "You're going to be searched." Naturally, anybody that gets in my car, now, is searched, and I don't care if he has been searched fifty thousand times, you know, exaggerating a bit. If he's getting in my car, when I'm inside with him, he's going to be searched. This is a common good safety practice. That's it.

He refuses to put his hands up on the back of the wagon. So I grabbed his big right paw and I slap it up on the back of the wagon, and my partner's got the other one, and we searched him. He's not struggling. He's jerking a little bit, but it's all for the crowd, which is about 30 strong now. You know, shucking and jiving individuals, teen-agers. I said, "All right, get in the wagon and sit up front." He turns around and he has one step on the wagon. He steps up on it, and he says "What?" "Get in the wagon and sit down up front," you know. If we have to stop fast and somebody's in the back, it's kind of painful, you know. He turns around and he says, "You make me get in." This is typical . . . Anyway, he turns around facing me up on this one step and I say, "All right, now, get in." I'm going to push him back and close the door. The man is immense, and I don't particularly want to fight him. At this point, he grabbed me by my badge and my shirt, and yanks me, and I went right over the top step and right into the wagon. We're both inside now. In fact, both my shins were skinned, in that I didn't step on the step, I went right over the top of it. And the beef's on. All I want to do is get out of that wagon . . . I'm like one of those rubber balls on the end of a paddle, because he's throwing me around like nothing, you know . . . So, finally, I gave a big yank, like this, and he comes in on top of me, and I whack my head on the lock up on the front of the wagon, and I can feel the blood trickling down my neck. So I figured, "Fellow, the hell with you." I was mad—angry, I don't think I was mad. My head was split open. I put the wood on him as much as I could.

You will note that the officer is again persevering in the face of obvious danger signals; that his inflexibility and his tendency to classify people again produce an inevitable clash; that he sees himself again as a giant-killer, and that he again resorts to extreme force in a moment of panic. To complete the parallel, consider the brief after-play which occurred several minutes later, while the wagon was under way.

. . . So we're going in, and he says, "White fella, someday you're going to be alone on that street, and I'm going to kill you." And I tell him, "Mr. Smith, I'm going to put one right through the middle of your head." Not ashamed to admit it. Cold, hard facts. Mr. Smith can break my arms off and serve them to his family for dinner if he wants to, and I won't fight him again; I'll kill him first.

The other of our two contenders, the boy who had assaulted this officer, has been expelled from several schools, in every case for fights involving serious damage to other children. Typically, these fights started with persistent harassment of an opponent, in a cumulatively degenerating game.

Concerning the incident with the officer, the boy expresses the view that the responsibility for this conflict would have to be shared. On the one hand, he described the officer as a "pretty tense guy." At the station "he got us in this room together, and he was writing everything up; and he comes in, and he gets his cup of coffee. He's kind of shakey, and you could see his neck muscles were all tense and everything, and he says, 'If you'd just told me your name and everything, this never would have happened!' " The boy remarks that the officer is "still trying to get something out of me. He's stubborn; he's going to have to change." At the same time, the boy admits, "I guess I wasn't flexible either, and that's the main thing that happened."

The boy summarizes at least part of the pattern of his own violent involvements as follows:

s: They're always the same. Like the one I got into with the policeman was a matter of communication. He accused me of doing something wrong. I wanted to know what I did wrong, and he wanted to know my name. Both stubborn, we—neither of us wanted to give in.

And curiously enough, if the officer could describe his own pattern of violence, he would probably provide the same type of characterization. Our incident thus represents a collision between two organisms of very similar construction.

Out of the Bushes and Into the Frying Pan

Late one night, a call goes out over the police radio summoning several units to the scene of a noisy party. The celebration is taking place in a recessed valley, surrounded by parking lots and heavily trafficked roads. Officer Gains is the first to respond to the call. He relates:

> Upon arriving on the scene I take the high road, turning off the lights on the police car and got out, turned down my radio, and got out of the car and looked down into this little valley and there was approximately, oh, to the best of my recollection, about twelve to eighteen juveniles there, in their late teens—eighteen, nineteen, and in their twenties. And they had, they had these big gallons of Gallo wine jugs and they were drinking and playing on the bongos. It was a group of male Negroes, male Indians, male Mexicans, and male Whites. And there was both female and male. And the girls were scantily dressed, like they were having a pretty good orgy going on down there. And I get back on the radio and call for cover. So they block off the other side of the park so that we can make, shall we say, an adequate raid on the group.

Having assessed the situation, Officer Gains embarks on a one-man operation, which brings him into contact with young Gomer Smith, who is leaving the scene of the festivities:

> Well, I get out of the police car after I call for cover and I head towards a stairway coming up from this little valley. And I'm behind a bush and I see a subject coming up the hill, staggering, and it looks to me like the subject is very intoxicated and I just waited and remained silent till the subject got, you know, got approximately ten, fifteen feet away from me, and I put the flashlight on him and I tell him to stop and I've got him in a state of fright. And I put the flashlight on myself so he knows who it is, that it's a police officer, and the first thing that comes out is, "What the fuck do you want, cop?" And I tell him he's under arrest for 647E, for being drunk and also disturbing the peace.

Officer Gains, at this point, has a prisoner on his hands, and he is worried about protecting the secrecy of the impending raid. He is also concerned about the possibility of a riot. Meanwhile the prisoner is giving every indication of wanting to escape, and of being willing to override the objection of his captor. Officer Gains is, therefore, keeping one eye on the crowd, and another on his charge:

> . . . And at this time, I get a glance out of my eye where he's standing up and he's coming towards me and he takes a swing at me. And as he takes a swing, using his weight, I grab his arm, and I flip him right down on his back and I pile on top of him. And I've got my hand underneath his chin like a semi, oh, throttle to keep his mouth shut so the group won't come up there. And I've got a hammerlock on him and I put the handcuffs on him, and all of a sudden, "What the fuck are you doing? Don't hurt me, I quit, I give, I give."

Officer Gains meets his prisoner's effort to escape with substantial force, and as a result has him securely in custody. Unfortunately, the scuffle has alarmed the celebrants in the valley, and most of them have scattered to safety.

The officer's prisoner, in the interim, feels that he has been subjected to a sudden, unprovoked, arbitrary, and brutal attack. He sees his own reaction as an instinctive response to the physical assault, as well as an expression of his desire to be elsewhere:

I: You were just walking through the park minding your own business, you say?

s: That's right.

I: Did [the officer] say anything? He didn't say one word?

s: He just came out.

I: What was the first thing he said?

s: Jumped out and tried to grab me, so I tried to run, myself. Started kicking me when he had the handcuffs on me.

i: You were trying to get away, you say?

s: Yeah, I wasn't going to stay there.

i: Was he a uniformed officer?

s: Yeah. Blue uniform. I didn't know who in the hell it was first.

i: So first, you didn't know he was an officer?

s: First I didn't, no.

i: But it became quickly obvious that he was an officer, cause he had this uniform and badge?

s: Yeah.

i: At what stage do you think you may have hit him?

s: I don't know, my reflexes, you know . . . When someone jumps on you, you know. Before some guys tried to jump out and scare me, I just reflex. Natural reflexes. You just jump up and start hitting them. I don't know. It happened so quick.

On the surface, this relatively mild encounter would appear to contain its own adequate explanation for the conflict. A young man is taken by surprise and he panics; an officer feels compelled to use force to retain a prisoner in custody. Of course, we are not precisely sure why the officer decided to endanger a major raid in order to take an innocuous-looking prisoner, and it is not entirely clear why the young man did not resign himself to his fate. But we can chalk up these details to human error and to impulse.

In order to arrive at a less situation-bound explanation of the interaction, we must review the past records of our contenders for other incidents of a similar nature. In the case of the officer, for instance, we discover that he has been repeatedly assaulted, and that the precipitating events have invariably been relatively minor. The following incident, for example, is one such case. The officer is sitting in his parked car, and:

> . . . I'm taking a statement from a victim of a vicious armed robbery. He was hog-tied and stabbed. Bleeding. And I had

a complainant or a witness who I was taking a statement from. We transported the victim to the hospital via the ambulance and I was, or the witness was, in the back seat of the patrol car, and I was gathering the information about the incident. I had one friendly witness at the scene who would talk, nobody else would talk or tell me a thing that happened about the incident.

And I was taking a statement from this gentleman and approximately a group of six male Negroes went by several times, yelling obscenities toward me or towards a police officer in general, like, "Look at that fucking cop; hey, dude, let's get that dude; hey, look at that motherfucker over there talking to that fink." And this went on for several minutes after four or five passes. And I decided about this time that some action should be taken.

So, I called what I thought was the ring leader, or the one instigating all this over to the patrol car, with negative results. So I got out of the patrol car and went over to this one subject, whose name I believe was J——— G——— Well, right away I get a bunch of static from him like, "Fuck you; cop; what do you want, cop," and all this noise, as I'm trying to get some information out of him . . . the name, whereabouts . . . So I take him along with two other male Negroes because three of them split the scene right away; they ran. I made them kneel down beside the patrol car.

I tested to get on the radio, and the witness in the back seat of the patrol car was a little anxious and excited about other people being around and I just ignored him. I was more concerned about these three subjects who I placed under arrest before I brought them to the police car for profanity and disturbing the peace.

Again, a major operation is in process, in the sense that the officer is securing information from an important witness about an important crime. His attention shifts to a group of teen-agers who (he feels) are casting aspersions on the police force, and he decides that "some action" should be taken. The action he takes is drastic, but not overly effective. Two of his three prisoners escape, his important witness is no longer interested in testifying, and Officer Gains becomes obsessed with the need to retain his one remaining charge:

s: . . . He was about ready to make his exit, and I latched on to him.

i: He started to run and you grabbed him?

s: He started up to run.

i: How did you grab him?

s: I grabbed him . . . I just grabbed him, I don't know how.

i: On the shoulder or around . . . ?

s: I think it was the neck. I don't know if I had him by his clothes, but a struggle started to ensue and finally I got a hammer lock on the subject and I dragged him back to the police car . . .

Again, the officer has felt compelled to do something physically extreme to retain what little is left of the self-defeating and embarassing situation he has created. This sequence becomes more obvious as the situation creates additional pressure and embarassment. Now, the officer's reaction becomes almost bizarre:

s: . . . And then the crowd started gathering. Maybe twelve male Negroes were in the crowd, and there were people looking out of the windows, and there was a shouting match going on back and forth and J., the one I had the arm lock on, started saying, "Let's get this dude, get this cop." Well, I started to get a little more scared or afraid and I started to put a little more pressure on the boy's arm and he started yelling for a little more assistance and his brother came up and attempted to grab J. away from me. And I was backed completely into the back seat of the patrol car, with J. right in front of me. So I put out my foot and I give a thrust out, and I kicked, I think it was J.'s brother, right in the chest, knocking him back approximately, oh, halfway across the street. And I told him if he came anymore, I'd break his brother's arm.

Officer Gains, it seems, is prone to take precipitous action in the face of short-term provocations, at the expense of more serious business. He also acts in defiance of considerable risk, and he resorts to violence in awkward efforts to extricate himself from impossible situations of his own making. A third illustration may make the pattern even clearer: Officer Gains is on patrol, and he encounters a group of teen-agers who excite his curiosity. He recognizes one member of the group, and he therefore feels that it would be easy to ask a few routine questions. He asks them, and a girl belonging to the group objects:

I: So, really, you wanted to stop and talk to them because there was at least one guy you knew and you wanted to talk to him about the situation?

S: Right.

I: The girl immediately starts to say some profanity about you?

S: Right. I asked her, I said, "Hold on a minute, I want to talk to you." And she says, "Fuck you, cop," and this was the straw that broke the camel's back.

I: Well, what do you think about when somebody says that?

S: You can't take it personally. This is something that—you know, I'm called so many names out there, and your own vocabulary is, turns into . . . you're a garbage mouth really because you're with it, you talk their language, and so, this doesn't bother me. But this was something—well, this was a personal affront to general law enforcement authority. I knew this girl before. No respect for her parents, a pure incorrigible, and so this is the straw that broke the camel's back. She was going . . .

I: So at this time you get out of the car and you say, "You're under arrest."

S: Right.

Again, there is a relatively minor provocation (profanity directed at the police force, as Officer Gains sees it), and his response is to proceed to an immediate arrest. The problem is that the girl he has arrested takes one look at the police car and decides that she does not want to go to jail:

I: Now when she gets to the car, she decides that she isn't going in?

S: Right.

I: And is she saying anything at this time?

S: She's just saying she's not going in. She's not going to go downtown.

I: Are you saying anything to her?

S: I can't recall, but I think I was saying, "Yes, you are." And I mean, it was just a . . .

I: Sort of a Mexican standoff?

S: Yeah.

I: So you're trying to push her in various ways to try to trip her up so she'll go in, and these don't seem to work out so well.

S: I'm trying to play it as cool as possible, mainly because of the crowd that had already gathered.

I: What would you have done if there wasn't a crowd there?

S: I wouldn't have played around. She would have gone. I would have put her in the way I did the last time, no and's, if's or but's about it. If you have a crowd, you have to play with the crowd and public opinion.

The officer again feels compelled to use force in order to follow through on the difficult situation he has concocted, but the force is comparatively mild because of the presence of witnesses. The girl is finally convinced—not by the officer, but by her friends—to get into the squad car. But as she sits watching the officer write his report, the arbitrariness and seriousness of the predicament, as she sees it, make her extremely angry. She reacts by leaning over the front seat of the car and tearing out the microphone. The officer becomes aware of the fact that the situation is now out of his control, and he becomes alarmed:

s: . . . I get ahold of the mike, and the mike's laying on the front floor of the car and she's got the box (my report box) and has got ahold of that, and I'm trying to keep that down . . . she's throwing everything out of the box, the penal code, all my reports, there was maybe 400 pieces of paper and assignment cards, ticket book, everything went out of the car piece by piece. And she started to swear at this time, "I'm not going," and I was a great distance away from the car . . .

i: You said she was getting mad here; she's not insane, she's mad?

s: She's been had.

Finally he subdues the girl, but not before he himself has sustained serious injury, and not before considerable reinforcements have had to arrive to aid him. Again, his role in the promotion of violence has been to take sudden action against a person emotionally unprepared for this type of contingency. And again, he resorts to violence when he is faced with the helpless rage of his victim.

But what of our friend Gomer Smith, Officer Gains' opponent in the first incident we described? Smith, we may recall, had tried to make a precipitous exit when he saw Officer Gains emerge from the bushes. When the officer moved to detain him, Smith lashed out at the officer, claiming that his "'reflexes" had gained the upper hand. Smith has had several violent encounters in his career. He recalls one, for instance, which took place one evening while he was walking home with his fiance:

s: . . . We were walking down 14th Avenue and these guys drove by and started calling my broad a whore, and so I picked up a coke bottle and threw it at 'em and they stopped. And they jumped out and just, you know, started firing on me, so I started fighting back. And I knocked one down and two jumped back, and I picked up a paper rack and broke it over their heads.

1: Over their heads, or one of them?

s: Yeah. I started hitting them with the rack and then they split. The guy lay there and I just walked away and left him there.

As in the incident with the police officer, Smith here sees himself the subject of an unprovoked assault by superior forces. This aspect of the situation, he maintains, makes him especially angry:

1: You must have been pretty mad when you picked up the paper rack.

s: Well, I . . . one against three.

The same theme of battling against unprovoked agression by "bullies" runs through a fight Gomer Smith had in a prison yard one afternoon:

s: We's standing by the barracks. Wait a minute. This colored guy, you know . . . He's been cutting in line on me at lunch and stuff, you know.

1: Always in front of you?

s: Yeah. I didn't give . . . I didn't care, you know. But this one time he come in, right in the door and he try to smart off to somebody, you know. Like he was a big tough one, you know. So he just runs up to me and calls me "fat boy" or some shit, you know. So I just hauled off and hit him. Some of his partners were there.

1: Did he say anything else?

s: No.

1: Had he said anything before to you?

s: Naw.

1: But he had bothered you? He had cut in?

s: Yeah.

I: Now, at the time that he said "fat boy" . . . were there a lot of people standing around?

s: Yeah.

I: How did you feel then?

s: Just got pissed off, you know. I don't like people to push me around, that's all.

Here Smith is quite explicit about the fact that the main precipitant of violence for him is an effort by anyone, especially a person who conceives of himself as having status, to use him unfairly. Smith sees this kind of thing in the episode with Officer Gains, as well as in other incidents:

I: . . . You say you don't like people pushing you around or that you hit this guy because he was pushing you around. You feel the same way about officers?

s: Yeah.

I: Did you feel the same way about these three guys that came along and hollered at you while you were walking with your girl?

s: Yeah. I felt the same.

I: Have you felt the same way in the other fights you've had? That people were pushing you around and you got in a fight with them because you want to stop them pushing you?

s: Yeah.

In our interview, we asked Smith whether he could recall having had any fights in his life that were not due to someone "pushing him around." He responded that he had been involved in some acts of violence in efforts to help his friends, and he cited the following illustration:

s: Like see, one time up in the park, these three guys walked

through the park, you know, four of them . . . And they were
drunk, you know, and they stuck one of my friend's little
brother's face in the water, you know. And so my two friends,
their two brothers, you know, this little kid, they were walking through the park looking for him. I was sitting up on the
hill with my girl friend, you know, and I saw them fighting,
so I just went down and helped them.

Again, we note, the opponent is a person who can be defined
as a bully and the object of the game is to try to counter unwarranted abuse.

The interaction between Officer Gains and Gomer Smith is
thus a familiar situation for both contenders. Officer Gains,
whose contribution to the incident is probably the major one,
reacted to Smith as he routinely reacts to people whom he views
as irritants. Smith, on the other hand, categorized the officer's
action in a class (which generally provokes him to violence) of
unfair harassment by an arbitrary aggressor. The incident, therefore, represents the collision of two violence-prone modes of
response to violence-prone modes of provocation—each characteristic of the man involved.

A Question of Manhood and Honor

Sometimes the response of two parties to each other is such that
it inevitably produces reciprocal misconceptions. Each person
comes to see the other as representing what he views as hateful
or threatening or humiliating or fear-inspiring. As a result, he reacts negatively, and the other person reciprocates, which reinforces the original preconception. The confrontation that finally
takes place is between two symbols rather than between two real
people. The following arrest report described an episode which
represents an encounter of this type.

Arresting Officers responded to a call of a family fight. Upon
arrival, suspect was in front of his home. Arresting Officers
attempted to talk with suspect to find the cause of the dis-

turbance. Suspect was very belligerent and obnoxious. Suspect had hands in the coat pocket of a long overcoat. Arresting Officers were exercising courtesy and patience. Suspect would not even tell Arresting Officer his name, age, or anything. Arresting Officers asked suspect to remove his hands from the pockets. Suspect told Arresting Officers; "I don't have to tell you shit and I don't have to take my hands out of my pockets." Suspect was ordered to take his hands from his pockets and show what he had in his pockets. Because of the attitude of the suspect and the nature of the call, Arresting Officers felt it was imperative that suspect remove his hands and so suspect was again ordered to remove his hands. Suspect restated "I don't have to do shit." Arresting Officers were forced to force the suspect to remove his hands. In doing so suspect struggled and resisted and had to be forced into police vehicle. Suspect willfully delayed and obstructed Arresting Officers while attempting to discharge their duties by refusing to remove his hands and refusing to give name or any identification. After being placed in police vehicle, Suspect screamed "You white m——f——s, etc." Suspect was ordered to cease the screaming and he only screamed that much louder. Suspect would not quiet down and Arresting Officers had to get in the back seat with the suspect when he further resisted and again force had to be used. Suspect then stopped screaming and yelling profane language such as "m——f—— etc., etc., etc." And only talked, did not scream. Suspect still refused and resisted by not giving name, birthdate, etc., and would only reply with more abusive language, stating he "Did not have to give you shit." Threatened to urinate on the seat if he were not allowed to get out of the patrol car. During the entire time the suspect kept threatening Arresting Officers by saying, "Me and my Black Brothers will get you. If I go to jail for anything, Oakland will burn just like Watts. We have plans for Oakland, Richmond, Marin City and all those. Me and my Muslim Brothers will get you, Whitey."

Two officers were present in the incident, but only one became involved in physical conflict. The report was written by this person, and as a result it is as much of a subjective history as it is an objective account. The officer covered the same episode informally in our interview, and here again he stressed the extent to which he preclassified his opponent as soon as he found him sitting in the front seat of his car:

s: . . . He said, "I'm on private property, you can't do anything to me." And I asked him if he'd step out of the car, we just wanted to talk to him, see if we could find some answers to this. And so he got out of the car and he had on a long trench coat, rain coat, and he stuck his hands in the pockets of this trench coat. And he constantly kept saying, "You can't do anything to me, I'm on private property." And his attitude bothered me a little bit, so I asked him if he'd take his hands out of his pockets.

i: In what way did it bother you?

s: Well, it bothered me in the way that I thought he would become more irritable, and I wanted to see his hands. I felt that his hands in his pockets were a threat to me.

i: You felt he possibly had a weapon?

s: Yes. I had no idea what he had in his pockets and his attitude was such that I figured that he might be carrying a weapon. So I said, "Would you take your hands out of your pockets, please." And he says, "Why, you think I have a gun or a knife?" I says, "Well, you take your hands out of your pockets, there's no question about it, don't even have to bother with it." He says, "I'm not going to take them out." And I said, "Take your hands out of your pockets, 'cause I want to see your hands." He told me he wasn't going to take them out and he kept his hands in his pockets and he moved them towards me and so I told him one more time, I said, "Take your hands out of your pockets." And he said something like, "Make me, you can't make me, I'm on private property, you can't do anything to me." So I felt that with his attitude this way, I felt that it was imperative that I take the man's hands out of his pockets. So I grabbed one arm and my partner grabbed the other arm and we pulled his hands out of his pockets and he started to fight. So we wrestled him and I got him in an arm lock and we took him across and put him in the back seat of the patrol car. At this time we decided that we were going to arrest him for interfering with an officer, not resisting, but interfering, because he was obstructing us in doing our duties. We felt that we had to see his hands, so we put him in the back seat of the patrol car and he went wild. He was sliding back and forth across the seat and kicked the glass and beat on it with his hands and screamed.

1: Was he screaming when you took his hands out of his pockets?

s: He just kept saying that we couldn't do it, he was on private property.

1: But you did do it. Was he abusive at all at this time, would you say?

s: Well, he became abusive as we took hold of him.

In this description, we see that the officer becomes irritated by what he views as unforgiveable defiance of his authority ("his attitude bothered me") and on this basis classifies the man as a troublemaker. This category implies the type of person who is likely to become more troublesome, and who therefore must be neutralized ("I thought he would become more irritable . . . I felt that his hands in his pockets were a threat to me."). The officer becomes stern and inflexible ("You take your hands out of your pockets, there is no question about it"), and when this produces no results, his stereotype of the man becomes reinforced. He also seems to feel that at this stage he must assert police authority at all cost ("I felt that it was imperative that I take the man's hands out of his pockets"), and must use physical force. It is at this juncture—and only at this juncture—that the civilian becomes violent ("He became abusive as we took hold of him.").

When the civilian's violent reaction occurs, the officer sees it as directed, not at himself, but at the police force, and at the institution of law and order; he also sees himself as the target of a one-man black nationalist riot. This conception emerges in a description of the prisoner's behavior after he was transfered into the wagon:

s: He screamed all the time and it was all vile, vulgar language and it was all directed at the white motherfucking police. And how come we were all so stupid, and didn't any of us have any education. That policemen in Berkeley were much better policemen because they had two years of college and that he was going to get his black brothers and they were going to burn Oakland and . . .

i: He just had all sorts of general suggestions?

s: Social reforms.

i: All right, now, you just think that he's trying to cause trouble. At any time along the line are you worried about this developing, besides the immediate problem of handling him? You don't see any problems?

s: No indication from the crowd in the street, but I don't doubt for a minute that he's going to do it. He mentioned several times that he was a Black Muslim and that he was going to get his black brothers and that I would be the first one that they got. His abuse was more directed at me than at my partner and he said that he'd find out where I lived and he'd burn my place and he'd get me.

This same conception of the issue, as one of a physical contest involving status, honor, and the social role of the police, becomes explicit in more general discussion of civilian–police confrontations:

s: I feel that it couldn't be personal. The guy doesn't know me. Chances are very slim that I've ever seen him before. I probably don't know him from Adam, so I can't possibly feel that it's personal to me. It's directed at law and order, at . . . not justice . . . Things, today, are growing so that the trend is, rather than correct a man when he's done something wrong, is to tell him that he's done something wrong, don't do it again. I can remember when I was a kid, if you talked to a police officer like I've been talked to, you would either wind up in the hospital or your folks would have you down at the jail and find out why. Now, I'm not saying that you should go out and beat up all the citizens, but I'm saying only that the respect for law enforcement is gone, not diminishing, it's gone. There is no respect for law enforcement at all.

The officer feels that the ideal solution for police–community problems is a physical fitness training program during which officers would learn to inspire physical respect among the civilians they encounter:

s: The goals of this kind of program would be, like I say, physical fitness and mental fitness, which would give a guy confidence. This is one thing that makes people aggressive. They lack the confidence; they don't feel that they can handle a situation. They feel inadequate to handle a situation when a guy fights with them. Some of the guys come on like they've never had a fight. They don't know how to handle themselves. Where it's knock the guy down or you'll get knocked down, it's not necessarily size that counts, or muscle. We have a lot of guys that are health fanatics, who lift weights; don't do anything else. And I think if a person checks, he'll find out that weight-lifters wind up on the injured list possibly more than anybody else because their muscles are not tooled for running, stretching, wrestling or anything else. They're toned for lifting and I feel that maybe weight-lifting should be a part of this program, but it should be, as I say, a part of it, not the complete program. I really feel that this would build a man's confidence, it would also build his appearance. We wouldn't have so many officers who couldn't handle a situation because they're just not physically capable of handling it.

The other officer involved in our incident also seems to feel that the turning point in the interaction occurred when physical force was used on the civilian. Force was used when the suspect's hands were removed from his pockets, and it was employed again when the arresting officer slapped his prisoner unjustifiably in order to quiet him down:

s: He started yelling in the car. He was quiet before, hadn't been loud, although he had refused to cooperate. There's a lot of people, and he is yelling so loud that M. told him to be quiet. We wanted to keep the situation a little bit calmer, had hand-cuffed him, and we finally ended up uh . . . M. had gone back and slapped him, not hard. Slapped him, trying to calm him down in the back seat, and he was yelling even louder. So we finally ended up taking him down to get him away from the address.

The second officer has an entirely different interpretation of the suspect's feelings from that of the first officer. He sees the civilian's reaction mainly as a method of saving his self-image in the face of a humiliating affront. The officer says:

s: As far as him yelling and becoming violent, I think it was mainly . . . a method for him to save face. Because he'd been put in an embarassing situation, 'cause he'd been taken down and searched and handcuffed; and it was the only way, I guess, he thought he could do anything to bring himself back up.

At another juncture in the interview, the officer makes this interpretation more explicit:

i: You say he was trying to gain face, regain face?

s: Well, I'd say, well, yes.

i: Was he doing it for himself, or was he pointing it toward the crowd there?

s: No, not to the crowd. I don't know whether he's trying to draw one or not, but he seemed to be awfully concerned at the time about being abused or being brutalized and, "Go ahead and hit me again, go ahead and hit me, and do what you want," and sounded like a bit of a martyr.

I: For his own benefit, basically, you say?

s: Yeah, probably.

What of the civilian? His description of the encounter brings out two important details. First, he reveals that the officer had already classified him as a "Black Muslim" at the point of initial contact. Second, he indicates that he merely perceived himself as dispassionately insisting on his rights, up to the moment where the officer resorted to physical contact, at which juncture he became very angry:

s: I was sitting in the driveway on the fender of my car, and the policeman come up and asked me what happened. I said, "I don't know." I didn't even know that they had been called. So they went and talked to her, and came back and was talking to me. I had a beard . . . he asked me was I a Muslim? And I asked him, "Have you ever seen a Muslim wear a beard?" So then he asked me to get my hands out of my pockets. I said, "Well, am I under arrest?" He said "No." So I said, "I don't see why I should have to take my hands out of my pockets. I'm not in the street and I'm sitting in a private driveway." And the next thing I know, they grabbed me. So they took me . . . each one of them had one of my arms twisted behind me, and they took me in the car. And then this one came around from the driver's side . . . Came around and slapped me. Up until that time I didn't get angry or lose my head or anything, till then.

The man also comes to see the situation at the point of physical contact as a challenge to a duel. He tells us that in the squad car, when the officer grabbed him, he shouted at the officer, "Why don't you stop the car and try that?" There is also some evidence that after the episode involving the removal of his hands from his pockets, a certain amount of baiting and challenging occurred:

I: Now, can you think of any reason at all why this officer would just come up and slap you?

S: Yeah, I think I know what. When he had my arms behind me, as I said before, I didn't get angry. Until he had slapped me. And I must have gotten angry when he put me in the car, and I said something to him and he said something to me, and he came around the side.

I: Do you remember what you said?

S: No, I don't remember.

I: Was it cussing him out or threatening or something like this?

S: I told him he was a stupid bastard.

I: At the point that they put you in the car, what were you thinking?

S: Well, when they first grabbed me and put my arms behind my back, you know, the first thought that came in my mind was if I had a chance, you know, to get loose from them, you know. Then I would have, probably most likely would have took them.

The motivation for the civilian's provocative behavior appears to have coincided with the interpretation of the non-participating officer. There is a question of self-image, in that the man places considerable weight on his manliness and inviolability. He is affronted both by the condescending aspect of being ordered around and by the fact that the officer initiates a physical contact without affording him an opportunity for retaliation:

I: Looking back on it now, if this were to happen again—if you and your wife were to have an argument, and she were to call the police and they drove up, how would you handle it now?

S: I don't know. If they came up and talked to me in a sensible way and I'm a man. Later I would probably cooperate, even though I felt that some things they asked me to do was unnecessary. If it was done in a mannerly way, but if I was approached the way that they approached me . . .

I: Let's take the part where you were sitting on the car with your hands in your pockets, and one of the police said, "Take your hands out of your pockets." How could he have put the message across, you know, that he was afraid you had a knife in your pocket, in such a way that you would have complied with it? Or was this alternative open to him?

s: If he asked me to take my hands out of my pockets, I would ask him again why. And if he told me that he thought I had a weapon or something, or if he wanted to search me to see if I had a weapon, I would take them out. But he just said, "Take your hands out of your pockets." And I said "For what reason?" And he said, "Just because I told you to." Then I would probably do it the same way.

Our man relates several other incidents in which he became involved because someone touched him, or because he was given an order, or because someone did not sufficiently acknowledge his manly status. Although the man's role in the episode with the officers was relatively passive, his perception of the officer's initial act and his exaggerated feeling of being violated does represent a reaction which is far from purely situational. Just as the officer reacted to the civilian because he pre-categorized him as a challenge to law and order, so the civilian classed the officer as the type of individual who deliberately emasculates his fellows. And as a result of these pre-categorizations, each man was inspired to play a part which precisely corresponded to the misconception of his opponent.

We have tried to suggest in our discussion so far that the violent incident is cumulatively created by persons involved in it. As each sequence progresses, it takes on violence-prone connotations, and it displays reactions to match. We have seen that violence-prone connotations do not spring out of the incidents themselves, but pre-exist in the shape of unconscious assumptions. We have shown that these assumptions are both personal and social: they are personal, because they embody stable frames of reference; they are social, because they relate to other people. We assume that such assumptions take characteristic forms in the minds of Violent Men. What are some of these forms? We turn to this question in our next chapter.

5

The Violence-Prone Person:
A Typology

According to our analysis, we ought to be able to make sense out of a violence-prone person by studying his involvements in violence. We should be able to reconstruct the man from a sample of his violent acts. Why? Because we expect the situations that provoke a man to be stamped out of a common psychological mold. We expect his agressive acts to be guided and shaped by needs they subserve. We expect them to mirror characteristic models of conduct, salient feelings, and special sensitivities and needs. We expect them to express a man's "personality," in the technical sense of the word.

This view entered into our analysis of police incidents in Chapter 2, and we have tried to add flesh to it with illustrations linking encounters to persons in Chapters 3 and 4. In Chapter 4, we tried to show how the violent incident can provide an arena in which the recurrent concerns of two violence-prone persons can compete. In Chapter 3 we suggested that if only one participant in an incident is violence-prone, he would most likely shape the incident; it would be he who would feel provoked by the other person, and it would be he who would interpret the problem posed between them as calling for a violent solution.

We now arrive at the point where we are ready to test and expand this thinking through an analysis of the information obtained from the main body of interviewees. These statements derive from individuals who, as an aggregate, constitute probably the most prolific originators of violence of any group its size. This small number of people has been collectively responsible in the course of their lives for an immensely disproportionate share of the interpersonal aggression we have witnessed in California. Unless the trends are individually reversed, many of these persons will continue to generate strings of violent incidents to enrich our hypotheses and to provide us with newspaper headlines.

We interviewed 75 persons in our inmate and parolee samples. Four sets of the interview tapes became unavailable (could not be processed, could not be adequately identified, or were technically imperfect). The remaining 71 interviews were transcribed into a standard format, consisting of incident diagrams and checklists. Each such package was then submitted to a "study group" of the kind described in Chapter 1. The "study groups" questioned the veracity of two interviewees, but summarized the information for all 71 persons. The summaries took the form of personality sketches or pattern descriptions, in which the objective was to provide an informal but systematic picture of each interviewee's approach to his violent involvements, as it emerged from facts he had provided us.

Our last task was to try to evolve a typology that could reliably and validly accommodate the patterns of individual interviewees as we saw them. The typology, which will be described and illustrated in this chapter, was derived through a process of grouping and content analysis. Preliminary definitions came into existence deductively, were revised through cumulative classification of pattern summaries, and were then conceptually refined. The final definitions were applied in a formal analysis of the sample, with each interview assigned to the category which appeared to best describe it. These categories became the "primary themes" of the violent persons being classified.

In a second review of the pattern summaries, we assigned subsidiary categories to any case in which additional classification appeared to enrich the description (where the "primary theme" did not completely exhaust the pattern description). Such subsidiary categories proved useful in less than half (29 out of 69) of the cases, and appeared indispensable to none of them.

The reliability of our classification was tested by submitting a stratified subsample of 36 out of our 69 cases to a research psychologist for independent coding. Since we wanted to simultaneously test both of our grouping methods (the "study group" summary as well as the typology) the data were re-analyzed in the form of interview data rather than of pattern descriptions.

THE TYPOLOGY: A PRELIMINARY CHARACTERIZATION

Our classification consists of ten categories, each describing one approach to interpersonal situations that promotes the exercise of violence. The total code is intended as a catalogue of ways of relating to people which carry a high probability of degenerating into contact of an aggressive nature.

We can characterize one group of our categories as encompassing essentially self-preserving strategies, with violence used to bolster and enhance the person's ego in the eyes of himself and of others.

This type of activity can take many forms, and we shall merely sample them. Our classifications include:

1. *Rep Defending:* A category comprising persons who are allocated by public acclaim a role that encompasses the exercise of aggressive violence.

2. *Norm Enforcing:* A self-assigned mission involving the use of violence on behalf of norms that the violent person sees as universal rules of conduct.

3. *Self-Image Compensating:* Various types of compensatory relationships between low self-esteem and violence, comprising:

    a. *Self-Image Defending:* A tendency to use aggression as a form of retribution against people who the person feels have cast aspersions on his self-image.

    b. *Self-Image Promoting:* The use of violence as a demonstration of worth, by persons whose self-definition places emphasis on toughness and status.

4. *Self-Defending:* A tendency to perceive other persons as sources of physical danger which require neutralization.

5. *Pressure Removing*: A propensity (largely resulting from limited interpersonal skill) to explode in situations with which one is unable to deal.

Our second grouping of categories may be described as comprising persons who see themselves (and their own needs) as being the only fact of social relevance. Other people are viewed as objects rather than as persons whose needs must be taken into account (or must be countered or anticipated). The typology includes:

1. *Bullying*: An orientation in which pleasure is obtained from the exercise of violence and terror against individuals uniquely susceptible to it.

2. *Exploitation*: A persistent effort to manipulate others into becoming unwilling tools for one's pleasure and convenience, with violence used when other people react against this effort.

3. *Self-Indulging*: A tendency to operate under the assumption that other people exist to satisfy one's needs—with violence as the penalty of noncompliance.

4. *Catharting*: A tendency to use violence to discharge accumulated internal pressure, or in response to recurrent feelings or moods.

Table 5.1 lists the distribution of primary themes among the 69 members of our sample whose data were deemed valid. The categories are relatively evenly distributed over the institutional and parolee samples, and in the discussion that follows these subsamples are pooled. Among all four groups of interviewees, incidents of violence within institutions and violence in the street were obtained, but in the prison samples the ratio favored intramural incidents. This fact, which is partly a function of the emphasis of our interviews, proved irrelevant to the classification of individuals, although it may affect the relative distribution of types. Before we turn to this problem, however, we can describe our typology, and present one or two illustrations of patterns classified under each type. For this purpose, I shall follow the order suggested by the ranks in Table 5.1.

Table 5.1 Classification of Types of Violent Persons
Primary Themes Only (N=69)

In Rank Order		Frequency
SELF-IMAGE COMPENSATING		
Self-Image Promoting	19	
Self-Image Defending	9	
Total		28
Rep Defending		10
Pressure Removing		8
Exploiting		7
Bullying		4
Self-Defending		4
Self-Indulging		3
Norm Enforcing		3
Catharting		2

VARIETIES OF SELF-IMAGE COMPENSATING

Self-Image Promoting

Fully one out of four members of our sample could be cate-gorized as a "self-image promoter" in our classification scheme. According to our scheme, a self-image promoter is a man who works hard at manufacturing the impression that he is not to be trifled with—that he is formidable and fearless. He goes out of his way to make sure that people understand how im-portant he is and how important it is to him that he is impor-tant.

His fights are demonstration matches, and they are designed to impress the victim and the audience. The impression left is presumed to govern future interactions with him. He is worried that if he does not follow this course of action he will be mis-taken for a weakling or a coward. He also suspects that, if he did not "come on strong," he would be a logical candidate for victimization. Since he is so afraid of the possibility of being seen as weak or insignificant, one deduces that he suspects he is weak or insignificant.

The self-image promoter equates manhood with the advertised desire or willingness to fight. He involves himself in the affairs of others (usually uninvited and sometimes against overwhelming odds) because he sees such occasions as proving grounds and because his exaggerated self-esteem tells him he is needed. He tests people to see what he can get away with. If they fail to react, he concludes that his word is law; if they fight, he feels accepted among those who settle their differences at high noon on Main Street. But since he is unsure of himself, his efforts are frantic; he irritates others deliberately and pounces on them over-eagerly when they respond. He does not permit retreat or peaceful resolution of conflicts.

The self-image promoter may sometimes merely defend his self-image, but the affronts he responds to are prearranged. In other words, he manufactures situations in which his involvement or his status are likely to be questioned. The distinguishing feature of this type is that he behaves in such a way that predictable objections must arise to his behavior. When he is psychotic, his irrationality assures him an unacceptable superior status. In his blander guises, he self-righteously steps on people's toes or demands unwarranted respect. This game not only risks conflict but invites it.

Ideally, for the definition to apply, the person who is being classified ought to go out of his way to become known as an individual of considerable toughness and potency. At the same time, he ought to leave the distinct impression that he himself was not convinced of his own worth. The following word portrait reveals the sense of inadequacy of the self-image promoter more clearly than most of our cases. This case summary, like all the others transcribed in this chapter, was prepared by a "study group" comprising social scientists and nonprofessionals. The procedure for arriving at these summaries is described above (Chapter 1, pp. 24 ff.) .

This man has been flooded all his life with strong feelings of not being able to be what he should be.

He hasn't been able to phrase in any positive sense what he ought to be, but he has done a tremendous amount of thinking, verbalizing and struggling with what he wasn't.

He has particular difficulty in handling verbal exchanges—as he sees it. He has also been very scared, especially as a youth, that if he got into physical combat he would not be able to take punishment. It seems at least plausible to assume that a great step took place in his life when he was actually able to start challenging people and to engage in physical conflict. He talks about a phase when he almost knew that he was going to get licked and usually did get licked, but that he became man enough to take the beating. He feels that here he was able to express something rather than just play the coward.

In this kind of involvement, it got so that he was able to win battles. He could then anticipate that with some selection one was able to win. It was a shift from trying to get some feeling of adequacy out of purely negative performances.

The chorus is important to him. There has been a series of involvements where he has to some extent sought a reputation. There is a further element in the violence that gets back to his earlier preoccupation—a feeling of guilt, of being scared and of a lack of worthwhileness. It bursts forth, at times, in expressions of violence.

He remarked: "It drives me wild that I ain't any good or ain't the guy I ought to be"—and he tries to prove himself wrong.

He proves himself wrong by going out of his way to provoke fights to show he isn't afraid. He tackles the first "bully" he meets in a juvenile institution; he calls another one "punk" shortly thereafter. He arrives at a party mad at one of his friends and proceeds to show him how well he could have licked him by assaulting the first man he comes across; he bluffs a pressure clique in prison to demonstrate how brave he is, even though he confesses intense fear. And in every instance in which his little demonstration succeeds he feels great. As he puts it in relation to one victim, he was tempted to stand on the man's chest and "yell like Tarzan." There are a few moments of regret—such as after he has beaten his wife knowing she was right, but by and large he feels good both after picking a fight and after stomping his opponent.

We speak of "promoting" one's self-image, to distinguish this type of person from the man who merely "defends" his self-esteem; however, the distinction is often difficult to apply. In practice, the blustering tough is often the man who most easily reacts when his performance is questioned by the audience. But such reactions are not really passive; where they are not engineered or initiated, they are certainly welcomed, in the sense that the man sees conflicts as opportunities to be eagerly encountered. Following is a case of this kind:

> We have an awfully powerful young man here who conceives of himself as something of a human tank—who feels that he is undamageable and that anyone who tackles him is going to go out of commission. Picking on him means several things, depending on the mood he is in. If he is angry or tense or depressed, it takes very little to pick on him. In other instances, he may give the person an awful lot of latitude, particularly if he defines the person as the sort of individual he feels it is beneath his dignity to clobber, such as a diagnosed sex pervert.
>
> He attacks when he feels that some aspersion that counts is being cast on him as a person and as a tough person. This happens, for instance, where after his arriving at a prison (while relatively young) he is whistled at in the yard. Following this encounter, he goes and broods for awhile and then comes out seeking the people who whistled at him, making them confess that they are sorry, and then beating them up.
>
> In various incidents that he tells us about he is quite specific about the fact that he just doesn't teach people a lesson—he puts them out of commission. He doesn't just vindicate himself—he destroys people. Even in one case where somebody comes and stabs him in the arm, he is very proud of the fact that with his bare fists he reduced this person to a condition where he had to be carried away in a stretcher.

In several instances where someone foolishly tried to hurt him, he tells us that he immediately turned around and broke the person's jaw.

It sounds like a broken record, "I turned it off, and broke his jaw." There isn't much time wasted here on verbal discussion. By and large the sequences are, "somebody says something to offend me, I provide the person the opportunity to challenge me to a duel and then I make mincemeat out of him." In other words, he puts the other person in a position where he can justify viciously attacking him. He very seldom feels sorry for what he has done, including killing his father's common-law wife in an argument or beating and knifing his father. He feels no remorse because he has already decided to his own satisfaction that violence is not only justifiable but necessary.

One statement he makes which might tell something about what goes on in his mind as he approaches these situations, is the statement that he has "never lost a fight." It is obviously quite important to him not to come out at the bottom, and he starts his fights knowing that he will come out on top. He is apparently conpensating physically—where he knows that he can come out on top—for any encounter where there is some question about his being the victor.

Several of our self-image promoters appeared to be swimming against the tide, in the sense that they were either consistently unsuccessful in creating a favorable impression or seemed unable to assess the odds against them. Some demonstrated a propensity to challenge the wrong man at the wrong time all the time. In other instances, the promoting effort itself had a somewhat pitiful appearance, in that much thunder and grandiloquence appeared wasted on minute issues. Prisons, of course, are notoriously productive of this type of relationship between form and content. In depriving inmates of standard sources of identity and self-esteem, prisons vest trivial substitutes with considerable emotional connotations. It is for this reason that "staring" at a fellow inmate can prove fatal in prison or that lives are taken over two packs of cigarettes. It is thus also possible to find inmates whose existence revolves around games of domino, as in the following case:

> We have two images we can invoke for this man. First, there is an element of the wild and woolly west about him. There is some swaggering and drawing. Secondly, somewhat inconsistent with the first, we have the image of a young man who is trying to keep his head above water. What happens specifically is the following: Our man has the image of people here and there in the world around him who are likely to pick on him and who are not fair. In the face of such people, he feels it incumbent upon him to rise to the challenge and to provide a good show. Now, admittedly, the people whom he fights don't appear to be particularly vicious, nor do the issues appear very monumental. These are really not Main Street duels but side street duels. The most prominent of the fighting issues is cheating at dominoes. Typically, we have a situation where our man spots the evil one in the shape of another person cheating and he promptly calls the man's attention to what is happening. Then he decides that he isn't going to let it pass. His feelings are hurt, and you have a kind of spiral in which he stages a fight. A small fight will do, and when it has taken place he walks away reasonably satisfied because he has made his point.
>
> One or two other reasons for fights which are equally trivial are, for instance, an occasion in which he has occupied somebody's seat in the television room and where the other person comes along to reclaim it. He assumes that an unreasonable request is being made of him. Again he decides that this is the occasion for a duel and he draws as the other person makes a move toward his gun.
>
> Another occasion arises where we have him receiving a request that he can't meet, but he answers it in such a way that the other person feels victimized. When the man comes back to clarify the matter he gets the usual wild west type treatment, and the fight is on.
>
> There is an involvement of others in this man's fights in

the sense that there is some need that the show-down should be public and that everybody realize that our man is a fighting champion. But then the amateur battle takes place where there are bound to be few persons, because it is really a type of symbolic act.

By "symbolic act" we mean that the point of the fight is to demonstrate to our man's own satisfaction that he cannot be crowded, monkeyed with, challenged, cheated, unfairly treated, pushed. When he feels that someone is thus playing unfair, he feels that he must take a stand, that he must fight in order to show himself that he is no one's fool. There is no need to hurt, draw blood, do damage, destroy. A gesture suffices.

The duels are small time—they have a "spitball or marshmallow at thirty paces" flavor. But then, the issues are small. And this is the case, because our man lives in a world of minor detail. Where the world of others includes momentous battle grounds for matters of valor, power, prestige, or love, our man plays dominoes. He plays dominoes full-time, and it matters to him that no one should pull anything sneaky on him in this serious, important game. If someone does, he draws attention to it testily, and makes sure that the other understands that the gauntlet has been thrown. We call him the "Domino Kid."

Besides self-image promoting, the other form of self-image compensating we found in our sample—also relatively frequently—was the pattern of self-image defending. We should stress again that we see these subtypes not only as being psychological cousins, but also as making up a continuum along which distinguishing marks are matters of emphasis. Thus, the "defender" as opposed to the "promoter" would be *primarily* responsive to slights, whereas the "promoter" would prefer to initiate conflicts demonstrating that he couldn't be meddled with.

Self-Image Defending

The self-image defender is a man who is extremely sensitive to the implications of other people's actions to his integrity, manliness, or worth. His violence arises in the form of responses to challenges, retaliations to slights, or reactions against aspersions to his advertised self-conception.

Some self-image defenders react at once—or even anticipate what they perceive as challenges or insults. Others first worry about the implications of what has been done to them. (During the delay, they may either work up courage or develop evidence to hang the victim.) But there are those who not only attack a person long after the offending incident has escaped the latter's mind, but may even do so repeatedly. Another variation is to let one or two affronts pass, while watchfully waiting for the decisive one.

The self-image defender fights duels in the medieval or Western tradition. He may respond to challenges or may throw his glove at the offending party, sometimes to the latter's considerable surprise. In some instances, this type of person may even contrive a potential conflict situation to test the proposition that others will slight him. He can do so with full awareness, because self-image defenders are often conscious of their doubts, of their feelings of unworthiness, and even of their self-destructive moments.

When this type reaches psychotic proportions, the self-slighting part of the self may be compartmentalized and may take the form of voices that tell the person he is worthless. Another psychotic stratagem is to manufacture the cues that inform the individual that other people hold him in contempt. In summary, self-image defenders are perpetually on guard against the probability that others will denigrate or belittle them. And the reason for their stance is that they suspect that the point is really a valid one.

Again, there is a dimension of social skill that cuts across the type, in the sense that some individuals are more apt and successful defenders than others. In some cases, we have evidence that the person selects with care the individuals against whom to retaliate and discriminately picks the most strategic time and place for vengeance. In other instances, we see persons who almost seem to be at the mercy of their challengers or who show a distinct trend in the direction of choosing the wrong opponent and the least effective setting for survival. Following is an instance of successful self-image defending, if success is measured in terms of the ability to commit aggression with a minimum of risk:

This man makes a great deal out of not much in the way of unusual incidents. One has the feeling that he is careful about with whom he makes much out of a trivial incident. Part of it is in sizing up the ability and intent of the potential opponent. He tends to make a fuss over the way the other is acting, and arranges a great deal of verbal exchange without violence ensuing. In such a case, he will continue to crowd the exchange, but when there is a threat of violence he will back off. It seems, however, that this leaves him with a sense of disturbance, of not being the person he should be—so he can't just leave the situation. In one incident, he waited six months before he finally goes back and takes the victim by surprise. The violence resulted from the initial situation, which made him look somewhat of a coward in not responding to the challenge that was offered.

In almost every incident, there is a backing off and then a sort of skimming around with this, before he eventually does something, provided he can fix the time so that he can get away with it. One possible exception to this occurs when he is stalking a man and the man turns around and punches him and makes him look quite bad. But here it seems plausible that he himself actually came from behind. Even so, this is a clear incident where he crowded the other person because he couldn't let the thing go, in terms of his concern about not being the coward which he seems to demonstrate fairly frequently that he is. He wants to show that he is not backing out. "I am tough, but this isn't the time or place," is the line. And then, eventually, he strikes.

In one instance, he is victimized because something is stolen and it is returned, but he doesn't let it go. In the second incident, he is accused of staring at somebody whom he has not been staring at, and when the person makes an issue of it, he proceeds to escalate the matter until he has challenged the person. In another incident, he victimizes somebody else and a third person intervenes. He backs off, as he always does when the going gets rough, and then subsequently challenges the person who intervenes. He postpones the fight but ultimately attacks the person with fists. So, what we have here is a series of delaying moves, a fencing method, a lot of hoopla and noise and a lot of talk surrounding what essentially ends up in a back-stabbing.

By contrast to this description there is the pattern we sometimes refer to as "small-time defending," which is extremely unproductive, if not completely self-defeating. In the following case, it occurs with an individual whom we have cross-indexed as primarily a self-image defender, and secondarily, a self-image promoter. The reason for this cross-classification is not so much ambiguity as the fact that there is a preliminary step of "throwing one's weight around" preceding episodes that are essentially clumsy reactions to perceived affronts. We also note that this individual shows a mixed pattern in the temporal nature of his defending acts; at times he reacts instantaneously, whereas on other occasions he broods and works himself up to his act of vengeance:

This man is a not very astute, small-manner retaliator. He tries to throw his weight around and he doesn't have much, and when he is challenged in terms of not being treated as someone who has considerable weight, he resorts to immediate violence. It appears to be difficult for him to try to handle things verbally or even to try to pace his act of violence so that things will be to his advantage. Instead, he reacts immediately to the experience of degradation, initiating the violence himself without any apparent notice of the likely consequences of his being overpowered and seriously hurt. And he does tend to prolong these kinds of involvements—which in one case actually leads to his killing somebody. Specific incidents that illustrate the pattern include the following contrasting situations: A. The type of situation in which somebody says something to him which he can conceive of as degrading, such as throwing him out of the room or telling him to be quiet. Here he attacks, even in instances in which his own somewhat clumsy handling of the preceding events almost invites the other person to degrade him. B. The type of situation that we have referred to as involving time; the best illustration of this, combined with clumsiness, is a series of encounters with an officer who calls him a degrading name—calls him "Sunshine" in spite of the fact that he shows the officer the name that's printed on his I.D. card. Only after this has been going on for some time, and after a final precipitating situation in which the officer refuses to let him take a shower in the gymnasium, does he proceed to an encounter with the officer by walking past him without showing his I.D. card, thereby inviting certain self-destruction. Obviously, in a situation like this, it can be argued that the person is out of control. Once the gauntlet has been thrown at him, once he has engineered the situation in such a way that the gauntlet is thrown at him, he feels compelled to charge in—and he charges in with considerable anger. He charges in to certain, intense difficulties, as in the situation with the officer, and in battling a person much larger than himself. And this appears to deflect the intensity of his reaction to the flaunts that trigger these incidents, and the intensity of his feeling of shame and degradation.

The following case again illustrates the stewing and brooding that precedes retaliation among several of our men. In addition, the pattern shows the continuity we often observe between abnormal and normal reactions in the same person. In some cases, "sane" and "insane" violence seem to serve the same ends; in other instances, forms of abnormality are used as part and parcel of the person's standard reactions to the world. In the following case, for instance, the "self-image defending" includes a heavy component of paranoia, which feeds "evidence" to the man that he is being affronted or slighted:

> The man states himself that he has paranoid feelings. He cites a series of incidents in which, without any provocation from the other party, he gets the impression that he is being

laughed at or belittled in different ways, and he invariably responds with violence to defend himself against the belittling. In one particular incident, in which he leisurely fights before a crowd, he then turns on the entire group as if to demand reassurance and to ask if anyone thinks what he did was foolish, with the obvious intent to beat the hell out of them if they did think anything like that. Although he claims to feel relief after any given violent incident, he retains long time grudges. His vendettas tend to go on interminably with at least some of the parties with whom he's had violence.

We have a rather consistent picture here of his getting the feeling that people have contempt for him, or have a lack of respect for him. He wants to do something to try to handle this lack of respect, and the *one* thing that he does is to resort to violence. He admits to a series of fights where he was just sitting somewhere and imagined that someone was staring at him; there are other instances in which the thing which was questioned by the victims was his manliness. This occurs, for instance, in one situation in which he has just told his girl that he's not going to supply her with money to gamble with and a person at the same bar offers her money—thereby implying that he cannot take care of his woman; there is another incident, for which he served a great deal of time, in which he killed the girl he was living with because he felt he had evidence that she was unfaithful to him. There is a whole string of incidents involving a young man who had informed on him, and in this case not only did he assault this individual (like he did his other victims) without any warning whatsoever, but kept on doing this time after time, until the victim finally apologized and said he wouldn't repeat his infraction. So what seems to dominate him, among other things, is a kind of need to save his self-image and a need to hurt anybody who in any way whatever could cast aspersions on it.

Violence as a Social Obligation

The next most frequent pattern we find in our sample is that of rep defending, where violence is the fate entailed in a role; in other words, where the person commits violence because his social position, physical size, or group status obligates him to do so—a matter of "noblesse oblige," so to speak. This sort of person is expected to have violent involvements, and he has therefore come to expect the same of himself; he is aware of his role and of the need to defend it or to sustain it or to live by it. He knows he must champion his people, execute the guilty, and put on a good show. He may not derive much joy from this special awareness; some gang leaders, for instance, may try hard to negotiate, and some muscular "gorillas" may discourage aspiring youngsters who feel impelled to challenge them. But the assumed obligation pursues such persons relentlessly and hard.

Some "rep defenders" contribute actively to their own destiny; they may enjoy the spotlight, arise with alacrity when summoned, do their job with an extra dash of vigor, and take more bows than the audience demands. They may, at the slightest provocation, pull out and display their collection of accumulated scalps. But even where the "rep defender" goes out of his way to follow his star, his various involvements tend to remain a corollary of an assigned role rather than an expression of an internal need. Violence occurs on behalf of the role, or to maintain it, or in terms of obligations implicit in it.

From the description we may note that in superficial details the rep defender resembles the self-image defender. The rep defender rises to challenges and sees himself as the bearer of the sword in situations in which others are content to sit on the sidelines. The distinguishing feature here, however, is that this conception or self-definition originates externally, in society, rather than within the person. And the rep defender plays from a position of strength rather than of weakness. He starts with a knowledge of his own charisma, of his social support, of his loyal following and acknowledged physical power. Although his violent actions strengthen his "rep" or establish it, this reinforcement is a by-product of the violence, rather than its aim. The intent is to comply with social obligations or to satisfy the audience.

It is in the case of the rep defender that the "chorus" is

uniquely important as a cause of interpersonal conflicts. In some instances, we have evidence that in the absence of other people, a particular rep defender may even show a distinct pacifistic streak. Following is a case in point:

> This man can be described as a somewhat reluctant and pussy-footing champion. There is a rep motive in his action, but it is pursued cautiously, and in some instances, half-heartedly; and it appears as if in quite a few of these incidents he has to be pretty well pushed, or in one or two situations even tricked, into fighting.
>
> The pattern is one of trying to avoid fights, and he does appear to consider the probabilities of successful completion of his fights in deciding what action to take. The situation occurs repeatedly that he is either outnumbered, or that the odds don't look favorable. And in such instances he tends to arm himself or to get reinforcements. In one or two cases he tries rather clumsily to prevent the fight from occurring by restraining one or another of his more enthusiastic followers.
>
> He has one incident which takes place in an institution, in which he goes through a series of steps in response to somebody having made a racially derogatory remark to him, and then finally the fight breaks out in a situation in which the chorus is present. In this same sequence where, potentially a fight could break out, it doesn't. It appears that at least one reason for this is because he and the other person are alone at this point.
>
> There are several gang fights here. And these are not the stereotyped kind of gang fight (in which two groups of people challenge each other, and then proceed to make good on their challenges), but rather take the form of an initial effort to get along and one or two misunderstandings which finally result in a fight. In an instance in which the other gang does take the aggressive role in a somewhat underhanded fashion, the fight never really does get off to much of a start before the police arrive.
>
> In summary, what we have with this gang leader is an effort to do the very minimum of fighting that is necessary in order

to maintain his position in the gang, and a reluctant effort on his part to follow through on the aggressive overtures of his followers—when he has no other choice.

Most rep defenders seem less passive and hesitant and less dependent on direct social reinforcement. The individual defender will carry his obligations with him into any situation in which members of his group are not involved. The "chorus" is implicit and invisible—its strains may be heard in the background, but it need not be present; the actor has adopted his role, and he plays it without support or acclaim, as in the following:

The man appears to be defending his status as a gang leader, which in turn is expressed in his defense through violence of the integrity of his gang (which is his racial group of friends). There is no effort, as in many other situations of this kind, to try to justify violent acts in terms of some kind of code of justice. In other words, he does not argue that people are taking advantage of his friends, therefore, he fights. Rather it is that they are his friends, and he needs them, therefore, he fights. He is undoubtedly seen as a source of strength and support and is willing to help create and keep this image as a tower of physical strength for the group. It does appear, though, that he's not just a strong-arm-member of the group, but is actually a leader, and this leadership is maintained through his ability to use force to help the boys—to help protect his boys and take care of his boys.

Part of the man's role, which he maintains and defends, is to be someone who backs up his word—or rather, the game that he is in. He also maintains an image for his friends to the effect that he'll back up the games they are in. In keeping with this, he doesn't do much that one would consider sneaky (such as backing out of involvements in order to retaliate later). In his case, there is an ability to, or commitment to meet challenge with physical action. There's only just enough delay here to suggest that the man isn't completely foolhardy in trying to handle himself.

Even in the one or two instances where this man is not fighting for or with his gang, the pattern remains the same. He feels protective (a friend tells him that a bully has been beating up his little brother in prison) ; he determines to intervene and fight (he vows to settle the matter once he is imprisoned again) ; he goes about making good on the resolution (having been imprisoned, he locates the guilty party, arms himself, and invites the other man for a conference in the man's room) ; he plays fair (when the other man asks that the matter end at this stage, he agrees) , but firm (when the other man then arms himself to turn the tide in his favor, he stabs the other man) .

On the border between rep defending and self-image compensating are persons who have acquired some reputation, but who are sufficiently unsure of it or of themselves to feel the need to stretch public acceptance and credulity. Here is the "small-time" leader who seeks "big-time" acclaim and the acknowledged amateur pugilist who promotes a reputation of professional championship.

Following is an illustration of the pattern. Here is a man (classified as primarily a rep defender and as secondarily a self-image promoter) whose reputation is a stepping stone to more grandiloquently shaped fantasy. The man's past reputation—which is inherited (his father is a distinguished Indian chief) — carries him only to a point, and it is here where pathetic efforts at self-aggrandisement begin to affix patches to his frayed mantle:

We have decided that this man is a gunsel—an individual who plays kid's games in a man's world, where others are playing for keeps. Now, B-24 is an Indian and is known to have had some status in the Indian world before he came to prison— and he spends considerable time and effort to capture some status in prison. When he can't do this with actual confrontations he is not above embroidering those situations he has been involved in—in order to impress us with his importance.

Some of his incidents sound highly implausible; for instance, it always takes six guards to subdue him when he has gotten out of line. Those incidents that do have some plausibility about them involve his punishing somebody accompanied by at least one and usually several friends. In other words, it appears that he does want the reputation of being tough and violent, but when it comes to actually getting involved in violence he sees that he has sufficient reinforcement at hand so that he can get the reputation of being tough, without the risk.

There is absolutely no question that this man is recognized as somewhat of a leader by the Indians in prison, and he is using these Indians to help him accomplish his purpose by helping him to acquire a reputation for toughness. He can do this, because Indians as a group are known as tough. This is not to say that some of the Indians who have been used by him don't recognize this, or that they may not use him for the same purpose. But it does mean that he plays this game consistently, single-mindedly, and better.

Where we have admixtures of rep defending and self-image promoting, as in our posturing chief's son, it is the historical sequence which may determine the primacy of one category or the other. If the individual first "builds" a reputation, which is next accorded him and which he then defends, one would have to define him as primarily a self-image promoter. To the extent to which the person starts with an assigned role, which he tries to convert into a more substantial one, the classification should credit him with the advantage of his starting capital.

Panic in the Corner

Probably a majority of violence-prone persons may be classed as deficient in verbal and other social skills. In some instance, violence is clearly related to clumsiness, as in cases of armed robbery where the bluff is unconvincing, or in situations where forcible rape substitutes for courtship and seduction.

The most general and direct relationship between vulnerability and aggression is possibly that found among persons who use violence as an expression of helplessness, or as a last-minute effort to obliterate situations to which they are unable to respond. This type of violence is interpersonal when the "sore loser" wants not only to tear up the game but also to destroy his opponent.

Such is the case with our "pressure remover," the type of person whose repertoire of available interpersonal strategies is limited, or at least insufficient to cope with some situations. Where others may be able to solve a problem through nonviolent techniques, such as verbal persuasion, the pressure remover feels himself smothered, walled-in, or subject to overwhelming odds. He may try to cope with this dilemma with brief, desperate, half-hearted, floundering moves, but it is usually clear that he had arrived at the bottom of his resources before he started.

The object of violence is to remove the horns of the dilemma, or to destroy its source. The dominant feeling tone is one of irritation, helplessness, panic, or blind rage. The violence has a desperate, lashing-out character.

The victim is told that he has been crowding beyond the limits of what is bearable or what can be coped with. He may have received a prior warning (such as "stop!" or "I refuse to argue!"), but this may appear innocuous despite its undertone of despair. The victim may not even realize that his plausible arguments or reactions are being perceived as nagging or pushing or boxing-in or threatening. The "discovery" comes at the juncture where, in lieu of an expected countermove, there blossoms an effort at complete physical annihilation.

The simplest version of pressure removing is the effort of verbally unskilled persons to terminate altercations in which they feel unable to respond. Here violence not only expresses frustration but also represents a brusque and inadequate summary of the argument the person cannot verbalize. In addition, it constitutes an effort to suspend the offending level of interaction. The following pattern contains several instances of this sort of violence:

> The object of this man's fights is to eliminate a source of irritation, which generally consists of verbal materials. The reason this kind of material proves irritating to him is because

he himself seems incapable of handling his end of the argument. Now, even when the action that precedes the fight is
initiated by him he can't follow through. As, for instance, in
a situation in which he has issued a command to a homo-
sexual to curtail his sex life—the next step being an encounter
with a friend of the person to whom he issued the command.
And in this situation the only means he has at his disposal to
cope with logic and the effort to persuade him to desist is to
tell the friend to stop arguing with him. And he does this in
various ways, including turning away. It is only when the
other person persists in talking to him that he gets angry (as
he invariably does in such situations) and hits the other man.
In some instances, our man is subjected to all kinds of talk,
which gradually builds up an irritation to anything. In other
instances, there are only relatively short conversations where
he simply doesn't know how to respond other than to hit the
person. In some cases the argument isn't even directed at him,
or at least not by the party who finally gets involved in the
violence. The most unusual instance of this kind is a situation
in which his wife subjects him to a great deal of irritating
talk about her ex-husband and he finally is very murderously
inclined. He explodes, but not at his wife so much as at the
ex-husband, whom he hunts out and shoots. In a relatively
minor incident of the same kind there is a conversation which
is not directed at him but in which he feels involved.

What happens is not necessarily that he wins the resulting
fights, because his anger is such that he doesn't really sit back
and calculate the odds. Despite the fact that he is a very large
man, he in one instance attacks an individual even larger than
himself, and in at least two other incidents he tackles a person
who has a great many friends, and as a result gets hurt. But
the satisfaction for him—irrespective of the physical outcome
of the fight—is always the removal of the irritation. There is
the fact that where a response might have been expected from
him it is now silent and peaceful again, and he can go about
his business.

More complex versions of this pattern are characterized by

diversified settings for helplessness. The range of situations in which the person feels impotent may be so wide that at first glance the pattern may seem nonexistent or obscure:

> The group doesn't really have awfully much to say about this man, possibly because his pattern, if any, is somewhat evanescent. The one common denominator in his incidents appears to be that he acts violently when he perceives himself in a corner, or when somebody's doing something to him that threatens him. He reacts to threats which come in different shapes. The first incident, for instance, involves a situation in which he and a partner are burglarizing a motel room, and discover it is occupied by a woman. When she screams, they try to quiet her down by administering a well-placed blow on the jaw. This doesn't do the job, so they keep on beating at her (with the same objective in mind) until they have pretty well beaten her to a pulp. The obvious purpose of this action is not so much to hurt or to retaliate as it is to get this disturbing agent to stop disturbing.
>
> The same kind of flavor permeates an incident which takes place in the institution, in which the victim keeps on nagging at our man, trying to make him admit that he made a mistake in placing a bet on a sports event. And it gets to the point where he doesn't see any way of stopping this verbal incursion except with force.
>
> In three instances money is involved; in one case he has placed a bet, and in the other one he's appropriating money in a burglary, and in the third case, he has money being taken away from him while he's playing drunk in a bar. Again, this is an occasion in which he uses force because he doesn't know how else to get out of the situation (where his money is being taken) .
>
> It looks as though the reason why he uses force in order to extricate himself in situations like this, is because he does not dispose of the verbal skills that would constitute alternatives to force. This holds for the motel room scene, for instance, in which probably some less drastic ways of quieting the lady might have been attempted. It holds for the situation in which

he finds the other man with his hands in his pockets, and it certainly holds in the situation where he's having the slight altercation with his friend.

We would like to note that the money element is present even in a relatively dramatic incident that occurred two weeks after we interviewed this man. Here he obtained some publicity; what is involved was his common-law wife shooting him after an altercation which dealt with financial matters.

It is interesting to note the ironic twist to the events referred to at the end of this summary. Obviously, lack of social skill can be a two-edged sword; not only can it produce violence as a substitute for talk but it can also inspire explosions directed at the inadequate person by other people who find themselves unable to reach him in more conventional ways.

The Cost of Consuming People

Our typology contains several categories of persons who manipulate others as if they were objects. The most "normal" or "adult" form of this enterprise is probably that of the "exploiter," who is relatively mature because he does not take pathological pride in human suffering, nor adopt the social perspective of a suckling infant. Exploitation is an avocation, in which skill and energy are invested in convincing other people to supply commodities or services without reciprocation. Violence results from the unwillingness of at least some target-persons to freely enter into this type of transaction.

If a person wants to live a parasitic existence, in which he can enjoy the possessions and the labor of his fellows, he risks the possibility of having to resort to violence. Heretofore cooperative associates may rebel, and presumably easy marks may acquire new confidence and wills of their own. Well-meaning spectators and other busybodies may intervene to spoil a plot and complicate the game.

Exploiters are persons who actively engage in the enterprise of using others as objects to satisfy their needs. They are aware

of the fact that their preferred relationship to people runs head-
long into the needs of these people, so that radical techniques
must be used to insure reluctant compliance. The exploiter
makes no assumptions about the human universe rotating
around him, intending to be of service. This does not mean, on
the other hand, that the formulas evolved to circumvent the
intended victim's reluctance need be successful. Often, the exploiter jumps over-readily at the assumption that his routine cannot fail; often, his routine is clumsy and should never have
been permitted off the drawing board and past the rehearsal
stage. The less socially adept and perceptive the exploiter, the
greater the likelihood that he will have to invoke violence, or
that he will meet unexpected violence which he must counter.

The exploiter characteristically also does not view violence
as the necessary or desirable means to gain control over others;
on the contrary, he stands on the threshold of conflict like the
cook who has followed directions but who has burnt the roast.

The following pattern shows an exploiter who is sometimes
assaulted by his victims and sometimes reacts with violence because he prefers to keep his manipulations confidential. He reacts to accusations which publicize his role as a clumsy cheat and
does some self-image defending at this stage. The violence in
these sequences is presumed to convince spectators that the
accusations are undeserved; it is also obviously intended to
punish the victim for spoiling the unilateral game:

> This man's pattern appears to be one of taking advantage of
> others through procedures such as cheating in gambling, short-
> changing, blatantly running out on his wife, informing, and
> eventually using up his credit with the victims of his cheating
> efforts. He tries rather clumsily to ward off any open attack or
> reprisal, but when cornered, does fight. Once he senses that he
> might have the upper hand in the fight, he becomes extra
> aggressive and extra vicious. There's some feeling there of hav-
> ing lost status by the fact that his cheating has been uncov-
> ered. He may be trying to get back some sense of his own
> manhood or some sense of his own worth by being over-aggres-
> sive in a situation where he can look somewhat powerful.

In the sequence of events, it seems that once he is caught and people are ready to accuse him, or it's blatantly clear that he's been cheating, he isn't able to confess or he doesn't just run off and terminate the game but still tries to deny his role, and this leads to his getting in a corner, becoming aggressive toward the victims, and promoting the ultimate conflict.

This aspect in the pattern comes out in the interviewing process also, because in most instances one has to infer the dishonesty from circumstantial evidence. For instance, the police mysteriously arrive after his wife has damaged two of his teeth with no mention of his having done anything to her, and in two cases in which he is attacked after having gambled, there's no mention of any possible provocation for these attacks, although it is obvious he must have been cheating. And in an incident in the prison stockade, the first indication we have of his having been an informer, is that somebody comes and calls him a snitch, after which, as usual, he gets vicious.

A somewhat more cold and calculated—almost chilling—version of the pattern is embodied in the following description. In this case, we have a cool practitioner of applied violence. There is strikingly little social awareness in this exploiter, in the sense that other people are viewed by him as manipulable objects, pure and simple. There is also, in this person, a self-consciousness about violence which (as in our other example) borders on sadism:

> This man is a user of violence as an instrument to achieve personal ends. These ends change from one incident to another, and they usually involve a victim who is not prepared and is taken systematically by surprise. In several of the incidents, our man has gone about the business of exploiting other inmates—violence comes in when this situation degenerates. The most flagrant case involves a game which he and a partner play on loan sharks, in which they send their victim back and forth between each other when he asks to be paid, with the hope that payment need not occur. This apparently works in some instances but there finally comes a man who gets wise to what is transpiring—and he is promptly stabbed.

The coldest instance of instrumental violence in this interview is one in which our man wants to be transferred, picks himself another inmate almost at random and assaults him—and as a result gets transferred. In several of the incidents the inmate culture reinforces his role. This occurs, for instance, where our friend learns that a new inmate has informed on his brother and everybody is telling him to murder this man, in retaliation. He does end up stabbing the man—not with the intent to kill him but to bruise him. A couple of incidents are minor, but this doesn't deprive them of information value. For instance, it turns out that our man cannot just walk away from a situation in which somebody sat down on his chair in the television room; he has to use violence, he feels, because otherwise people may have contempt for him. He definitely feels that when he is standing as a look-out for a friend who is collecting debts it is his obligation to intercept and fight the victim when he flees.

It appears that with him violence seems necessary and proper. We have here a man who uses every opportunity for violence provided him. And he not only strikes first, but he is extra careful to be systematic in the preparation and execution of his violence.

The Joy of Inflicting Terror

The most unpleasant type of violent person (both from the vantage point of society and that of the victim) is undoubtedly the bully, who goes out of his way to be unfair, unmerciful, and inhumane in his violence. Empathy with the bully's perspective is difficult because of the fact that he derives satisfaction from the suffering of others, and because he is intent on protecting his immunity to the point of cowardice. One generally assumes that this type of alien disposition must spring from very strong motives which push the person to abandon otherwise universally held premises and feelings. The most probable motivating force is intense fear. This seems reasonable because of the fact that it is fear that the bully goes about generating in other people, and it is fear over which the bully makes such a point of exercising control.

The bully is the artisan of violence, for whom force is a tool or an instrument self-consciously employed to inspire terror and to increase pliability. Violence is the coin of the realm, and the balance of trade is maintained in one's favor.

Bullies may espouse quaint power-centered theories and may claim to follow simplistic approaches to the process of influence, but the bully is really the man who enjoys the experience of exercising effective violence—and the clue to this disposition is the habit of invoking violence wherever it can make an impression to be savored. What is wanted is the physical and psychological effect of violence on other persons, which can cement the bully's conviction that there is nothing to fear in fear itself because it is, after all, always present in others.

Bullies are not calculating and cool, effective and impressive, although some of them occasionally give that appearance. The bully makes his own task easier by not risking even encounters; he picks on weak people because the effects of terror are most easily secured with them; he gives no quarter, because lenience takes away the edge or full measure of his enjoyment.

The pure bully uses violence to secure power, obtain goods and services, and keep others in their place or at a distance. Violence is invoked as a tool in a variety of situations, because the means are more important than the ends. This polymorphous exercise of violence distinguishes the pure specimen of bullyhood from the bully (exploiter), who has the same strongly motivated faith in violence, but who is more specialized and pragmatic. The bully (exploiter) uses violence to secure cooperation from his victims; he uses it exclusively for this end, and uses no other means. What makes such persons primarily bullies is not only that they go out of their way to use violence but that they reveal a disproportionate emphasis on its use. Thus, they will selectively approach victims who are particularly helpless, or they will expend considerably more viciousness than the "exploiting" part of the job requires. Bullying is wasteful. What matters to the bully is not that violence "works," but that it impresses and damages and intimidates.

With the bully (exploiter) as opposed to exploiters (bullies), the classification problem is one of emphasis. We have a person classifiable as primarily a bully if he is primarily a dispenser of violence—if bullying is his main dish, and the exploitation is his gravy.

The following description of a "classic" bully not only contains all the elements we have mentioned (including those suggestive of the dynamics of this pattern) but also illustrates the relationship of the bully to some of our other types. We see the bully as an exploiter who gets carried away with his more drastic tools, but also as a perverted caricature of the self-image defender. It is possible that the magnitude of the bully's reaction reflects a degree of personal inadequacy much more pronounced than the self-doubts of other violent persons:

> Without making a value judgment, we think it would be fair to say that this man is a consistent, unmitigated, low-level heel, who has never had what one could describe as a fair fight. The pattern in a variety of situations (starting with a few boyhood escapades, and terminating with adult felony assaults) involves his taking advantage, unfairly, of somebody who is in a weakened position. As a second step, he will, when the other person gives some indication of weakness (begs for mercy or asks him to stop), accelerate his violence, and he here describes himself as becoming angry. And at this point he resorts to walking over the person's chest, or stomping on his face, or doing any number of other things that are obviously extremely cruel.
>
> One consistent pattern with him is that he will do almost anything to create a situation in which the other person is at a disadvantage before he strikes. He will use deception; he will maneuver the situation physically. And as soon as he has achieved the objective of being able to surprise the other party, or being able to place a blow which creates an immediate advantage for him, he proceeds—but not before. He will also use people other than his victims. There is one classic instance of this in which he makes a pact with a girl to fight a person who is hunting for him, and then leaves the girl to

do all his fighting. This episode not only illustrates his tendency to use people, but also exemplifies his outlook toward
the female sex, where we even have two or three instances in
which he shows no hesitation about fighting girls. And he as-
sesses them pretty much like he does his male opponents.

The general way in which violence occurs with him is that
he evaluates instantaneously a situation in which it becomes
possible. It even occurs in instances in which the other person
involved, the potential victim, is in the process of complying
with demands, or is in a conflict with him in which he had
previously obtained the upper hand, but now somehow the
tables can be turned, and advantage can be taken of this. And
this second type of situation is important in that before the
fight starts he might have experienced fear, and part of the
reaction may be against his own fear. As a matter of fact, fear
is a kind of theme that runs through the sequences in a variety
of ways. It occurs very directly in any situation in which the
other person does, objectively speaking, have the advantage,
and he can't do anything about it. Then he has no compunc-
tion whatsoever about running, about giving up. It occurs in
that he initially fights, as we have indicated, when he himself
has experienced fear, and it occurs very blatantly in a situation
in which the other person shows fear; that is, in which there
is this request for mercy, or some other indication that the
other person is afraid of him; and then he becomes extremely
furious, and he shows no mercy whatsoever. And what one
might infer from this is that in all of these situations what he's
really doing with his violence is handling his own fear. That
is, he is a bully in the classic sense—a person who acts extremely unmercifully toward others because of the fact that he
himself (as he introspects) feels terribly small and disadvantaged.

The Omnipresent Threat

Whereas the bully goes to great pains to fight fear in himself,
the next most frequent type, the "self-defender," cultivates fear,

and uses violence to deal with people he fears. This does not mean that some of the threats in the self-defender's life are not concrete, objective, and urgent; but, since they occur repeatedly, we must suspect creative effort. At minimum, the self-defender must have a propensity to appear in the most dangerous places at awkward junctures; more usually, he counters vague insecurity by locating it where he can grapple with it, among dangerous people who surround him.

Self-defenders commit their violence as a means of attaining safety, or refuge, or the neutralization of danger. They fall on a continuum from accurate probability-assessment to complete subjectivity. On the one end of the continuum lies the person whose ability to diagnose real danger is rivaled only by his skill in systematically coping with it; next comes the precipitant practitioner of the "first strike," who attacks first and asks questions later (often too late to profit from the innocence of the replies). There is also the individual whose obnoxious demeanor gives him a penchant for making enemies or for creating unfavorable social situations. Further along the continuum is the person who easily panics, or whose fantasy is peopled with powerful and aggressive enemies. Lastly, there is the "paranoid self-defender," who is engaged in a continuing battle against an awesome conspiracy of his own creation.

The strong element of fear as the person's almost exclusive motive is exemplified by every one of these patterns; it shows us how precarious the existence of the typical self-defender really is; he may secure momentary peace by coping with specific threats, but he always discovers another danger lurking around a nearby corner. The following is an extreme case.

> This man shows a pattern which is dominated by basic fear of doom and the conviction that others are trying to kill him. He sees in many of the personal exchanges that he has become involved in threats upon his life. Once he perceives this threat, he panics. He becomes enmeshed in extreme violence in an effort to handle this panic. He seems to resort to violence as a way of being assured that the other party is not going to kill him—at least, that is the way he feels. It seems ironic that he

engages in the very thing of which he is scared to death. Now, in the last incident, it almost looks as if there is a flaw in his pattern, because here is an incident in which he is almost convinced that he is going to kill somebody and he doesn't kill him but feels that the price that the other person pays for not getting killed must be to provide him with assurance, in the form of statements that can be believed, that the incident is concluded. The point is that he can be reassured here.

We have noted in this man the kind of game which occurs both inside and outside the institution. When he is young he charges his brother with a rock because he is convinced that his brother is going to kill him (with a small baseball bat). Also outside, he shoots and kills the wife of a candy store owner because she screams when her store is being held up. Again, he has the feeling that he is going to get killed, so he is going to get her first.

In prison, the same kind of thing happens when he gets the same feelings. Usually, of course, there is not really any occasion for him to fear for his life, but he gets the feeling that he is wronged and he reacts with anger and becomes very dangerous at this point. Even the slightest statement that could possibly signify the possibility of somebody having designs on him, mobilizes this very intense fear. He then feels the need to defend himself against his "attackers" and he charges in and commits violence.

The Liabilities of Adulthood

Whereas most of us learn at an early age to at least take into account what others want, some adults continue to base their lives on the premise that the only purpose of other people is to cater to them in every possible way. This type of orientation can eventually produce a tantrum, when the patience of even the most nurturing providers becomes exhausted in the face of patently ridiculous demands and expectations.

We call such persons "self-indulgers," because they view the world from the vantage point of infants, and toddle about their way expecting to find a crib or breast around every corner. Unlike the case of the exploiter, there is no intent here of deliberately taking advantage of others. There is, rather, the view—which is held naively and in good faith—that one's own wishes must invariably prevail. This premise is given the status of a natural law.

The self-indulger thus procedes good-naturedly on the assumption that his own welfare must be of primary concern to others. He deals with his acquaintances and relations on the basis of this assumption. There is no concern here with the needs of other people, because these are irrelevant to the basic scheme. Information about the views and desires of others is not perceived. Their discontent is never noted until it has blossomed into full rebellion.

When the moment of truth arrives, the self-indulger sees people suddenly and mysteriously turning on him and feels compelled to deal with unprovoked aggression. His indignant reply reflects the magnitude of his hurt. At long last he must assimilate—with wonder and indignation—evidence of the unreliability and perfidy of man.

The almost comically naive orientation of the self-indulger becomes obvious when we examine concrete incidents in their careers. The following pattern, for instance, includes the most casual defiance of all manner of social convention, with a reaction of pained surprise in the face of predictable consequences:

> This man is very much concerned that the world may not be a place which has reasonable respect for humanity in general and for some humans in particular; yet he appears to approach his own interpersonal relationships as if the world ought to let him do anything he wants, anyway he wants to do it, at any time he cares to do it. He becomes very upset when the world does not live up to these expectations. Incidentally, the way the world treats him would be much more manageable from the philosophy that he expresses about the way the world is, but it appears that, at least implicitly, he's upset when the Southern police don't treat him (a Negro) as if he had extra privileges beyond his regular privileges. He double parks in

front of them, threatens them, and crowds the system, to say the least. He's concerned when his wife finds him with another woman; but even when, as far as he knows, it's been his transgression, he becomes very upset at her being annoyed about this.

Things do not seem to happen immediately but rather, over a period of time. There's some brooding, and some working out of the position that there's been unfairness done him and that there is the need to punish. Then he gets into the violence trying to handle the fact that people are not treating him as a deserved privileged person. In addition to this procedure, there seems to be an overwhelming elephantine quality about him. He has a penchant for associating with ineffectual persons in futile efforts to commit unmanageable transgressions; then, when he gets himself into a corner, he tries to extricate himself in ways that are doomed from the beginning. But he somehow still manages to extract from these experiences nothing but a continuing feeling that the world is an unfair place. This feeling then leads him to act violently. He plays his clumsy acts on a great variety of stages; in prison he stupidly challenges two other inmates, and flaunts the guards. In burglaries it is both his partners and his victims; in his marital affairs, his wife. It appears that this man simply has a penchant for doing the wrong thing and has the nerve to punish others for his overwhelming awkwardness.

The Burden of Dispensing Justice

There are some persons whose violence is ostensibly in the public interest and in the service of society—although the service is rendered informally and voluntarily, sometimes over the protests of its beneficiaries. This type of person—the "norm enforcer"—acts as a one-man posse, who feels that he knows when rules have been violated; his conception of how violators must be dealt with is primitive and direct, and invariably involves his active participation. There is a superficial resemblance to rep defending in this pattern, because violence ostensibly occurs on behalf of others or in the common interest. The real parentage of this type, however, is the self-image promoter, who feeds his self-esteem by drawing attention to himself. When he interferes in the affairs of others he advertises his role rather than their problems. "Justice" serves as a convenient excuse for ostentatious interference. Unfortunately, this often is the only motive on record, and we must infer the self-doubt which we assume really inspires the performance.

Whereas rep defenders are elected to responsibility, "norm enforcers" enter their career on a self-appointed basis. Strictly on their own, they undertake the task of becoming the conscience of society and the insurer of its integrity. They exercise violence as a matter of principle rather than as a social obligation. They do not require others to come to them for help or for advice (no one does); they do not need anyone to nominate them as champions or to recognize them as spokesmen for their people (no one does); they are convinced that the job needs to be done and that they must do it.

These men perceive themselves as arbiters of dispute, as slayers of dragons, as protectors of the weak, and as dispensers of justice; they define themselves as policemen, prosecutors, judges, and executioners. They patrol their beat alertly searching for black knights carrying off maidens. They attack any abuser of power or violator of decency they spot, often without much prior notification. And although they may view themselves as exercising whatever due process is due, this is seldom the way they are perceived by others.

Their public image is that of unpredictable aggressors and of interlopers in the affairs of their peers. Because their entry onto the stage is unplanned and unannounced it leaves the villain abused, the onlookers confused, and the hero or victim ungrateful.

The following illustration shows that norm enforcers may sometimes operate in private encounters (involving relatives and acquaintances), while at other times they pretend to arbitrate relatively public and large-scale conflicts:

> This man appears to fit the "defender of justice" pattern; particularly for friends and for his own brother. He perceives

himself as having a reputation to maintain as one who does not let people take advantage of his special friends and family. As soon as he perceives that the other party is going to resort to violence, he sets out to arrange the situation so that he will get in the first blow. He does not necessarily start every incident with the instigating of violence. He does make an effort to establish his reputation as a defender of justice on a verbal level. His first effort would be to get the other party to plead guilty. If such happens, then no violence need result. But if the other party will not plead guilty, and admit that he had committed an injustice to his friend or brother, then the man will set up the situation in rather elaborate form so that he is almost certain to win and so that he will have the opportunity for the first blow in the violent exchange. He also (to be consistent with his reputation) goes to extreme lengths to make this move so as to be referred to as an executioner. He is a protector who uses real violence and does not hesitate when the consequences of this violence include actual murder.

In one of the incidents, he is in one institution, and his brother in another. A new inmate arrives, claiming to be the brother's friend. Subsequent information reveals that the man is not only making a false claim, but that he even owes the brother money. When our man demands to be paid, the other puts him off; he also goes about the place asking for a knife. Despite the fact that the evidence indicates that the knife may be intended for other creditors, our man takes no chances; he invites the other for a cup of coffee, and—once safely in the crowd milling around the dispenser—he stabs him.

Aggression as a Therapeutic Agent

Our final type consists of "catharters," who attack others to release accumulated emotions, so that the identity of the victim becomes a matter of incidental importance. Cues and incentives to violence are in the "catharter's" mind, and the external occasions for it are arbitrarily selected; in this sense what goes on seems to fit the traditional picture of the indiscriminate exploder, for whom violence liberates accumulated tension. But this is not completely true as a statement of what occurs, because the timing of violence is always tied—and systematically tied—to specific feelings and needs; moreover, this kind of violence is purposive violence: the "catharter" is a person who has learned that by becoming aggressive at key junctures in his life he can successfully cheer himself up.

In other words, for "catharters" violence is not really a social response. Violence satisfies a personal need, rather than being a way of reacting to others. A precipitating incident generally starts when the person notes in himself urges and moods that he interprets as a call to arms. He then sets out in search of conflict, and generally finds some, because he will go to any length to manufacture a situation is which he can claim that violence is appropriate. "Appropriate" here can mean as little as that someone walked by him and made himself available as a victim, but it can also entail an elaborate ritual of "picking a fight" or justifying aggression.

The feeling tone preceding this game may range from depression and tension to boredom and desire for excitement. It may arise out of disappointment and frustration, or emerge out of a slow evening on Main Street. The resulting conflict tends to be emotionally tinged to match. It can vary from grim and intense to devilishly lighthearted and "fun and games." To the victim, of course, the distinction is academic, because he faces the problem of being attacked without apparent cause. He—as well as most bystanders and observers—usually concludes that they have experienced flagrantly irrational behavior by an obvious maniac. However, the reason why the play is cryptic is simply because the aggressor is the only surviving member of the original cast and because the rest are hastily hired understudies who have not been supplied with the script.

The following illustration represents the "lighthearted" extreme of the type, in which the motivation for violence is boredom and the desire for entertainment. Other forms of the pattern feature more negative emotions, such as extreme tension and bitterness. No matter what the feeling, it impels the person to aggressive activity, because he has come to associate this with relief and peace of mind:

It looks as if the main fights, or at least the most dramatic sets of sequences of fights, occur with this man when he wants to amuse himself, or himself and others, by spontaneously attacking casual victims whom he happens to encounter. One fairly spectacular sequence of this kind consists of him pulling drivers out of cars that patronize a drive-in and assaulting them physically. And a second sequence occurs as he and a friend go from one party to another on a weekend, antagonizing people. In the course of this expedition they assault gas station attendants, their host at one of the parties, and a set of guests who happen to arrive on the scene at another.

While in prison, our man appears to be somewhat careless in baiting several people in succession in such a way that by the time he's finished, his situation looks precarious to an outsider.

The role of others in this man's involvement is not always the same. In some situations there is team work involved and he appears to enjoy a kind of camaraderie with another violent individual. And there is some team spirit in this kind of sport. In other situations he's an entertainer, acting for an audience. In still other instances he gets himself into a violence-prone situation, counting apparently with the support of people who, assessing this same situation, decide that they don't wish to become involved. And then he proceeds anyway; since he has, at this point, no real option. There also appears to be some tendency for him to gain an unjustified feeling of immunity. That is, it looks as if he does not take very careful stock of the odds in several of the situations in which he encounters violence.

Another point is that after the sequence of events begins, he won't back out, he won't change his strategy until he's either knocked out or the fight's over.

It also appears as if, in at least some of the situations with this individual, the word "strategy" isn't as applicable as the word "fun." That is, there is a kind of spirit of enjoyment and levity about the proceedings. And it is as if he doesn't take account of the fact that the victim may not share the enjoyment as much as he and his friends do. (Although in at least one instance, the enjoyment was so infectious that one victim got into the spirit of the game before he was flattened.) There appears to be some evidence here that at least in the majority of instances violence for this man might be an end in itself. The clearest situation where this occurs is at a party where the guests discover that another set of guests is arriving, and our hero announces that whoever they are, he's going to lick them. And as soon as the first of the new group of guests arrives, our friend hits him in the face with a mop that he happens to have been mopping the floor with.

PROBLEMS OF VALIDITY

Do the classifications we have proposed correspond to reality? The question is fair, but it is difficult to answer. Typologies, after all, are invariably fictions. Whenever we group complex items, such as people, we bring together only some of their attributes. With respect to other features, the in-groupers may differ as much as do their fellows at large. Moreover, the properties a typologist honors are the properties he thinks are of interest. These qualities rarely stand out in the eyes of beholders— or in the eyes of the individuals being typed—as essential or central.

The aim of our study was to make sense out of violence; our typology classifies people in terms of their propensity to violence. True, violence here is part and parcel of a person's social orientation; but that does not greatly change the matter. Although we record general characteristics, these are always characteristics related to violence. This means that other qualities are neglected, and some of these can be important. Any of our types can bring together saints and sinners, idiots and geniuses, schemers and obsessed men. The types can be pure in our terms only, while being conglomerates with respect to more important matters.

Granted this fact, one can ask whether we have validly accomodated our objective. Have we accurately classified people in terms of the forces that shape their violence? Again, our reply must be inconclusive. For one, violence (like any other form of human conduct) is a brew of many ingredients, all of which in some sense define it. We have focused on some information only—the type of information that documents the sort of explanation we favor. Ours is a typology of interpersonal orientations, because such is our theory. Our portraits may look plausible to someone who shares our view of aggression as a byproduct of social conduct. But anyone who feels that violence is born in childhood, or that it is situationally determined, may question the validity of our characterizations.

Theory and potential controversy enter elsewhere also. Clearly, our types are not merely groupings of observed facts. Frequently, they describe relationships among facts, and they even postulate causes for behavior. The validity of such clinical inferences can be only indirectly established, and it cannot be substantiated by pointed at the data we have collected.

We stand on more solid ground when we defend the integrity of individual classifications. Within the limits of our categories, we have some safeguards against arbitrary assignment of persons to types. We benefit from the fact that our typology is derived from case materials prepared by professional and nonprofessional staff. This method insures against narrow pre-classifications. Nonprofessionals have intimate acquaintance with the data, which permits them to screen out characterizations that are theoretically plausible enough, but that are incompatible with the experienced acts of comparable people in comparable situations. (Such "real life" experiences, of course, are not necessarily generalizable, and social scientists can help guard against the temptation of making too much of unique encounters.)

But what about the "facts" we have collected—the data themselves? Can we assume that these are valid? The chances are probably excellent. Our peer interviews were designed to gain the trust of informants, and we have evidence that the procedure worked. Often, our nonprofessional researchers learned that their presence made interviews possible. Many of our subjects were candid to the point of self-incrimination. The sample included offenders of notoriety, who had in the past proved impervious to official questioning. One such inmate spent several days regaling us with detailed descriptions of unrecorded transgressions, some of which we informally verified later.

In most cases, our code-numbered interviews and the coded record transcripts were found to supplement each other. As a rule, an interviewee would furnish us with at least one or two incidents already noted on his dossier. The details on record, to be sure, rarely provided information to fully explain the person's violent involvements. Causes were noted, but they tended to cover information needed to attach and to gauge blame, or to arrive at a casual understanding of precipitating interactions. Thus, the record often tended to give an impression of heterogeneously and malevolent motivated violence where we found patterns.

But we did encounter instances where the official record was factually more accurate than our interviews. Some rapists and chronic sexual exploiters would not talk with us at all. Several who did exercised prudent censorship in describing their involvements. They tended to limit their narratives to episodes less shocking and reprehensible than those on record. We found in such cases, however, that the interview accounts reflected the same exploitive orientation that permeated the material on the record—and usually the victims proved similar in kind. The following case concerns one of these persons, whom we classified as an exploiter (with a secondary theme of self-indulging) :

> Here is a man who unmercifully takes advantage of women, and then gets extremely indignant when they show the slightest resentment. His record, which he does not discuss with us, is a long and redundant series of episodes in which he sexually assaults a collection of women ranging in age from kindergarten to senescense. (And in which, in a large proportion of instances, he also has the gall to extract money from his victims.) In addition to this he has another game that he plays with married women, forcing his attentions on them and then extracting blackmail money from them by threatening to tell

their husbands that they submitted. The episodes he does discuss with us show the same patterns in a slightly less blatant fashion. In the first of these sequences, he ostensibly helps a female in distress by evicting her common-law husband, but then it turns out that his real motive was to move in as a substitute, and when this scheme is unsuccessful he becomes extremely annoyed with the intended victim.

In another instance of unmitigated gall that he relates, he steals his current flame's complete bankroll, gambles it away, becomes indignant when she questions him on the subject, beats her up and then lies down to sleep on her bed. Here he is painfully surprised in more ways than one when he wakes up to find himself cut to ribbons.

A similar episode takes place in another context, involving a lady whose acquaintance he made and in whose case there is a more attractive and younger niece residing at the same address. And as soon as the lady goes to the kitchen to prepare coffee for him, temptation lurks and he gives in. That is, when she returns from the kitchen, she finds him in the process of seducing her niece. Again, of course, he is the object of some indignant attentions which he fails to understand.

In other words, there is a consistent tendency on his part to view women as objects for exploitation. And then the added factor that any resistence whatsoever on the part of his victims is viewed by him as provoking and as unjustifiable. It is of course one of the consequences of the kind of game he plays, that he has repeatedly come to the attention of authorities. However, there are many episodes that precede each of the unsuccessful encounters that end him in prison.

Building on Fabrication

We have excluded from our typology the two interviews whose validity was questioned by our nonprofessional colleagues, and whose substantiation through recorded information wes not satisfactory. Following is the text of the study group summary of one of these two interviews:

There are three indications that this man was fabricating most of the information he supplied us with. First, this is the impression of an interviewer, who records that "it was too bad this guy was such a liar"; the interviewers felt that here was a blatant effort to impress them. Second, we would expect serious displays of public violence of the kind claimed by this man to be matters of public record—and we don't have a single incident officially noted in his parole file. Third, there is the internal evidence.

This man claims to be a vicious kind of superman, an avenging killer. The image he traces for us is that of the man who in cold blood avenges injustice at its source, by putting a gory end to those responsible. He walks into a juvenile institution—he says—and is nudged by a guard. Next thing he is standing in the Warden's office, explaining to the Warden about necessary changes. The Warden pays insufficient attention to the message, and is knifed. The rich fantasy life behind this episode of grand vengeance also permeates other stories. For instance, there is the gang fight, ended by our man with a shotgun—brutally used on the leader of the rival gang. Again, the image he conveys is of a definite, cold-blooded, brutal act.

He also claims to enjoy violence, and he certainly enjoys talking about it. He endows his incidents with an almost orgasmic quality, and builds up to the climax in a series of delicious delays. The violence, or the telling of it, is exciting.

There is one incident which rings true out of the group, and here the man admits stabbing someone by mistake. He assumed a knife that was being manufactured was intended for him, and it wasn't. The suggestion also is, judging by the mass of scar tissue on his face, that his experience with violence may not be that of the conquering dispenser of Justice, as he claims—but rather of a man who repeatedly has been taught the error of tackling the wrong people.

It would be hasty to discard this type of information as useless, even though our facts are probably largely fictitious. In dealing with this person, it is no doubt important that his fantasy life is peopled by acts of cynical brutality and bloody retribution against authority. There is directionality and pattern here which rests as securely on psychological foundations as would the bloody acts being described. In fact, the sense of inadequacy and some paranoid flavor are highlighted by the need to fabricate the information. By virtue of the individual's membership in our sample, we know that he has been involved in acts of violence; we can presume that these have a far less lofty aspect and definitive outcome than those with which the person credits himself. The discrepancy is one which could be of considerable diagnostic and therapeutic importance in more intensive work with this individual.

In other words, even fabrications, when subjected to the type of analysis we have suggested, can provide testable hypotheses and potential means for the production of personal change.

But What About Reliability?

Our entire picture, of course, would fall into the realm of poetry if an independent judge could not duplicate the classifications. At best, our typology might constitute insight without applicability; at worst, it could imply that we had focused on irrelevant or idiosyncratic variables.

The independent rater (Dr. Jeanne Block) did not find the classification task a particularly easy one. She reported that the coding did not resemble other types of judgment; although clinical experience was applicable, it had to be refocused, because the person's use of violence—rather than his general orientation—was at issue. Dr. Block also reported that the choice of one primary category was in several instances a difficult one to make.

Thirty-five interviews were independently typed. The results of this operation showed 7 out of 35 judgments to yield major discrepancies; in 16 instances, the types corresponded exactly, and in 12, closely related or functionally equivalent categories were used. This last group requires comment and has the most important implications for the nature and scope of our typology. We shall, therefore, discuss it first.

The Problem of Thematic Emphasis

More than half of the twelve "related" classifications involved two categories; the first of these is that of self-image defender, which in four out of six instances was transmuted by the coder into self-image promoter. In one of these cases, the classification read "norm enforcer (self-image promoter)," but we can include this in the group because of the fact that norm enforcing is clearly a specialized subclass of promoting.

The preferential use of the "promoting" label indicates that our rater saw in most self-image compensation some initiative in the shape of readiness to fight, or some extra satisfaction with the opportunity for violence. Whereas this does not invalidate the conceptual distinction between advertised pugnaciousness and overeager responsiveness to slights, it does show that this distinction is hard to apply. The self-image compensator is rarely a pure defender or a pure promoter; if he tends to *react* to slights, it is also true that he does so with alacrity, so that the initiative for the conflict becomes difficult to assign; further, responses to perceived challenges tend to add up to an aggressive stance. Conversely, challenging involves goading people into reactions that can be "defended" rather than "promoted." Finally, there is coder preference. Our rater seemed oriented toward initiative on the part of the self-image compensator; she thus placed the weight primarily on the promoting effort, rather than on the defending acts.

The second group of functionally related discrepant classifications involved pressure removers, three of who were converted into "self-indulgers (pressure removers)" or, in one case, into a pure self-indulger. The link between these themes is a chronological one. By and large, pressure removing is the last resort used in self-engineered dilemmas. Most often, the type of person who operates at a level of maturity in which he expects others to comply with his needs (or at minimum, who assumes that they will refrain from being obstacles in his path) is most apt to blindly explode when he encounters what he sees as non-amenable and non-cooperative people. Our original classification focused on this final act, whereas the rater placed heavy emphasis on its presumed antecedents. Again, the discrepancy revolves around differential attention to the actor as against the incident, in a standard chain of related psychological events.

PATTERNING PROBLEMS: THE COMPLEX VIOLENCE-PRONE PERSON

We have noted that in 7 of our 35 cases, independent classifications produced pictures at variance with the original coding. In some instances this difference was clearly attributable to different weights assigned to different aspects of a given person's violence. Thus, two of our rep defenders were seen as bullies (by the rater) because in both cases victims were manhandled and were fairly thoroughly and systematically destroyed. The type of individual classified here unquestionably took his rep defending sufficiently seriously to raise the possibility that it provided him an excuse for the joy he derived from administering punishment. In a case like this, a secondary theme is not a standard solution, because the question is one of ambiguity rather than of intersecting motives; what is at issue is whether conflicts are imposed on the person and he *then* gets carried away, or whether he gets carried away in situations that he can legitimize as a product of his "rep." Such alternatives would have to be resolved through appropriate interview questions.

In addition to divergences such as these, which result from ambiguities in the data, there are others that seem produced by the fact that the violent individual is a man of unusual and considerable complexity. Here we have the rare person who with each stone kills several motivational birds, so that it becomes virtually impossible to pinpoint and isolate one target for his violence.

The extreme is furnished by a member of our sample who also happened to be one of our research workers. His original classification (based on a "study group" summary prepared with his own participation) was self-image promoter, with secondary themes of bullying and rep defending. The rater, however, decided that the man was a pressure remover, with admixture of exploiter. In other words, half of our typology was ultimately invoked in attempting to describe this one man's violence.

How is this type of classification phenomenon possible? We turn to our study group summary, where we find the following excerpts:

1. (Self-image promoting) : There was—the group noted—a persistent theme "of coping through force (and force here means essentially a show of force) with people who haven't sufficiently caught the point that here is someone that one doesn't want to mess with." Again, "one factor in our man's violence are hostile spectators who are warned 'here is someone you don't meddle with,' and people who are to be impressed in terms of recognizing the status of this kind of activity."

2. (Bullying) : The group noted that in many of the fights "the terrorizing can become fairly drastic, and can take the form of physically neutralizing the opponent and continuing to harm him beyond what is necessary to put him out of action." Furthermore, "there is also the continual presence of the weapon, combined with the way in which fights are set up, both of which seem to indicate that the effort is really to physically harm the other person—not to permit him to escape by saving face in some fashion or by concluding the matter peacefully."

3. (Rep defending) : The group noted a "secondary" aspect to the man's violence, "which consisted of protecting the members of the clique, or members of the team, or the extended family, or simply friends if they require strong arm protection." There was also mention of an omni-present "chorus of friends who receive the impression that their interests are being adequately protected."

4. (Pressure removing) : The rater noted that our man "can't stand people crowding close," and that he "doesn't know when and how to stop." The group also recorded this second reaction and located it principally in youthful or early acts of violence; in these early incidents (according to the group) "the action

degenerates because, after the terrorizing, he is really somewhat clumsy"; the resulting violence is thus "unintended." The group and the rater both saw the subject angrily responding, in unscheduled ways, to accumulated pressure. The group, however, felt that the pressure represented crowding behavior come home to roost.

5. (Exploiting) : The rater pointed out that the subject "exploits his friends and sacrifices them to his needs... three times his friends are hurt as a result of his acts." The group also noted these facts but attributed them to a propensity for clumsiness and an inability to control self-demonstration efforts. Thus, the group described one youthful adventure, in which our man went out of his way to carry a gun to a party, where "he unnecessarily uses the weapon and finds himself hurting several people who strictly speaking didn't have to be hurt," simply in order to carry through.

We here find that part of the reason for discrepant classifications is a difference in interpretation and weighting of identical facts, including instances in which the rater concentrated on a theme prevalent in some incidents which appeared to drop out in others. This possibility points up the variable of change over time, which in a few of our violence-prone persons could make it desirable to permit a more complex classification, with successive stages in the development of one individual's violence represented as overlapping but different categories.

The picture also suggests that there are some violence-prone persons whose complexity demands a relatively multidimensional categorization for accurate representation. Although most persons in our sample appear to be adequately covered by means of one (or, at most, two) recurrent themes, there are a few whose games are more sophisticated. Here a more generous catalogue of themes can both increase validity and insure that the type is as reliable as is the person it represents.

RESULT OF THE RELIABILITY STUDY

Clearly, the major moral of our re-classification venture has been that our typology can be communicated and that it can yield comparable results in diverse hands. Given the complexity of the concepts involved and given the fact that we employ nine (or ten) categories, one could live comfortably with considerably more than seven errors out of 35 classifications.

Of course, when we speak of "seven errors" we assume that we can concentrate on the phenomena referred to rather than on the labels we use for them. We can thus accept our coding nuances in the classification of self-image compensating, and we can accommodate the career-oriented versus incident-oriented variations we have found in the classification of the self-indulging–pressure-removing sequence. The transition from one such label to the other could easily be bridged with one or two explanatory phrases, or by standardizing the instructions, or by awareness of the coder's bias, or by increasing multiple-classification. The point is that the labels are functionally related and that the concepts referred to are the same, so that the transition is provided for.

A different situation exists in the seven negative cases we referred to. In some of these there is recognizable ambiguity, and the remedy here would be to suspend classification until questions could be clarified with the interviewee. (If the ambiguity is not obvious, two independent codings would make it so, as in the above cases.) The remaining instances seem to consist of persons who make violence serve more purposes than the one or two that are characteristic of the average violence-prone individual. These multi-variate practitioners of violence need not be confused with men of polymorphous violence, as envisaged in the "indiscriminate exploder" model. Whereas the traditional conception of violence denotes an asocial exploder, the person we refer to makes violence serve social objectives; whereas the traditional violent man is unpredictable and random, our complex practitioner replicates his violence, with the many elements that enter into it. Rather than being the exception that proves the rule, this problem child is merely the exception that embodies the rule, and does so with such a vengeance that he makes rules difficult to apply.

6
The Anatomy of Violence

In Chapter 5 we presented the substance of the typology used in this study. We cannot maintain that the types we isolated exhaust the universe of violence, but it can be expected that an extension of the classification would not alter its nature.

What is the shape of violence-proneness as we have begun to describe it? And how is the type of violence we have described related to other forms of violence? What bearing does this description of violent personalities have to collective violence, such as riots? What are the similarities, if any, between people who are recurrently violent and those who explode insanely once in a lifetime? In the following pages, these questions will be explored. We shall attempt thus to extend the findings and to place them in context.

First, we shall consider the nature of the beast we have isolated and its place in psychological functioning.

THE IMPLICATIONS OF THE VIOLENCE-PRONE PREMISE

We have suggested that two types of orientation are especially likely to produce violence: one of these is that of the person who sees other people as tools designed to serve his needs; the second is that of the individual who feels vulnerable to manipulation. These two perspectives, when we examine them more closely, become faces of the same coin: both rest on the premise that human relationships are power-centered, one-way affairs; both involve efforts at self-assertion with a desperate, feverish quality that suggests self-doubt.

Of course, this description does not fit all cases. Some of the rep defenders, for instance, initially respond to a draft, instead of promoting their own reputation; some self-defenders react to a human jungle in which they are unfairly asked to survive; pressure removing sometimes represents little more than feeble-mindedness. But even in these instances, experiences with violent encounters teach the person to respond overeagerly, suspending the dictates of equity, ignoring the norm of reciprocity, and asserting personal autonomy at the expense of others. Such, it appears, is the nature of the violence-prone game.

The violence-provoking incident typically consists of several stages: first there is the classification of the other person as an object or a threat; second, there is some action based on this classification; third, the other person may act—if he has the chance—to protect his integrity. At this juncture, the violent incident reaches its point of no return. The initial stance of the violence-prone person makes violence probable; his first moves increase the probability of violence; the reaction of the victim converts probability into certainty.

The extent to which violent incidents are predetermined depends on how aggressive the aggressor feels. If his violence-propensity is substantial, he may insist on conflict; if his requirements are modest, the victim may be left with pacifying moves. For instance, a mildly scared individual can be reassured; a person who feels somewhat inadequate can be satisfied with flattery or a show of humor. But if the aggressor's ego demands blood, the victim may find himself pursued remorselessly, no matter what he says or does. Hemingway illustrates this in an episode involving two professional killers (Max and Al) toying with a restaurant owner (George) and his patron (Nick) :

"You're a pretty bright boy, aren't you?"

"Sure," said George.

"Well, you're not," said the other little man. "Is he, Al?"

"He's dumb," said Al. He turned to Nick. "What's your name?"

"Adams."

"Another bright boy," Al said. "Ain't he a bright boy, Max?"

"The town's full of bright boys," Max said.

George put the two platters, one of ham and eggs, the other of bacon and eggs, on the counter. He set down two side-dishes of fried potatoes and closed the wicket into the kitchen.

"Which is yours?" he asked Al.

"Don't you remember?"

"Ham and eggs."

"Just a bright boy," Max said. He leaned forward and took the ham and eggs. Both men ate with their gloves on. George watched them eat.

"What are *you* looking at?" Max looked at George.

"Nothing."

"The hell you were. You were looking at me."

"Maybe the boy meant it for a joke, Max," Al said. George laughed.

"*You* don't have to laugh," Max said to him. "You don't have to laugh at all, see?"

"All right," said George.

"So he thinks it's all right." Max turned to Al. "He thinks it's all right. That's a good one."

"Oh, he's a thinker," Al said. They went on eating.

"What's the bright boy's name down the counter?" Al asked Max.

"Hey, bright boy," Max said to Nick. "You go around on the other side of the counter with your boy friend."

"What's the idea?" Nick asked.

"There isn't any idea."

"You better go around, bright boy," Al said. Nick went around behind the counter.[1]

The probability of violence in violence-provoking incidents is tied to the extent to which the aggressor indulges in pre-classification or selective perception. For instance, many of the participants in our police incidents scan human contacts assiduously for the possibility of threatening implications. They do so

[1] Reprinted with the permission of Charles Scribner's Sons from *Men Without Women*, pp. 378–379, by Ernest Hemingway. Copyright 1927 Charles Scribner's Sons; renewal copyright © 1955 Ernest Hemingway.

with varying degrees of intensity and with differing abilities to "spot" suggestive information. The actions of other people are eventually classified as either non-challenging (safe) or as challenging (requiring action). Because of the dreaded consequences of error, the scales are far from evenly weighed: with greater or lesser distortion, potentially harmless encounters become transmuted into "unprovoked" onslaughts by "vicious" bullies. And at this point, the time-worn formula of the weak ego prescribes an aggressive confrontation. If this confrontation consists of direct aggression, it ends the incident; when it does not, the other person must somehow cope with the affront to which he has been subjected. His response is likely to lead to violence, because it usually feeds into the hypothesis that provides the aggressor's rationale for offensiveness.

For several reasons, the probability of violence in personal encounters increases with each new act of aggression. Violence is habit-forming. Aggressors discover that they can satisfy new and unsuspected needs by becoming aggressive. They also learn to view themselves as participants in violent games. Most importantly, they start seeing elements of past violent encounters as they approach fresh situations and begin to respond routinely. They seek and find consistency of self at the expense of their victims. Richard Wright illustrates this phenomenon in his description of the murders committed by Bigger, the hero of *Native Son*. Both killings were motivated by panic and by the desire to escape danger. The first—which was almost accidental— resulted when Bigger tried to quiet a drunk girl, to avoid being discovered in her room:

> Mary mumbled and tried to rise again. Frantically, he caught a corner of the pillow and brought it to her lips. He had to stop her from mumbling, or he would be caught. Mrs. Dalton was moving slowly toward him and he grew tight and full, as though about to explode. Mary's fingernails tore at his hands and he caught the pillow and covered her entire face with it, firmly. Mary's body surged upward and he pushed downward upon the pillow with all of his weight, determined that she must not move or make any sound that would betray him. His

eyes were filled with the white blur moving toward him in the shadows of the room. Again Mary's body heaved and he held the pillow in a grip that took all of his strength. For a long time he felt the sharp pain of her fingernails biting into his wrists. The white blur was still.[2]

The second murder was in many ways parallel to the first. Like the first, it was designed to rid Bigger of a girl who threatened to impede his escape. Again, Bigger had nothing against his victim and merely wanted to insure his safety. And the danger was the same, with the discoverer of the first incident still perceived in the shadows of the second.

Bigger, however, had changed. Having killed once, he now saw himself as a taker of life when the occasion demanded it;

A sense of the white blur hovering near, of Mary burning, of Britten, of the law tracking him down, came back. Again, he was ready. The brick was in his hand. In his mind his hand traced a quick invisible arc through the cold air of the room; high above his head his hand paused in fancy and imaginatively swooped down to where he thought her head must be. He was rigid; not moving. This was the way it *had* to be. Then he took a deep breath and his hand gripped the brick and shot upward and paused a second and then plunged downward through the darkness to the accompaniment of a deep short grunt from his chest and landed with a thud . . . How many times he had lifted the brick and brought it down he did not know. All he knew was that the room was quiet and cold and that the job was done.[3]

EVOLUTION OF THE VIOLENCE-PRONE PREMISE

Although the logic of violence may emerge from the practice of violence, it probably originates most frequently in interpersonal relationships early in life. Thus, manipulative efforts mark the

[2] R. Wright, *Native Son* (New York: Harper, 1949) , p. 74.
[3] *Ibid.*, pp. 200–201.

failure of socialization somewhere between unbridled infancy and the assumption of social responsibility. Self-assertiveness or defensiveness suggest that one's upbringing has been deficient in stability and emotional support, thus making it difficult for positive self-perceptions to develop. In both instances, brittle egos spend their adult years in belated efforts to buttress themselves at the expense of other people, and these efforts become productive of violence.

Of course, a brittle ego is a relative construction; some situations can shatter selves of steel, while others cater to the lowest levels of maturity. The young police officer out on his first beat faces all kinds of problems with which he is unprepared to cope. And what of the "fish"—our Sam, for instance—entering the prison yard for his first time, expecting to be terrorized into a state of emasculated slavery? And what of the fact that both the young officer and the young fish have learned that they are entering a world in which power is the only voice that carries, and in which attention to the feelings of others is a dangerous weakness?

Situations promotive of violent reactions undoubtedly exist; individuals are faced with human relations problems of almost insoluble complexity and serious personal import. These problems awaken fear and a sense of inadequacy; violence-prone solutions advocated by persons who are presumed to be experienced and sophisticated are persuasive. It would almost follow that these solutions would be adopted.

It would *almost* follow, that is, except for the circumstance that these solutions involve violations of the integrity and the aspirations of other people, and that this circumstance can be plainly inferred. It is obvious that the mythology of violence-proneness at minimum requires the short-circuiting of rules of procedure, or calls for precipitous aggressive action with little inquiry into its justification. And it is because violence is primitive that the most successfully socialized persons among those exposed to a potentially explosive situation will resist premature acceptance of the violent formula of survival.

The willingness to adopt the violence-prone mythology of survival distinguishes the members of our sample from other inmates or police officers or slum children or unhappily married men. It distinguishes them as persons with a starting capital of insecurity or egocentricity available for investment in violence-promoting premises.

Unfortunately, as the game of violence unfolds in our interviews, it appears to be insidious in its cumulative character. Once a person discovers that the ego can be buttressed at the expense of others, the discovery seems to be recurrently applied. The routine, moreover, gains from both success and failure; its stability rests on the fact that it feeds on personal insecurity, rather than on the reactions of victims and the sanctions of authority. The task of re-educating the violence-prone person is thus one of considerable magnitude and a challenge worthy of the best of the social sciences and helping professions can offer.

THE SUBCULTURE OF VIOLENCE

We have made much of the role of violence-prone premises or assumptions in the creation of violent incidents. We have seen that persons who tend to interpret situations as threatening, or goading, or challenging, or overpowering can turn harmless encounters into duels, purges, struggles for survival, or violent escapes.

To be sure, the propensity satisfies personal needs; it resolves doubts about self-importance, it brings social prominence and respect, and it preserves a consumer role in personal relations. But these ends can be achieved in other ways—sometimes with considerably less risk or consequence.

Violence-prone premises tie neatly into immature personality patterns, but the connection is not inevitable. Some use violence as a crutch, and others do not; some use violence as a weapon, and others do not. The question is, what accounts for the difference? Where do violence-prone assumptions have their origin—where are they learned? One explanation would be that violent alternatives may be accidentally discovered and that, once violence has been exercised, the experience transfers to successive encounters. But this explanation is too related to chance. It seems easier to assume that in some segments of our society violence-prone premises are widely accepted and that they are available for adoption by susceptible individuals.

This type of explantaion has been advanced by Marvin Wolfgang, and has been expanded in Wolfgang and Ferracuti's treatise *The Subculture of Violence*.[4] The basis for the idea is a statistical one: it rests on the finding that some groups are more prone to use violence to solve their problems than are other people. For instance, Italy has several localities in which it is customary to retaliate against private affronts, and in some parts of Mexico citizens are apt to settle their disputes with physical combat. In the United States, young men who have grown up in Negro ghettos have learned to be dispensers (and victims) of violence.

Such situations can be labeled "subcultures of violence" because they imply a code which prescribes violent conduct and which is passed on—through word and deed—from one generation to the next. Why is violence thus taught and why is it learned? In some cases, the reason is sociopsychological. American and Mexican slums, for instance, contain many homes in which the mother is of considerably more consequence than the father, who may be rarely in evidence. In such homes, the masculine role may not seem imposing, and growing boys may feel compelled to evolve physical means of demonstrating their manhood. Violence here becomes one of the facets or vehicles of the well-known *machismo* syndrome.[5] In other subcultures, emphasis on violence can originate in transformed social customs or group relationships. Family feuds and tribal rivalries, for instance, can give rise to a tradition of retaliation, as in parts of Italy. Frontier justice can be transformed into a system for

[4] M. Wolfgang and F. Ferracuti, *The Subculture of Violence: Toward an Integrated Theory of Criminology* (London: Tavistock, 1967).

[5] Most of the literature on *machismo* exists in Spanish-language publications. Erich Fromm, in an unpublished study of the character structure of Mexican peasants, has established the relationship between assertion of masculinity and mother-dominated homes. Among American delinquents, the masculine "toughness" value has been described by Walter Miller, W. B. Miller, Hildred Geertz, and H. Cutter, Aggression in a boys' street-corner gang. *Psychiatry* (1961), 24: 283–98.

privately punishing presumed offenders. And nonviolent career lines may often be unavailable.

Whatever the origins of the subculture of violence, it exists in the form of values, beliefs, and attitudes held by its members. These may relate to all manner of situations, and may prescribe appropriate conduct for them. Violence is one such form of conduct, and it is permissively viewed. That such a doctrine is prevalent does not mean, of course, that every person residing in a given geographical area will be equally subjected to it, nor that everyone exposed to these assumptions will adopt them. Violence-proneness is restricted to the select minority within the subculture who have fully assimilated its violence-prone teachings and who live by them.

For these select persons, a wide range of situations would be defined as justifying aggressive responses. Violence-prone people do not merely espouse violence as a doctrine or philosophy, but they tend to see the world in violent terms and respond to it accordingly. In the words of Wolfgang and Ferracuti, "variations in the surrounding world . . . [would] have a greater chance of being perceived and reacted upon . . . as menacing, aggressive stimuli which call for immediate defense and counteraggression." [6] In the American Negro ghetto, for example, "a male is usually expected to defend the name and honor of his mother, the virtue of womanhood . . . and to accept no derogation about his race (even from a member of his own race), his age, or his masculinity. Quick resort to physical combat as a measure of daring, courage, or defense of status appears to be a cultural expression . . ." [7]

Members of the subculture of violence perceive themselves as aggressive; they see opportunities for violence in the world around them, and they play stereotyped violence-prone games. An example of stereotyped violence is the procedure known as

---

[6] Wolfgang and Ferracuti, *op. cit.*, p. 157.

[7] M. Wolfgang, *Patterns in Criminal Homicide* (Philadelphia: University of Pennsylvania Press, 1958), p. 188. A systematic study of this pattern is described in Short, J. F., and F. L. Strodtbeck, *Group Process and Gang Delinquency* (Chicago: University of Chicago Press, 1965).

"playing the dozens," which is popular in the slums and in prisons. "The dozens" is a form of verbal interaction designed to test one's own equanimity, to produce rage in one's opponent, and to build up a rationale for physical violence. Ralph Berdie describes one form of this interaction as follows:

> One of the tormenters will make a mildly insulting state- ment, perhaps about the mother of the subject, "I saw your mother out with a man last night." Then he may follow this up with "She was as drunk as a bat." The subject, in turn, will then make an insulting statement about the tormenter or some member of the tormenter's family. This exchange of insults continues, encouraged by the approval and shouts of the ob- servers, and the insults become progressively nastier and more pornographic, until they eventually include every member of the participants' families and every act of animal and man. . . . Finally, one of the participants, usually the subject, who has actually been combating the group pressure of the ob- servers, reaches his threshold and takes a swing at the tor- menter, pulls out a knife or picks up an object to use as a club. That is the sign for the tormenter, and sometimes some of the observers, to go into action, and usually the subject ends up with the most physical injuries.[8]

Stereotyped violence-prone games appear in many forms in subcultures of violence. They also have elements in common. A striking parallel to "playing the dozens" for instance, is the dueling among German university students, and jousting among medieval knights. The character of the latter is evidenced by the prescribed sequence of insults preceding each encounter. T. H. White amusingly makes this point in describing the clash between King Pellinore and Sir Grummore, in *The Once and Future King:*

> "Suppose we'd better have a joust, eh, what?"
> "Yes, I suppose we had better," said King Pellinore, "really."

[8] R. F. Berdie, Playing the Dozens, *Journal of Abnormal and Social Psy- chology* (1947), 42: 120–21, p. 120.

"What shall we have it for?"

"Oh, the usual thing, I suppose. Would one of you kindly help me on with my helm?" . . .

As soon as they were ready, the two knights stationed themselves at each end of the clearing and then advanced to meet in the middle.

"Fair knight," said King Pellinore, "I pray thee tell me thy name."

"That me regards," replied Sir Grummore, using the proper formula.

"That is uncourteously said," said King Pellinore, "what? For no knight he dreadeth for to speak his name openly, but for some reason of shame."

"Be that as it may, I choose that thou shalt not know my name as at this time, for no askin'."

"Then you must stay and joust with me, false knight."

"Haven't you got that wrong, Pellinore?" inquired Sir Grummore. "I believe it ought to be 'thou shalt'."

"Oh, I'm sorry, Sir Grummore. Yes, so it should, of course. Then thou shalt stay and joust with me, false knight."

Without further words, the two gentlemen retreated to the opposite ends of the clearing, fewtered their spears, and prepared to hurtle together in the preliminary charge.

"I think we had better climb this tree," said Merlyn. "You never know what will happen in a joust like this." [9]

The subculture of violence thus prescribes certain rules for the exercise of violence and also equips its members with motives, attitudes, and perceptions which produce the games in which these rules apply.

Fannin and Clinard, who studied the self-images of lower-class and middle-class delinquents, report that it is usual for the lower-class boys to see themselves as tough, powerful, fierce, and fearless. It is also usual, according to them, for these boys to want to become even tougher, harder and more violent than they are. The boys further feel that their prestige depends on

[9] Reprinted by permission of G. P. Putnam's Sons from *The Once and Future King* by T. H. White. Copyright 1939, 1940 by T. H. White; © 1958 by T. H. White.

advertised ability and willingness to fight, on physical superiority over others, and on general fearlessness. The interesting point is that the delinquent boys do not uniformly live up to the prescription, nor do they have similar conceptions of their own activities. Fannin and Clinard explain:

> the range of such conceptions appeared to run typologically from the "bruising marauder" to the "fearful warrior." The former is a boy who is constantly proving his toughness by fighting unrelentingly at the slightest provocation, or who initiates brawls because he "likes to fight." His perception of ridicule, or the merest hint of disbelief about his masculinity, is extremely acute and he will settle the matter immediately by force. He is looked upon with respectful apprehension by his peers as a "nut," "crazy bastard," "a real goner," and as "dangerous" because he is always stirring up trouble; he is, in short, a disliked deviant.[10]

How does this observation relate to our typology? We assume that the true member of the violent subculture—at least in the American slums—would be quite eclectic in his motives for violence. But we also assume that true subculture membership is comparatively rare in real life. We know that even persons with common backgrounds are somewhat differently reared and that individual preferences always govern susceptibility to general norms. The subculture of violence should thus consist of individual variations on subcultural themes. These variations should reflect both the subculture and the private views and problems of each individual. Wolfgang and Ferracuti themselves indicate that "differential personality variables must be considered in an integrated social-psychological approach to an understanding of the subcultural aspects of violence" [11]

Personality can intersect with group norms in one of several ways. For one, personal needs will dictate how well subcultural

[10] L. F. Fannin and M. B. Clinard, Differences in the conception of self as a male among lower and middle class delinquents. *Social Problems* (1965), 13: 205–14, p. 211.

[11] Wolfgang and Ferracuti, *op. cit.*, p. 160.

teachings are assimilated. Ultimately, it is the individual who decides whether violence is to be eagerly adopted, casually rehearsed, or totally ignored. And given the rewards of violence, weak egos are apt to assimilate best violence-prone lessons. Moreover, neighborhood definitions can leave considerable latitude for excitability thresholds, for preferences in roles, for variations in physical tactic, and for individual styles of response. Cultural definitions can reflect all manner of personal sensitivities and can accommodate every stage of maturity in interpersonal dealings. Thus, subcultural prescriptions for violence may not specify whether insults should be sought out or reacted to, whether aggression should take physical or verbal forms, whether the individual should lead or follow in matters of aggression. Whereas the subculture of violence promotes violence, it does not prescribe the violent encounters of individual members. The nature of the person's violent acts can therefore reflect both the spirit of the times and the unique contribution of his individual needs.

This is especially the case with persons who take to the "violence" in the subculture of violence with more alacrity and enthusiasm than their neighbors. It is these individuals, who meet the norm "thou shalt be violent" much more than halfway, who best personify the sociopsychological model of subculturally induced violence. For it is these persons whose needs are most felicitously responded to by the license to destroy which they feel is furnished them. And ultimately, these persons carry violence to such an extreme that even their subcultural coreligionaries may classify them as violence-prone.

COLLECTIVE VIOLENCE

No form of violence is more accepted and more damned, more ignored and more feared, than collective violence. On the one hand, the carnage of war—terrifyingly standardized and dehumanized and organized—has become an almost noncontroversial feature of the human landscape. Except for a minority who are often viewed as starry-eyed, civilized society condones the violence of war and rewards and decorates individuals who have distinguished themselves by inflicting death and destruction on the battlefield.

On the other hand, we encounter apprehension bordering on hysteria in relation to such forms of domestic violence as our recent urban riots. It is these displays of rage, with their sniping and arson and looting, which have occasioned declarations of bankruptcy and despair, calls of emergency, and demands for collective action, including counterviolence. It is these events that also have been dismissed as irrational in motive, or have been explained away with simplistic formulas emphasizing economic or historical determinism.

It is only very recently that careful investigation under government auspices—such as a study by the President's Commission on Civil Disorders (1968) —have pointed to some of the complexities in the motivation of collective violence.

The riot commission listed five "powerful ingredients" as "catalysts" of riots: (1) frustrated hope, generated by the civil rights struggle in the north and south; (2) a climate heavy with "approval and encouragement of violence"; (3) the frustration of feeling powerless to move the system; (4) a new mood— particularly in the young—of "self-esteem and enhanced racial pride"; and (5) the view of police as a symbol of "white power, white racism and white repression." [12]

Clearly, these factors comprise a package of sorts. Increased hope creates increased bitterness as institutions are found unresponsive; enhanced self-esteem can generate a determination not to accept disappointments as answers; alternative solutions can be sought, and these can take the form of increasingly self-reliant measures (especially, given the premise that legality is a cloak for oppressors). It is also understandable that if conventional justice and conventional society are perceived as unjust and hostile, "antisocial" violence can come to acquire a positive, rather than a negative, connotation.

According to this view, violence is a last resort. The person has problems—he seeks relief—he obtains no satisfaction—he becomes bitter. Since his direct demands yield no result, he is

---

[12] *Report of the National Advisory Commission on Civil Disorders.* (New York: Bantam Books; E. P. Dutton, 1968) , pp. 10–11.

forced into increasingly indirect, affect-laden, protest-oriented action. The Commission points out that riots are preceded by incidents that dramatize unredressed complaints or affronts. The Cincinnati disturbance, for instance, followed a period during which, "without the city's realizing what was occurring . . . protest through political and non-violent channels had become increasingly difficult." The Commission points out that "to young Negroes, especially, such protest appeared to have become almost futile." [13] In pre-riot Newark, "Negro constituents and their white councilman found themselves on opposite sides of almost every issue"; anti-police charges were made, but "no complaint was ever heard of again"; against opposition by Negroes, the city determined to name a white secretary to the board of education.[14] Such stalemates, according to the Commission, "were linked in the minds [of rioters] to the pre-existing reservoir of underlying grievances." The recurrent picture is one of a "cumulative process of mounting tension that spilled over into violence when the final incident occurred." The precipitating incident—usually involving the police—could then be of a relatively trivial nature, and yet trigger rioting.

The type of explanation offered by the Riot Commission is that of a "chain," in which unhappiness leads to unsuccessful efforts at redress, which in turn cumulates in despair, anger, and a sanctioning of violent solutions. Interviews with riot participants and sympathizers tend to confirm this view. By and large, statements at the scene of a riot are catalogues of unresolved grievances and cumulated feelings, and the riot emerges as an expression of impatience and an emotional discharge.

The Phenomenology of the Watts Riot

A review of press quotations from Watts rioters may serve as illustration of the feelings described by the Commission. Remarks made to Negro reporters during the Watts riot tend to cover a relatively small number of themes, some of which are:

[13] *Ibid.*, pp. 47–48.
[14] *Ibid.*, pp. 58–60.

1. *Police Brutality:* The rioters frequently referred to feelings against the police as the motive underlying their violence. They often talked of the police as their enemy, and they were bitter in discussing police-related grievances. It seemed as if the police had come to represent all manner of humiliations and mistreatment suffered at the hands of white society. One young man who had participated in the burning of a supermarket, for example, ventured the opinion that "the riots will continue because I, as a Negro, am immediately considered a criminal by the police, and if I have a pretty woman with me, she's a tramp—even if she's my wife or mother." An unemployed man, who admitted having repeatedly thrown rocks at the police officers, declared: "Maybe the people of Beverly Hills would riot too if they spent most of their life with a cop's club in their face. Or if they had to get out of an automobile with their hands over their heads to be questioned for doing nothing at all. We're not safe from police brutality even in our own home." [15]

The various rumors circulating about the incident that triggered the riot illustrate the extent of anti-police sentiment. Thus, one young rioter recalled that "the police struck a lady—and she was pregnant—and they broke her nose." [16] A Negro mother, standing outside her Watts residence, related, "I heard they beat an old woman over there— them police beat her half to death." She added: "You can't sit and take it forever, can you?" [17]

2. *Retaliation Against White Exploitation:* This was the motive implicit in most of the spontaneous remarks made by rioters in the course of their destructive activities and probably the most prevalently voiced rationale. Stores with windows carrying signs that identified their owners as "Negro," "Soul Brother" or "Blood Brother" were generally not

---

[15] *San Francisco Chronicle,* Aug. 18, 1965.
[16] *Ibid.,* Aug. 16, 1965.
[17] *San Francisco Sunday Chronicle,* Aug. 15, 1965.

looted or burned; [18] among white-owned stores, the first targets were reportedly those "whose owners had a reputation for gouging Negroes or for foreclosing mortgages." [19] And in the course of looting, "the first thing they [the rioters] went for is the credit records." [20] A female resident of Watts explained: "They're fed up with these whites cheating them out of their money—you know it ain't easy for people like us to get jobs, and we got to work hard for everything we get. Why should we let them cheat us out of what little we got? Let 'em loose a little bit now. Ain't it about time?" [21]

The rioters, in discussing the white Watts merchants, alleged that the commodities offered for sale in the ghetto were rejects from outlets in white areas, including stale food. These items, according to the rioters, were generally sold at much higher prices than elsewhere. Considerable resentment against white landlords was also voiced. One man declared while he was watching a burning building: "I wouldn't give a goddamn if they burned my house down as long as I could get this. Mine ain't worth a damn nohow. He's the one with everything to lose." [22] In general, the mood prevailing among those engaged in the destruction of white property was described as one of joyful vindictiveness. The anti-white "warfare" aspect of the proceedings is also evident from the fact that Negro nonparticipants were frequently informed that their inactivity implied treasonous partiality to "The Man."

3. *Unemployment:* Lack of a job was frequently mentioned as the cause of the riot, as evidenced by Governor Brown's complaint that when he asked people for the reasons behind the destructiveness, they "gave me no clues to the

[18] *Los Angeles Sentinel,* Aug. 19, 1965.
[19] *San Francisco Chronicle,* Aug. 21, 1965.
[20] *Ibid.,* Sept. 3, 1965.
[21] *Ibid.*
[22] *Life,* Aug. 27, 1965.

reasons, although they did describe the economic problems." [23] A speech by Martin Luther King in Watts was
interrupted with the shout, " 'I had a dream, I had a dream'
—hell, we don't need no damn dreams. We want jobs." [24]
Many Watts residents indicated that they believed unemployment to have been the chief cause of the riot. The *New
York Times* quoted a young Watts mechanic as proclaiming, "We've come to life. You get me a job and pay me—
we're satisfied. If you don't—well, we're not going back to
slavery" (Aug. 17, 1965). A woman explained that "this
wasn't no race riot. It was a riot between the unemployed
and the employed. We are tired of being shelved and being
told we don't want to work." [25]

4. *Hopelessness:* This feeling was mentioned by some as a
contributing factor to the riot. A young mother of four put
the case very eloquently, when she told Governor Brown:
   "I feel buried here in Watts with nothing to look forward
to ... Everyone has a deep feeling of lostness. There's no hope
out here in Watts, we're stranded. We want something to
look forward to. It's no fun cashing a county welfare check
every week." [26]
   A number of Watts residents discussed their past hopes
and failures. A young man who had migrated to Los Angeles
from Texas with his wife and three children explained that
he was working as a dishwasher. "People come here looking
to better themselves," he said, but "it ain't here for you."
A female evangelist interviewed by the same reporter indicated that "when the government says it's going to help,
but then there ain't nothing, it's disheartening to people." [27]
Louis Lomax wrote that "Negroes in Watts have a pa-

---

[23] *San Francisco Call Bulletin,* Aug. 20, 1965.
[24] *Newsweek,* Aug. 30, 1965.
[25] *Time,* Aug. 27, 1965.
[26] *San Francisco Call Bulletin,* Aug. 20, 1965.
[27] *New York Times,* Aug. 26, 1965.

thology of failure—they failed in the South and failed to find the promised land in Los Angeles." [28]

5. *Anonymity:* This appeared to be a condition which for some was dispelled by the riot. In one encounter a young Watts citizen asked Brown: "Had you planned to come down here before this?" "No frankly, I hadn't," Brown replied." [29] Another resident declared: "I don't believe in burning, stealing, or killing, but I can see why the boys did what they did. They just wanted to be noticed, to let the world know the seriousness of their state in life." [30]

Rioters felt that as a result of their actions, they would achieve collective and individual visibility. The one is exemplified by the statement of an old man, who said "the only way we can get anybody to listen to us is to start a riot." The other is implicit in the claim of an unemployed young man that "Negroes are ready to die for respect." [31]

6. *Lack of Identity:* This feeling was diminished by the riot, according to some participants and observers. A Negro graduate student who had returned to Watts at the time told a former teacher: "As a riot, it was a masterful performance. I sense a change here now, a buzz, and it tickles. For the first time people in Watts feel a real pride in being black. I remember, when I first went to Whittier, I worried that if I didn't make it there, if I was rejected I wouldn't have a place to go back to. Now I can say: 'I'm from Watts.' " [32]

James Farmer asked one young rioter how he felt, and the boy replied, "baby, I feel like a man." Another told him, "Man, this is instant renewal." [33] A Negro psychiatrist

---

[28] *Ibid.,* March 20, 1966.
[29] *San Francisco Call Bulletin,* Aug. 20, 1965.
[30] *San Francisco Chronicle,* Aug. 18, 1965.
[31] *Newsweek,* Aug. 30, 1965.
[32] *Life,* Aug. 27, 1965.
[33] *San Francisco Sunday Chronicle,* Sept. 3, 1965.

described the rioters as having developed "a feeling of potency." He said that "they feel the whole world is watching now. And out of the violence, no matter how wrong the acts were, they have developed a sense of pride." [34]

Riot-Generated Motives

It is clear that this type of testimony does not provide a full picture of riot motivation. For one, it omits or embroiders socially less desirable or constructive needs, such as the satisfaction obtained from destruction for its own sake, or from the use of violence to obtain stolen goods. Such statements also underrepresent the motives that are born from the riot situation itself. For instance, there are those who join destructive activities because of excitement generated by collective action, or as a means of entertainment, or as a response to opportunity.

In relation to one of the disturbances following the murder of Martin Luther King, *Time* magazine observed:

The majority of plunderers and burners in American cities last week were about as ideologically motivated as soldier ants. Many, to be sure, were venting the longstanding resentment of black Americans in a white society. But the Negro looters were predominantly driven by a combination of self-help and help-yourself. What of Martin Luther King? "His death just gave us an excuse," said Ronald Rudolph, 22, in Pittsburgh. "I never did dig the man much when he was alive." When a well-provisioned Harlem "liberator" was asked why he was stealing, he cried: "It's because they killed what's-his-name!" "You know why people loot?" explained one young rioter. "Because they ain't never, so long as they live, gonna have enough money to buy a color-television set. Man, I got big ambitions, but not much will power." [35]

[34] *Time,* Aug. 27, 1965.
[35] *Ibid.,* April 19, 1968.

The presence of other rioters is an obviously important factor in riot motivation, especially among people who become involved as the disturbance expands. Although latecomers might be motivated by grievances, these predispositions would be more likely to remain latent if it were not for the presence of an ongoing disturbance. It is a truism that an individual could never riot. The availability of like-minded companions and the example set by riot-initiators often facilitate the translation of despair into destruction and explosion.

One reason why violence comes so easy to rioters is that they can derive it from a common cause. They can see themselves individually laboring toward group ends. They can feel themselves partners of a joint enterprise. They can conceive of their own acts as defined and sanctioned by a larger effort. Every solitary marauder can come to regard himself as a member of a crusade.

In this sense, every riot is—in extended form—a violent incident of the sort we have described. The game is played between members of a frustrated group and the agents of white society. In the opening moves, black Citizen A makes demands and requests of white Social Agent B; these strongly felt aspirations take the form of physical or psychological requirements. The game revolves around A's discovery that his aspirations cannot be satisfied. Presumably, A can make a variety of efforts to gain his ends before he concludes that B will remain unresponsive. Moreover, he can make such efforts on various fronts. Thus, he can look for a job, and not find one; he can stand on street corners, and be chased off them; he can seek illegal sources of income, and be jailed. Ultimately, he concludes that the agents of society are his tormentor, and that he must act accordingly. When many persons arrive at this conclusion, a collective move to act in its spirit can be expected. [36]

The victim of collective violence thus symbolically represents persons and agencies who have remained unresponsive to group aspirations. In the Watts riot, we have seen the police as a

[36] H. Toch, *The Social Psychology of Social Movements* (Indianapolis: Bobbs-Merrill, 1965) .

prominent enemy, because police action is visibly repressive and because personal awareness can most easily focus on the sort of humiliation experienced in police contact. Moreover, the police have inherited their connotations from their role as instruments of forces already perceived as repressive.

A more general reaction, similar in kind, is the second theme we have mentioned. At the height of a riot almost any white person can be perceived as an enemy. This is the case because the riot participants have come to ascribe racial motives to the social agents with whom they have dealt. Repressive agents not only have been seen as anti-Black but have become viewed as the spokesmen for similar sentiments among white people at large. Hence, the broad retaliatory theme in the Watts riot.

The remainder of our list describes the substance of the discrepancy between expectations and failures. In the case of Watts, the list includes low status and the non-availability of means of achievement. This fact suggests that participants in the riot felt that they could look back on a very broad range of frustrating experiences. It also suggests that specific economic measures (such as the creation of jobs) would not now address the core of their problem, much of which revolved around self-esteem and the desire for psychological rewards.

One dimension of riot motivation which tends to be obscured by summaries of grievances is that of the permutations that these grievances achieve in the individual histories of rioters. The Watts riot no doubt contained individuals who stood as classic examples of the sort of sequence described by the Riot Commission. Persons who found no access to medical service; swindled consumers; frustrated job-seekers; subjects of police searches; forced school dropouts; commuting menial workers— such men and women could point to reservoirs of experiences that found direct expression in rioting. In other instances, the sequence might have been similar, but based on more unrealistic aspirations, including immediate access to a life of luxury and leisure. We also assume that frustrations totally unrelated to racial themes could become displaced in retaliatory violence, giving the Watts riot more psychological and existential overtones.

Obviously, some participants in group violence will be more conscious of its social objectives than others. But it is hard to conceive of any rioter who could be totally oblivious of the grievances shared by his fellows. Such a non-socially-motivated destroyer must at least be a self-conscious hanger-on to social protest. He must know that he is riding the crest of a wave which provides him with the false sanction of a large-scale revolt.

At the initial juncture of collective violence, the Riot Commission isolates a group predisposed to action by many unredressed grievances. Such persons arrive at the situation with a level of outrage sufficient to enable their participation. The motives impelling them to rioting, however, are not yet born. In the words of Ralph Turner, these are an "emergent norm." [37] They must be created, in the sense that the anger must attach itself to the precipitating event and must convert it into an unacceptable affront. Here it matters little that the actual situation may be a proper exercise of police power, or a minor dispute. The event is interpreted as symbolically related to grievances—hence, as the occasion for action. The ideal type of situation for this purpose is one of ambiguity, and it is filled with confusion, discomfort, excitement, rumor-spreading, and tension. The illusion which is created converts the discrete event into a collective insult—into a deliberate provocation that is repressive and intolerable. If this view is sufficiently prevalent, violence can be legitimized. A crowd becomes a mob, and the violence formula gains potency. And when this occurs, the intrinsically innocent situation has become transmuted into a time and place for destructive retaliation—into a "violent incident" of gigantic proportions.

The Precipitating Incident in Collective Violence

The Watts riot shows the role of pre-existing motives in shaping

[37] R. H. Turner, Collective Behavior. In R. E. L. Faris (Ed.), *Handbook of Modern Sociology* (Chicago: Rand McNally, 1964), pp. 382–425.

the perception of incidents that precipitate collective violence. It also highlights the fact (which we shall discuss later) that violent persons can contribute to the genesis of large-scale explosions.

The Watts tragedy took place during the week of Wednesday, August 11, 1965. The context and background fit the Riot Commission's prescribed pattern: Watts consists of small, congested, pre-war rental homes, and, in terms of living style, the Watts resident is only slightly better off than his peer in New York's Harlem, who typically inhabits a cold water tenement flat. Statistics confirm the underprivileged, but not rock-bottom, status of the Watts Negro; 30 per cent of the children in the area came from broken homes; the drop-out rate in Watts schools was more than twice the national average; only one-third of the residents had started high school. The majority of the persons living in Watts were migrants from the South, and most were unskilled. Not surprisingly, the Watts unemployment rate was more than triple that of the white community; more than half of the Negro families of Los Angeles were on relief; and 20 per cent of Negro families in the area earned less than $3,000 a year.

The riot occurred during an unusually hot period toward the end of the summer; for four days preceding the explosion, a heat wave combining temperatures of 90° to 100° and very high humidity had prevailed through the area.

On the national scene, the hopes of Negroes had been recently raised: For at least three years, the civil rights movement, with its sit-ins, marches, and other demonstrations had been in full swing. Negro voter registration in the South was initiated the very day on which the riot began. Locally, hopes had been squashed. For example, President Johnson's anti-poverty program had not become active in Los Angeles, in part because the mayor had been unsympathetic to some of its provisions. A hard-won state fair housing act was repealed in 1964 by a public referendum.

At the time of Watts, rioting had already occurred elsewhere— most dramatically in New York and in Rochester, the preceding year. Models were therefore available. Some local observers had pointed to Watts as a potential riot scene for several months, on the basis of resentments and bitterness encountered there, closely comparable to those in other riot areas.[38]

The events that triggered the Watts riot began with the arrest, on a drunk driving charge, of a young Negro named Marquette Frye. There were spectators to the arrest; their mood was one of amusement. If anything, their sympathies extended to the officer, who was clearly justified in making his case. Everything went lightheartedly until the trooper and his partner tried to place Frye into physical custody. The young man reacted with panic. Robert Conot reports that as the officers started toward Frye, he broke down completely:

> As he spoke to his mother, his voice broke. He was almost crying. Spotting the officers, he started backing away, his feet shuffling, his arms waving.
>
> "Come on, Marquette, you're coming with us." [Officer] Minikus reached toward him.
>
> Marquette slapped his hand away. "I'm not going to no son-ofabitching jail!" he cried out. "I haven't did anything to be taken to jail." [39]

As Frye's fear increased, so did his awareness that he was exposed in the eyes of his neighbors. Shame produced resentment, and resentment brought memories of past humiliations: "What right had they to treat him like this? 'You motherfucking white cops, you're not taking me anywhere!' he screamed, whipping his body about as if he were half boxer, half dancer." [40]

The incident had been converted into a tense, violent confrontation, and it was acquiring connotations susceptible to more general interpretations. Conot reports that the witnessing crowd—now including mostly persons who had only just arrived on the scene—became sympathetic to Frye. Frye's situation seemed to be that of a victim, and his fate mobilized feelings of indignation grounded in a common underprivileged past:

[38] *San Francisco Chronicle*, Aug. 16, 1965.
[39] From *Rivers of Blood, Years of Darkness* by Robert Conot. Copyright © 1967 by Bantam Books, Inc.
[40] *Ibid.*, p. 14.

The officers were white; they were outsiders; and most of all, they were police. Years of reciprocal distrust, reciprocal contempt, and reciprocal insults had created a situation in which the residents assumed every officer to be in the wrong until he had proven himself right, just as the officers assumed every Negro guilty until he had proven his innocence. The people began to close in on the three highway patrolmen.[41]

As the situation degenerated (Marquette's brother, Ronald, had become engaged in the dispute), another police officer arrived. This officer, like Frye, was a man susceptible to panic— a person who seemed prone to precipitantly aggressive action. Conot describes his entrance into the sequence in the following terms:

> Officer Wilson, as he arrived on the scene, riot baton in hand even before he had the kickstand of the motorcycle down, was confronted by an image of blurred chaos . . . he went into action with no more opportunity to assess the situation than those Negro spectators who had arrived late and assumed from what they saw that there was violent conflict between Marquette and the officers . . .
> Rushing toward Ronald and Lewis, and without speaking to either, Wilson jabbed the riot baton into the pit of Ronald's stomach. As Ronald doubled over, he jabbed again. Ronald rolled to the ground.
> With one adversary dispatched, it was but a half dozen steps to where Marquette was fending off Minikus. Wilson swung the baton. He caught Marquette with a glancing blow to the forehead, above the left eye. As Marquette turned instinctively to meet him, Wilson jabbed him hard in the stomach. Marquette doubled over.[42]

At this juncture, Ronald's mother, seeing her sons painfully beaten, indignantly intervened. As a result, the crowd was treated to the spectacle of an old lady forcibly pushed into a patrol car.

[41] *Ibid.*
[42] *Ibid.*, p. 15–16.

One member of the crowd later declared, "When that happened, all the people standing around got mad" [43]. Conot reports that there were isolated shouts of: "Come on, let's get them!" "Leave the old lady alone!" "We've got no rights at all—it's just like Selma!" "Those white motherfuckers got no cause to do that!" [44]

The situation degenerated even further after one officer complained that a young lady in the crowd had spit at him. Several other officers converged on the girl, and they apprehended her after considerable resistance. The picture of the girl's helpless struggle against overwhelming odds symbolized, for many in the crowd, the hopelessness of their own fate. This feeling, and the resulting impotent rage, is vividly described by Conot:

> In the manner with which the police had handled the girl the people saw, or thought they saw, the contempt of the white man for the Negro. They felt, collectively, his heel grinding in their faces. They were stricken once more by the sting of his power.
>
> "Goddam!" a woman called out. "Goddam! They'd never treat a white woman like that!"
>
> "What kind of men are you, anyways?" another challenged. "What kind of men are you, anyways, to let them do that to our people?"
>
> "It's a shame! It's a pitiful, crying shame!"
>
> "Blue-eyed white devils! We is going to get you! Oh, shit! We is going to get you!"
>
> "Motherfuckers!" It came from all sides of the crowd. "Motherfuckers!" [45]

The Riot Commission's "cumulative chain" had reached its last link. An incident had been generated which symbolized for those present every ounce of humiliation, every nuance of hopelessness, every hurt to pride, self-esteem, and loyalty possible. The fruits of second-class citizenship had taken shape: they had become sensitivities which turned private conflict into public is-

[43] *Time,* Aug. 20, 1965.
[44] Conot, *op. cit.,* p. 16.
[45] *Ibid.,* p. 21.

sue, which converted disputants into Oppressors and Oppressed; which metamorphosed a minor exercise into a morality play that promised intolerable victory to unspeakable evil.

To be sure, the transformation was not inevitable: some actors played their parts too well; some pawns proved ambitious, and hastened the plot. Frye's fear impelled him to present himself as a frenzied martyr; Wilson's pugnaciousness converted him into a caricature of arbitrarily exercised power. Tragedy might have been averted if one impulsive girl had been permitted to escape into the crowd. And there might have been no riot if one man had not felt more humiliated, more resentful, more excited, more impotent, more shamed, more desperate, more angry, and more compelled to act than his neighbors. It took one man, feeling what others felt and converting these feelings into action, to generate the last interpretation, the ultimate connotation, the irreversible inference—the crucial conclusion that violence was in order:

> Without conscious thought of his action he darted into the street and hurled the empty pop bottle in his hand toward the last of the departing black-and-white cars. Striking the rear fender of Sgt. Rankin's car, it shattered. And it was as if in that shattering the thousand people lining the street found their own release. It was as if in one violent contortion the bonds of restraint were snapped. Rocks, bottles, pieces of wood and iron—whatever missiles came to hand—were projected against the sides and windows of the bus and automobiles that, halted for the past 20 minutes by the jammed street, unwittingly started through the gauntlet. The people had not been able to overcome the power of the police. But they could, and would, vent their fury on other white people. The white people who used the police to keep them from asserting their rights.
>
> It was 7:45 p.m. Amidst the rending sounds of tearing metal, splintering glass, cries of bewilderment and shouts of triumph, the Los Angeles uprising had begun.[46]

[46] *Ibid.,* p. 29.

Once collective action has been initiated, it acquires a momentum of its own; even if people did not suffer from grievances, riots would attract and recruit participants. They would do so because they appeal to boredom, anger, frustration, desire for adventure; because they provide a ready-made opportunity to discharge feelings; because they furnish festive activity with the sanction of peers and under the eagis of principle.

As violent crowds form, bystanders are invited to join; if not, they find it natural to fill gaps in the ranks. Streets become an arena for heroism, a proving ground for bravery, a stage for protest. Boys can achieve manhood heaving rocks or defying police officers; men can acquire purpose through guerrilla warfare; groups can gain meaning through riot-connected projects. Benefits are provided to so many persons that there are few left to disapprove. At some point, nonviolence calls for special explanation and requires special motives. Violence becomes, temporarily, a way of life.

SOCIAL VIOLENCE AND PERSONAL VIOLENCE

In our discussion so far, we have only been able to hint at the relationship between collective violence and personal violence. At first glance, the two types of violence differ. Whereas the violent person approaches his encounters as a solitary agent, the rioter becomes mobilized as a member of a group; whereas the violent person has affinity for aggressive action, the rioter is a product of history; whereas the violent person provokes violence, the rioter seems to respond to a situation created to provoke him. The appropriate kind of analysis differs: while in personal violence we expect to find consistency within the individual, in collective violence we assume that people respond uniformly to a sequence of frustrating experiences.

But these divergences are less sharp after we examine the motivating patterns in riots. For one, we see that violent incidents must come into being to provide a focus for grievances. In the genesis of such incidents, individuals with violence-prone personalities play roles similar to those which they play in their other encounters.

We have seen that in a riot the man in the street can gain benefits usually reserved to the Violent Man. He can gain these benefits by availing himself of ready-made opportunities, which make violence possible for him. Riots contain provisions for the replication (in miniature) of several of our violent types. A person may become a rioter to promote his self-image, or to defend his status, or to remove pressure, or to release pent-up feelings. And the quality of riot participation is probably to some measure dependent on such preferred modes of adjustment, or on favored styles of relating to others.

On the other hand, the motives and perceptual content of a riot are restricted, compared to the rich tapestry of free lance violence. Most rioters are self-defined revolutionaries; many of them see rioting as vengeance; almost all are inspired by the fellowship of their comrades; and in all instances, they have a mythical, collective conception of the Enemy. We have also seen that in the development of riot motivation, economic grievances and social disappointments are prominent in the awareness of rioters.

Riots gain uniformity from the fact that they are institutionalized: The Ghost of Riots Past hovers like a friendly specter over each new outbreak; it provides historical sanction, and it furnishes vivid images of how and why to proceed. This kind of advance prescription reduces the room for individual initiative.

This does not mean that personality cannot express itself in riots. There is occasion for the display of personal style, and opportunity for the satisfaction of personal needs. Riot participation can be lighthearted or grim; it can be angry or playful; it can be fearful or calm. And the riot situation can be viewed in many different ways: rioting may thus be an act of revenge for some, and an emotional discharge, or an act of rebellion for others. Violence may serve as a vehicle to personal identity, or as a means to power or material gain. A riot can be many things to many people; some of its meanings may run deep or may extend far back into time.

In this sense, riots are less psychologically confining than are some other forms of collective violence, such as war. In battle, violence is committed because the individual's military vocation demands it. The soldier is instructed to follow destructive routines (such as shooting at moving targets or pressing a button that operates equipment to release a projectile), and he largely complies because he has learned to do so, because he respects his superiors, and because he accepts his role as defined for him. Typically, he gains no satisfaction from violence beyond those of efficiently discharging his obligations and of participating in the collective destruction of a concensually defined enemy.[47]

There are soldiers, to be sure, who seek out blood and gore beyond the call of duty and who gain considerable reward from the administration of death and destruction. There are those who volunteer for elite killer units that operate behind enemy lines and engage in assassinations or sabotage; there are others who prize assignments as snipers or scouts; and there are figures of heroic stature with a penchant for singlehandedly launching offensive operations in defiance of sensible odds. It is within the ranks of soldiers such as these that we find our violence-prone persons, those driven by the desire for physical action, those who seek a new identity or a bolstered image in the eyes of themselves and others. And it is these individuals—praiseworthy though they may be from the viewpoint of the military—who must be monitored and eventually resocialized for membership in the civilized community.[48]

[47] The extent to which mechanized and impersonal violence characterizes modern warfare is illustrated in the following description of an American bombing mission over Vietnam:

Harris lined up the target in the luminous cross hairs of his screen, threw two switches that opened the bomb bay and armed the load of 108 bombs. Over the radio, the impersonal voice of a SAC ground controller announced "seven minutes to 'hack' (bomb release point)." The count droned on until at hack, when Harris punched a black button and 30 tons of high explosives cascaded toward the ground more than 30,000 feet below us. There was no shock, no noise, no sight of explosions. Only the impersonal voice of the controller: "Bombs in the target area. That was a good run, fellows. Have a nice ride home and see you another day." Thigpen banked again and we were on our way back to Guam, six monotonous hours and 2,600 miles away. In a small oven in the cockpit the men began heating TV dinners. They had not seen their target, their enemy, or the effect of their mission, (*Time,* Aug. 2, 1968).

[48] J. Hersey, *The War Lover* (New York: Bantam Books, 1960).

Among men who engage in violence, there are monsters who fill the public mind with special dread and revulsion. These men stir the imagination, displace headlines, disrupt peace and tranquility, and inspire massive official action. And these men are not those who account for the bulk of violent damage, nor are they those who engage in repeated acts of destruction. They are, rather, the unexpected authors of violence that is irrational and senseless—the progenitors of acts that are blood-curdling and bizarre.

In the ranks of these ogres are assassins and those who lynch them; stranglers of women and torturers of children; practitioners of patricide and killers of offspring; and among them we find the quiet veteran who converts his home town into a target range. Such men strike fear for several reasons: for one, they cast doubt on the sanctity of life, because they assault victims who have done them no harm and who are frequently unknown to them; they raise questions about the meaningfulness and predictability of human motives, because their lives typically do not foreshadow their tragic fate. Frequently these are the mildest, gentlest souls, immune to anger and unconcerned with their surroundings. Frequently, they are shy, brooding, and shadowy, unnoticed until the moment when they explode into horrible prominence.

The most noteworthy feature about these persons may be their extreme nonviolent disposition. Edwin Megargee tells us:

> In case after case the extremely assaultive offender proves to be a rather passive person with no previous history of aggression. In Phoenix an 11-year-old boy who stabbed his brother 34 times with a steak knife was described by all who knew him as being extremely polite and soft spoken with no history of assaultive behavior. In New York an 18-year-old youth who confessed he had assaulted and strangled a 7-year-old girl in a Queens church and later tried to burn her body in the furnace was described in the press as an unemotional person who planned to be a minister. A 21-year-old man from Colo-

rado who was accused of the rape and murder of two little
girls had never been a discipline problem and, in fact, his
step-father reported, "When he was in school the other kids
would run all over him and he'd never fight back. There is
just no violence in him." [49]

This sort of picture represents, in many respects, the opposite of the pattern we found among typical violence-prone
persons. Whereas the average Violent Man becomes aggressive in
a wide variety of situations, the type of individual described by
Megargee does not; in fact, he is calm and unresponsive in
situations that would make most of us angry. It is as if he saved
his rage and resentment until the pressure becomes unbearable,
and until the dike of his self-restraint bursts. Although incidents
that finally trigger violence may be provocative, their role is
often minor. In fact, the precipitating incident may be irrelevant
and the victim incidental. It is useless to study actual explosions
to understand this type of violence. Instead, one must focus on
potentially violent encounters in which no reaction takes place.
It is among these nonviolent incidents that we can expect to find
the self-destructive patterns that ultimately burst into the open.
And we expect these patterns to be of a different order from
those encountered in other violent persons. Rather than comprising simple feelings and monolithic urges, these patterns should
simultaneously feature irreconcilable and opposing needs. They
should promote violence and restrain from it, and thus always require unsatisfactory and unstable compromise.

A fine example of this sort of pattern is the case of a wife-
killer reviewed by LeRoy Schultz. The man (Jim) carved up
his second wife, who had subjected him to an endless series of
unreasonable demands. Jim's previous marriage had included
the following sequence of events:

Then Jim came home by surprise one day and discovered
his wife in bed with a neighboring farmer. He said he did not

[49] E. I. Megargee, Undercontrolled and overcontrolled personality types in
extreme antisocial aggression. *Psychological Monographs* (1966), 80: (entire
No. 611).

know what to do and merely closed the door and returned to the fields and cried. He added that he could have done "something" as there was a loaded rifle in the room adjoining the bedroom. Jim never brought up his wife's infidelity and she, seeing so little objection, became more bold in her affair. The paramour began staying for meals and on several occasions stayed overnight. Jim voiced no objection and even lent the paramour money, seed and farm equipment, as well as labor. Finally, after this arrangement had gone on for three years, the paramour took a truck to Jim's farm while the latter was away, loaded up the household goods and livestock, as well as Jim's wife and four children, and took them away. Jim, though surprised at his wife's and children's absence, did nothing to find out where she was or to attempt to bring her back, nor did he ever approach his wife's lover.[50]

Jim murdered his second wife after she informed him that she also, had acquired a lover. This act not only placed her in the position of evoking rage in her own right, but also of inheriting the suppressed resentment of Jim's past. The pattern was more complex, however, because Jim did not marry his wives at random, nor did he treat them in a random fashion. Instead, he found domineering women, and he clung to them with desperate possessiveness. It was as if he demanded self-destruction on one level and resented it on another. He thus created both his aggressors and his potential victims.

Instances of violence may climax careers that are considerably more complex than Jim's and are less easy to break down into steps or components. But invariably the person's unreasonable demands on others—usually unspoken—create reactions with which he ultimately cannot cope. And he must then respond with blind and senseless rage, usually directed at innocent or accidental bystanders. Having finally given vent to his rage, the lamb-turned-lion generally reverts to his previous state of forced, tortured passivity. And his helplessness is at this stage made

[50] L. G. Schultz, The wife assaulter, *Journal of Social Therapy* (1960), 6: 103–11, quote at p. 106.

even more pathetic by the fact that he must face the unassimilable knowledge of his latent bestiality.

Such is one of the types of violence often described in headlines. Other patterns are even more bizarre and difficult to envision. They may show us twisted conceptions of self and reality; they may feature dark passions and episodic explosions; they may reveal captive souls, gripped by compulsions to destroy; and they may include men and women who live in feverish nightmares or in half-consciousness. Such individuals tend to be categorized by the law as "insane," because they seem oblivious to the premises of courts and prisons. Psychologists, in turn, talk of such people as "abnormal," because their lives do not follow patterns of conduct employed by the majority of men.

From our vantage point, such a person is simply more complex, and therefore less patterned, than our Violent Men. His doubt is deeper, his ambivalence greater, his perceptions more twisted, his objectives more conflicting. His violence is forged in chains of encounters that are cumulatively doomed from the start. Such a man attacks when he can stand no more, and he explodes with ugliness and senselessness, because he expresses a dilemma that has become insoluble. And—unlike our Violent Men—he explodes but once, because his violence provides him the ultimate proof of his failure.

7
Some Implications

The current concern with the problem of violence has increased the demand for explanations and practical suggestions. This climate calls for caution, because it makes us over-ready to supply simplistic formulas that imply easy remedy. On the other hand, we may be tempted to advance over-pessimistic appraisals that consign the problem to the realm of comforting unresolvability. The discussion of violence today contains both types of explanations and is suffused with suggestions that would solve nothing.

Explanations can become merely decorative and innocuous, as is the case with catalogues of correlates or causes. We are not helped when we learn that violence can be produced by biological, economic, demographic, cultural, and psychiatric factors. Such explanations are inadequate, because they have no consequences. In relation to a Violent Man, the import of diagnosis rests on whatever it implies for his fate, and for the fate of others in his life, such as his prospective victims. When a person's violence is attributed to anomalous brain functioning, the implication is that a physician can implant electrodes deep into the man's cerebrum, and can convert him into a raging maniac or a semi-comatose vegetable at the click of a switch. To the extent to which our man—now irreparably emasculated—*might* have been psychologically treated or re-educated, his diagnosis as an organic patient is obviously wasteful.

This problem cautions us to the danger of premature classification and disposition. On the other hand, there is equal risk in yielding to the temptation of remaining expansively diffuse. Especially in times of crisis, problems can come to be perceived so broadly that they cannot be tackled, and discussion takes the permanent place of action.

Violent Men do not respond to saber-rattling. They are not affected by public debates, by increases in police hardware, by generalized talk of violence in the press. They are not stimulated or inhibited by the level of violence on television, nor by disputes concerning the availability of weapons. To be sure, some isolated act of violence may be prevented because precedent doesn't furnish a model for it, or because a shotgun to execute it is not readily at hand. But ultimately, violence occurs because men find it satisfying and effective in achieving their ends. Violence can thus only be fought by removing the incentives for it, and by changing the motives that produce it. This requires close-quarter, face-to-face combat with real-life Violent Men.

VIOLENCE AND THE CRIMINAL JUSTICE SYSTEM

It is often brought home to us that we must know something about the personalities of offenders before we process them. We cannot subject to routine booking an alcoholic or an addict deep in a dream world of his own making. We have discovered the risk of releasing into prison yards bands of predatory homosexuals and raving lunatics.

If the goal of criminal justice is to rehabilitate, the need to consider personality attributes becomes greater than if we are merely guided by concern for the smooth operation of our police stations, courts, prisons, and probation systems. Most correctional clients prove no major embarrassment, but by the same token they are neither helped nor changed. To accomplish the latter objective, one would have to have different facilities available for different kinds of offenders, and one would have to distribute inmates to such facilities on the basis of special knowledge about them. One would also have to treat people at such locations with the aid of more refined knowledge than is now displayed in institutional settings.

In the case of violent offenders, the need for information is greater than it is in other offender groups. On practical grounds, violent persons are extremely troublesome. Many of them resist smooth handling, and when released, they commit the kinds of crimes that reflect adversely on our correctional machinery. To keep our system functioning, it is essential, in the case of these men, to take rehabilitation seriously. And the regeneration of Violent Men is difficult without information about the nature of their violence and of its psychological meaning. Whereas burglars and sneak thieves can be treated without knowledge of their antisocial conduct, violence is a symptom of social maladjustment, and the nature of a man's violence relates importantly to the techniques we must use to discourage it.

One must know more about a Violent Man than the fact that he is violence-prone. If we only know this fact, we are reduced to labelling him, and to secreting him away for several decades. In prison, the Violent Man often becomes a custodial problem, and he may dispense his violence more lethally, if less visibly. He creates a need for physical settings of a kind long recognized as outmoded. He contaminates other inmates and staff by enmeshing them in his violent games. And he must eventually be discharged—usually as a more bitter and dangerous man. If the Violent Man is a model prisoner, his first assault takes place after release into the street. In such a case, we have accomplished a successful act of storage and segregation. This result may be modest, but it is admittedly positive. The difficulty, of course, is that this result is unpredictable. As long as we only know that a man is violent, we have no way of sorting the nonviolent inmate from the pool of Violent Men.

But are Violent Men not deterred by prison? Nothing in our picture suggests that they would be. To the contrary, in fact: Violence feeds on low self-esteem and self-doubt, and prison unmans and dehumanizes; violence rests on exploitation and exploitiveness, and prison is a power-centered jungle. It is true that we try to teach inmates that the use of force can only produce more difficulty for them, but we make this lesson far from convincing. If a man harms others in a prison, where else can he go? What extremity of discouragement can we furnish him? Many of our own interviewees preceded their discussions of particularly vicious acts with the declaration, "What the hell, I had nothing to lose!" It is an ironic commentary that prison violence is concentrated in the maximum punishment units, where violent inmates are sent from the yard.

The deterrence argument for long sentences sometimes has it that Violent Men will harken to the fate of their imprisoned comrades. This assumption is implausible. For one, violence is private and personal. Violent Men form no community, have no affinity for each other, join no unions. Where they are members of gangs or neighborhood groups, their status and prestige tend to rest squarely on their known propensity to violence. This fact is not neutralized by imprisoning other members of the group. In fact, enhancing the risk of violence would no doubt function to increase its prestige value, and hence, the benefits derived from its exercise.

The chief reason for doubting the impact of deterrence on Violent Men, however, lies elsewhere. It rests on the fact that destructive behavior is the least loss-and-gain motivated conduct of all antisocial activity. The rewards and punishments of violence are measured in increments and decrements to the ego, rather than in terms of future well-being. The perspective of violence is short-term and impulsive, rather than calculated and future-oriented. The Violent Man measures his worth by the distorted criterion of his physical impact, rather than by his ability to pursue a life plan. He has no career to be threatened, no stake to be impaired by prospective imprisonment. Of course, he desires freedom, and he would rather be at large than in prison; but his violence is neither stimulated nor inhibited by such remote and general needs. It is curiously true that deterrence is potentially most effective with those who least require its impact—with rational, career-oriented, future-invested individuals of the kinds who populate the ranks of the nonviolent, law-abiding middle class.

Of course, there are purposes to institutionalization other than storage and deterrence. Ideally, a closed institution furnishes the possibility of carefully controlling a person's environment and of providing him with continuing support and sustenance. It also makes it possible to monitor the person's progress on a day-to-day basis, and to adjust for adverse changes if they occur. Here, it is obviously important to provide constructive support and positive programming. There are no advantages to settings with custodial orientations. To multiply such facilities under the headings of the War Against Violence is equivalent to fighting any other enemy through isolation and news management.

IDENTIFICATION AND CLASSIFICATION OF VIOLENT MEN

A Violent Man is a person who has a propensity to take actions that culminate in harm to another. Such a person can be validly and reliably identified only on the basis of his record of violent acts. By "record," I don't mean his police "rap sheet," nor his list of accumulated convictions. Such documents are fragmentary and incomplete and are confined to unrepresentative acts that have come to the attention of authorities. A man brought into court as a first offender may have initiated scores of violent incidents at home, in the school and in the streets; a repeat offender may have become, on one or another occasion, a victim of fortuitous circumstances.

On the other hand, many persons are currently classified as violent offenders who are not really violence-prone, in the sense of tending to inflict harm on others. For instance, the consummate robber is a professional who is usually skilled at avoiding the use of the weapons he may carry. Such a man must be separated—for purposes of treatment—from the unstable amateur, who may shoot, because of a propensity to be clumsy, boisterous, fearful, touchy, or sadistic. This type of person is a Violent Man, and he must be processed as such. For this purpose, he can be identified through systematic review of his past conduct.

Our law enforcement agencies and our courts must thus make it their business to secure data about their clients' involvements in violence—without regard to the severity or the legal significance of the incidents that are uncovered. This information can be obtained through sympathetic interviewing, through searches of school files, through field surveys and other fact-gathering techniques.

An exhaustive listing of violent incidents can identify a person as a Violent Man. When such an identification has been made, it becomes important to secure detailed information about incidents, so as to categorize the person in terms of the nature of his violence. It is this information which makes sensible disposition possible, provided, that is, that relevant treatment is available.

THE OBJECTIVES IN THE WAR AGAINST VIOLENCE

Violence is not an isolated phenomenon, socially or psychologically. "Subcultures of violence" have attributes other than violence-proneness; Violent Men are blessed and cursed with diverse qualities, many of which are unrelated to their destructive potential. To reduce violence it is not necessary to remake people, nor to remodel society. Our assignment is to rechannel or to redirect specific undesirable propensities, without prejudice to the integrity of the persons involved. A more wholesale approach would not only be wasteful but might magnify the very problem it seeks to eliminate. Violence feeds on low self-esteem, and it thrives on a sense of inadequacy. We would therefore have to make sure that we stress to Violent Men that they are not condemned as individuals or as classes of people, but that our concern about their destructive behavior is ultimately governed by our regard for their worth as human beings, as well as by our feelings for the victims of their acts. We must make certain that every Violent Man understands that he himself is the victim of violence—not only because society reacts against him, but because violence is self-defeating. The history of each violent person contains ample documentation to support this case.

Reducing violence among "subcultures of violence" is a difficult process, and our research contains little information relevant to the problem. When a group assumes that certain kinds of violence are appropriate and legitimate, it is obviously sterile to combat this assumption by arguing the case that violence is undesirable. Sermons and speeches that decry violence are viewed as ludicrous and insolent by violence-prone audiences. This is only in small part due to the fact that sermonizers and speech-makers belong to a society that itself sanctions violence (some-times vis-à-vis the very persons who are told to decry it). The main reason for cynicism lies in the fact that anti-violence propaganda takes no account of problems and needs that seem to require violence in the eyes of its practitioners. Nor does anti-violence propaganda take cognizance of the need to pro-vide substitute avenues for the achievement of group aspirations.

Frequently, society preaches nonviolence while simultaneously reinforcing conditions that make violence attractive to large seg-ments of the population. Ideally, social reform would have to go hand-in-hand with campaigns against subcultural aggression. Wolfgang and Ferracuti have pointed out:

> To intervene socially means taking some kind of action de-signed to break into the information loop that links the sub-cultural representatives in a constant chain of reinforcement of the use of violence. Political, economic and other forms of social action sometimes buttress the subculture by forcing it to seek strength and solace within itself as a defense against the larger culture and thereby more strongly establishes the subcultural value system.[1]

If the resources for direct attack on social problems are not available or not used, society is limited to the indirect strategy of rescuing members of violent subcultures from the common fate of their brethren, and of building them into subcultures that make violence unnecessary for survival. In the words of Wolfgang and Ferracuti, "The personality must undergo a pro-cess of weakening of the subcultural ties by means of one of a variety of techniques until allegiance is decreased and a new value system can be introduced." [2]

[1] M. Wolfgang and F. Ferracuti. *The Subculture of Violence: Toward an Integrated Theory of Criminology* (London: Tavistock, 1967), p. 299.
[2] *Ibid.,* p. 309.

This process, as I have indicated, does not require complete transmutation of a person, nor does it necessitate complete divorce from his erstwhile companions. Rather, it presupposes some remedial action directed at group aims that are invoked to legitimize violence. At minimum, it involves furnishing substitute means (such as constructive social action, or new career lines) for the achievement of these same objectives.

Unfortunately, however, the task of regenerating Violent Men is far from confined to their integration into nonviolent subcultures. Violent Men have propensities for violence that are built into their personalities and modes of functioning, and the difficult task we ultimately must tackle is that of reshaping or redirecting such propensities. The remainder of this discussion will address itself to this problem.

STRATEGIES FOR CHANGE

In planning strategies designed to change Violent Men, a number of considerations must be kept in mind: 1. The violence-prone person invites violence-prone interactions with other people. These interactions follow a pattern, in that they arise under repeatedly occurring circumstances, and in that they serve equivalent ends. The object of change must be (a) to reduce the needs and incentives for such games, or (b) to furnish alternative expressions or courses of action.

2. Violence-prone games tend to be played by men who feel unsure of their status or identity, and by others whose orientation toward people tends to be egocentric or exploitive. Such basic conditions should be specifically attended to.

3. Simultaneously, the task of the changer must be to provide each violence-prone person with insight into his conduct, in the sense of making him able to diagnose his own motives. Such insight must be accompanied with retraining, in that the person must be taught to respond to similar situations in different ways. Retraining must be accompanied by rigorous and reliable tests. As long as alternative behavior patterns are not firmly established, the person remains violence-prone.

4. It makes no sense to approach all Violent Men with the same remedial program; by the same token, it is unnecessary to tailor-make efforts at change individually. Violence-prone persons can be grouped in terms of the nature of their violence; persons who follow the same pattern of violence can be subjected to a common strategy of change.

5. Efforts applied to homogeneous groups of violent offenders are not only economical but may be expected to have enhanced impact, since group pressure can be mobilized on behalf of constructive change, so that "outsiders" are not viewed as primarily involved, and so that individuals can use each other to gauge their own condition and to measure progress.

6. On the other hand, violent games are interpersonal in character, and they can be best modified by involving in the change process not only the violent men themselves but also the partners of their games.

The Problem of Intervention

Two facts must be set against each other in considering the problem of rehabilitating Violent Men: 1. If one confines efforts to convicted violent offenders, only few acts of violence can be prevented, because most Violent Men are at large and are unknown to us. 2. The formal treatment of people who have not been convicted, and who merely have a "propensity" to violence, would be grossly unfair and would force unpleasantness on a substantial number of persons whose future violence is merely hypothetical. The first statement implies that we must make an effort to extend our attention beyond the ranks of those Violent Men sentenced to prison; the second premise excludes their institutionalization and raises questions about any programs involving involuntary processing, manipulation, or restraint.

It is obvious that we must take steps to improve our prediction methods, particularly with respect to young boys who will someday seriously aggress against others. But we cannot await the results of such studies, which are likely to consume many years.

In the interim, we must explore retaining possibilities of a kind that would invite participation and would not violate the integrity of its subjects.

Consider the case of a mythical lad who delights in forcibly relieving his classmates of their lunches, setting animals afire, and otherwise showing his faith in a two-fisted approach to interpersonal relations. Currently, the boy's life may be studded with summonses to the principal's office, threats of reform school, and impending disciplinary dispositions that carry a heavy nuisance value.

But it might be possible to offer such an individual the alternative of joining extracurricularly an activity or club involving contemporaries who have shown themselves similarly troublesome. In this setting, group discussions of violence could occur, violence-related games could be played, skits or plays could be produced, and behavior patterns could be generated that could meet the boy's requirements for self-affirmation, without its destructive consequences.

The young man thus might be recruited into a career as a performer, or as a member of team sports activities, or as a teacher's aide. Such nonviolent involvements, when combined with self-analysis linking them to destructive motives, could be effective—especially at this early stage—in heading off the development of a Violent Man. And civil libertarian objections would not apply to this strategy as validly as to more formal therapeutic efforts.

In the case of adult offenders, in whom convictions require formal dispositions, limits must be set in terms of rehabilitative requirements. At first, indefinite sentences are probably required, but these obligate us to insure (a) that the time is in fact used, and (b) that release follows rehabilitation. As soon as experience accumulates, success rates must be translated into maximum terms and paroles. Moreover, confinement must always be viewed as a last resort. Combinations of imprisonment and furlough time can be introduced to prevent stagnation, to ameliorate pain, and to test level of rehabilitation in real life.[3]

[3] H. Toch. Prison inmates' reactions to furlough. *Journal of Research in Crime and Delinquency* (1967), 4:248–62.

This is especially important for offenders such as Violent Men, whose contact with social reality is deficient.

Building Mature Personalities

Probably the hardest task we face in the rehabilitation of Violent Men is that of developing their interpersonal maturity, or—in psychoanalytic parlance—of building their ego. Some reshaping of personality undoubtedly would occur if we simply taught people to be consistently nonviolent. We have seen that the exercise of violence has a cumulative effect, so that the violence-prone personality becomes increasingly warped over time. It would stand to reason that the continued exercise of peaceful options—if we could teach it—could lead to a less immature outlook on life. Moreover, if we could resocialize violent offenders in groups, as an experiment in living with others, one would expect some carry-over in the shape of a less egocentric orientation.

But more direct effort must be expended on the task of converting Violent Men into men in fact, into persons whose chronological maturity is matched by more mature outlook and conduct. Achieving this transformation entails supplying self-esteem and self-assurance to fragile selves that are domineering, blustering, self-advertising, and afraid. It includes the development of concern and consideration among individuals whose outlook on humanity is self-centered and exploitive.

This task probably requires the participation of clinical professionals who stand in the forefront of their field as sensitive carpenters for brittle psychological structures. Authorities of the caliber of Redl, Wineman, and Bettelheim, who have demonstrated the ability to resocialize violent children,[4] should also be involved in the challenging task of restoring personalities at the height of their destructive careers. Institutional climates and

---

[4] F. Redl and D. Wineman. *Controls from Within: Techniques for the Treatment of the Aggressive Child* (New York: Free Press, 1952); B. Bettelheim. *Truants from Life: The Rehabilitation of Emotionally Disturbed Children* (New York: Free Press of Glencoe, 1955).

routines can be designed to permit clinicians to provide support for immature egos and to build into their patients the
controls they need for civilized dealings with others. This sort of
climate must include continued monitoring of personal reactions, with interview sessions designed to give every patient insight into his strategies for self-preservation at the expense of
others.

Group pressure and feedback can more than supplement professional skills in this area. Sociologists—and most notably G.H.
Mead [5]—have shown that the self is primarily a social product.
Interpersonal immaturity must be the result of deficiencies in
the way other people have supported (and controlled) the
growing person in his formative years. If the child is catered to
or neglected, the resulting man will view other people as instruments rather than as life-partners; if the child is unrecog-
nized and unloved, the man will be filled with self-doubt and will
be firmly convinced of his inadequacy.

Deficits resulting from such deficient socialization should be
redeemable through the restorative acts of people bent on re-
building each other.[6] Groups of Violent Men, given the task of
reeducating each other, should be able to function as a "therapeutic milieu." They could do this by reinforcing each other's
strengths, by helping each other in joint activities, and by each
analyzing the others' roles in the enterprises of their community.

The task can be facilitated by creating meaningful projects in
which the men can jointly engage, in which they can demonstrate proficiency, and in which they can practice cooperation
and interdependence. The role of each person in such team-
work could be reflected in results obvious to him, as well as in
the expressed esteem of his team members and supervisors.

Additional benefits could arise if the work assignments provided skills with market value outside the institution. And it is

[5] G. H. Mead. *Mind, Self, and Society: From the Standpoint of a Social
Behaviorist* (Chicago: University of Chicago Press, 1935).

[6] D. R. Cressey. Changing criminals: the application of the theory of differ-
ential association. *American Journal of Sociology* (1955) , 61: 116–20; O. H.
Mowrer. *The New Group Therapy* (Princeton, N.J.: Van Nostrand, 1964) ;
H. Toch, *The Social Psychology of Social Movements* (Indianapolis: Bobbs-
Merrill, 1965) , chapter 4.

desirable for the work to be such that the men can build on existing aptitudes and experiences. Although this shrinks the number of available possibilities, it means that rehabilitation can start at the apprenticeship stage.

The Context for Retraining

Probably one of the most direct approaches to the task of retraining Violent Men is to undertake re-educational programs in the context of violence-centered research. There are several advantages to linking self-study with subject matter concern. For one, the focus remains on the relevant theme. If the program is intensive enough, each man can become violence-conscious, to the point of sleeping, eating, and living violence. A related advantage is that of promoting self-involvement. Most violence-prone persons are opposed to violence in other people. A campaign against violence could be attractive to them and could constitute an acceptable means of entry into self-change.

This transition is not only seductive, but logically plausible. The awareness of the Violent Man often is populated with specters of negative pressures. These comprise power-centered relationships, omnipresent threats and fears, threatening and destructive intentions in others. The Violent Man assumes the necessity or desirability of violence in the sort of life in which he sees himself enmeshed. Attention to violence can help to sort this subjective component from social reality and can focus attention on the man's own role and his own contribution.

Another related benefit is the fact that in a research effort, the person can perceive himself as an expert, as well as knowing himself the focus of inquiry. This role can given him pride, furnish him with elements of a new identity, and even provide him with a few marketable skills. It can also introduce new meaning, in the shape of end products that transcend the person's own resocialization. These end products, moreover, are badly needed: case materials on violence are sparse, and the nexus between social environments and individual reactions to them are not easily bridged. Research into violence carried out by persons with experience in the world of violence can shape such materials.

Finally, inquiry is a respectable prelude to change; the transition is natural and easy. The first step toward self-examination is self-knowledge, and self-knowledge is tied to more general knowledge, encompassing the place of one's conduct in its social context. When such information has been acquired, not in the passive stance of the classroom learner but in the role of the information-gatherer and analyst, the next step, of applying the knowledge and of operationalizing its implications, can be more readily faced.

Another possible framework for the resocialization of Violent Men is that of social service work or philanthropic activity. This type of enterprise might be especially helpful in the reorientation of bullies, exploiters, and other manipulative persons. It might help them make a transition from "doing to" to "doing for," without sacrifice of "doing." Self-centered orientations could be undermined, as the person learns to evaluate himself in terms of the quality of the services he renders.

It is obvious that in this as in other types of programs there exists some danger of co-optation. A power-centered view of social relations can be easily translated into social service, as patronage politics and some social work efforts demonstrate. This sort of tendency can be undermined, however, if client initiative and involvement are stressed. Psychodrama, role-playing, and other techniques can be used to insure that altruism does not become transmuted into a system for dispensing gratuities or for accumulating credit.

The Creation of Violent Incidents

One of the difficulties in devising strategies for changing violence-prone persons, and in monitoring their change, is the problem of simulating relevant situations. Obviously, we cannot afford to place Violent Men into the testing grounds of real-life incidents. By the same token, there must be clear relevance and transferability in the trial situations that we are

able to devise. These must be subjectively equivalent to temptations and threats, goadings and pressures encountered in the tavern, the back alley, the home, and the prison cell. The stimuli
must be intense, realistic, and convincing. The person must
become oblivious of the make-believe character of the situation
and of its role as a measure of his rehabilitation.

Several techniques are available at this stage. One of these is
psychodrama, with scenes drawn from violent incidents in the
person's past, and from variations on these scenes. The person
can replay his own role, both constructively and destructively,
and also that of other participants in the same incidents. He can
discuss the implications of his behavior, after he has experienced
it from every vantage point. He can carry incidents back to various stages of their origin, and he can explore alternative courses
of action and their consequences.

Tapes, kinescopes, and other mechanical aids can be used to
keep reactions in awareness, and to focus on relevant aspects for
discussion. Such records are also useful for gauging progress or
lack of progress. The participation of other violence-prone group
members can provide tools for comparative analysis of various
kinds.

Counseling sessions can be tailored to create pressures that
matter. These pressures can be intense, and they can be meaningful. Having lived and worked with other members of the
group for a period of time, each man will regard the others as
important to him, and he will have formed special relationships
with some of them. Experiments carried out in such contexts can
have qualities similar to incidents in the street.

Two types of test situations can be devised; one of these would
revolve around working and living relationships, in which roles
can be assigned (involving power relationships, conflicts of interest, and issues of prestige and reputation) that carry violence
potential, whose consequences the group could evaluate. The
type of stress situations used in OSS training during World War
II contains models that could be adapted and used for this
purpose.[7] Inquisitorial interviews and group problem solving

---

[7] OSS Assessment Staff, *Assessment of Men* (New York: Rinehart, 1948).

ventures under frustrating conditions constitute examples of mock stress. Leadership and followership roles in these kinds of exercises can be interchanged, and each task can be followed by a review of interpersonal conflicts and their resolution.

Another promising type of test situation has been developed in self-help movements, such as Synanon.[8] Here groups convene in counseling sessions, and members subject each other to systematic cross-examination and prosecution. The substance of the person's defense against such tactics, and the nature of his reaction to attack can ultimately be subjected to constructive recapitulation. This second, reviewing phase (which is not prominently featured in the Synanon use of the technique) seems especially important, because it converts the interaction from one of unmitigated hostility to a constructive and didactic one.

Games as Violent Incidents

In several experiments currently under way in various institutions for juvenile offenders, simple retraining procedures based on principles of learning theory are being tried. These involve rewards for desirable conduct, such as completed work assignments, and they stress systematic praise and other signs of approval. First results indicate that the rewarded conduct becomes established after a time and the young inmate no longer requires external rewards when learning has occurred.

With adults, candy and coins may be merely a source of amusement in an atmosphere of dead seriousness, but they may be effective if taken lightly. No man likes to be treated as a maze rat, but most of us like to gamble. This fact makes leisure time important, both as a period for lighthearted testing and as an occasion for playful training. All manner of games could be devised, for instance, to make violence tempting and to reward nonviolence.

In general, commerically marketed children's games tend to emphasize competitive, retaliatory, amassing and aggressive solu-

[8] L. Yablonsky. *The Tunnel Back: Synanon* (New York: MacMillan, 1965).

tions, to a disquieting degree. Variations on some of these games could place the premium on more desirable conduct. The emphasis could be placed on negotiation, for instance, in situations in which warlike acts are standard options. Reality-testing could be encouraged in game form. Self-defenders could be involved in a game of danger, for instance, in which gains are accumulated by acting in defiance of potential threat and discovering that harm does not exist, or, to be more accurate, that it most often does not exist. Games for self-image promoters and reputation defenders could stress the definition of force as a manifestation of weakness. Self-image defenders could be rewarded for non-retaliatory conduct in the face of provocatory moves, in games combining "Dirty Dozens" with alternatives featuring nonviolent resistance.

Equity, justice, and fairness could be built into some games. In many current games, for example, the elimination of weak opponents is routinely rewarded. This condition could be reversed in games designed primarily for bullies. Players could be penalized whenever they moved aggressively against a position of weakness and could be rewarded for protecting a weak partner against a strong opponent.

The number of variations on socializing games is potentially large and only limited by the ingenuity of the designer. Commercial toy manufacturers should welcome the opportunity of becoming involved in the production of constructive games. However, there is no reason why Violent Men themselves could not be involved in the creation and building of anti-violence games. If playing is psychologically involving, knowing the principle of the game should not impair its effectiveness.

Although procedures such as these may seem playful and irreverent, they can perform a critical role in re-education. Violent Men play violent games because their nonviolent repertoire is restricted. Even when a violent person is aware of what he does, he rarely knows what he could do instead. In fact, such a man frequently assumes that violence is the only means available to achieve his objectives. Changing his needs is not enough; we must help him arrive at the discovery of new strategies for satisfying needs. Playful simulation enters here, because it represents a painless way to help the player abandon reactions that invite defeat or harm in favor of more constructive ones. Games may succeed where real-life situations fail, because there is little at stake, and there is small risk in rehearsing unfamiliar and untried moves. Simultaneously, games are ideal shorthand representations of life. They bring to the fore rewards and punishment that every Violent Man has encountered, whenever he is not immersed in his subculture of violence. And unlike life, games offer no opportunity to miss the point.

The Interpersonal Setting of Retraining

One of the ironies about Violent Men that we have repeatedly pointed to is that they not only play violent games but involve others in the playing of these games. Rep defenders *do* succeed in making innocent targets "lose their cool" and explode with undignified rage; self-image promoters *do* obtain responses in their efforts to challenge others to personal duels; [9] violent persons communicate their fear and resentment to substantial numbers of people and can thus be instrumental in initiating large-scale disturbances, such as riots.

Frequently, social environments are set up unwittingly to make the destructive task of the Violent Man relatively easy. Total institutions, such as prisons, often provide ammunition for the rationale behind violence; standard administrative procedures, such as police practices, can meet the Violent Man more than half way in his efforts to create an arena for violence. Often, the role taken by persons representing the controlling authority may trigger the playing out of a game that ends in violence. This role, which emphasizes physical and social distance, minimal communication, and a we-versus-they attitude,

[9] Thus teachers frequently become involved in violence-prone games with their students. See Wertham, F. The function of social definitions in the development of delinquent careers. President's Commission on Law Enforcement and Administration of Justice, Task Force Report: *Juvenile Delinquency and Youth Crime* (Washington, D.C.; Government Printing Office, 1967), pp. 155–170.

makes it all too easy for the instigator of the game to ignore individual differences among persons in the controlling role, to view them in terms of preconceived stereotypes, and to justify his behavior in terms of the stereotype. We may recall one of our subjects, whose core concern was defending his reputation as a fearless leader. One cannot, of course, be seen as fearless unless there is an enemy, perceived by others as both threatening and powerful, to attack. This man's way of maintaining his reputation among the inmates is to challenge the staff periodically, in defense of his peers. Since challenge invites retaliation and punishment, his attacks on staff are a proof of his fearlessness and he is able to maintain an unchallenged leadership reputation among the other inmates. Staff reaction to his provocations does nothing to discourage the playing of this game. In fact, it only increases its usefulness to him and makes him ready to play it again when his reputation needs to be bolstered.

Other persons use violent behavior to manipulate the controlling authority in a specific way. In these cases authority's reaction, which focuses on the violent act itself and not on its antecedents in the instigator's current experience, is readily predicted. It is this reaction which is the goal of the violent act. For example, an exploitive inmate wants to get out of a situation in an institution in which his game of taking advantage of others has been just about played out. He attacks another inmate in a way that brings minimal risk of harm to himself through the encounter but that makes certain the authorities will be informed. He knows the custody staff games sufficiently well to predict that this incident will get him transferred to another institution. He is right.

For still other persons, the low probability of being apprehended for a given incident built into the control procedures itself becomes an instigating challenge to play out some forms of violence-prone games. These games merely move around the authorities. If the instigator does not want to get caught while engaging in violent or violence-prone behavior, he can be assured that the probability of his being detected is (and even more importantly, is perceived by his peers as being) very slight. In our prisons, control staff admit tacitly (and sometimes openly) that they are not able to enforce regulations and to guarantee the protection of potential inmate victims. What they are able to do is engage in crude detective and spying intrigues with little chance of success for any given incident. The probability of "beating" the staff at any given time is therefore very high. Thus, the looseness within the control procedures and the lack of opportunity offered inmates to prove themselves as men in any other way than "beating the system" provides a climate in which these inmates concerned with proving their manhood rise to the challenge of playing out a violence-involved game.

What these facts imply is that training for nonviolence must involve not only Violent Men but also the standard partners in their violence-prone interactions, including peers, love-partners, authorities, and officials. This extended definition of retraining has multiple benefits. Not only does it alert nonviolent persons to the violence-prone sequences in which they become enmeshed, but it also brings the partners of standard violence-prone interactions into new, more constructive relationships.

Thus, law enforcement officials could be trained as participants in groups with multi-violent offenders who have assaulted officers. Participants in such training sessions could move from known role-playing games to games that spontaneously developed out of these. This would lead, covertly or overtly, to the officials identifying their own game participation for analysis.

In establishing such self-study training, it might be advantageous to work initially with staff and with violent offenders in separate groups, then bring them together as soon as the groups were reasonably comfortable with the method and its content. Such a procedure for working with separate interest groups with the intent of ultimately bringing them together was developed in a community action project conducted by the Youth Studies Center at the University of Southern California.[10]

In any event, as training programs for violent offenders are set up—most probably in the shape of special centers in penal

[10] H. R. Sigurdson, D. G. Dodge, Annette Gromfin, and R. Sanfilippo. Community education for delinquency prevention: Santa Monica Community Study. In *Corrections in the Community: Alternatives to Incarceration*, California Board of Corrections Monograph No. 4 (Sacramento, 1964).

institutions—it is desirable to involve outside staff in them as participating observers. Career correctional staff are often suspicious of new programs that veer from a philosophy of punishment and control, that appear to coddle offenders, and that seem to give scant respect to their own experience and training. Staff experience is as important as offender experience in the design of research and development. If program development is likely to involve shifts in staff functions and roles—and it inevitably will—then it is important not only that staff be involved in shaping the direction of new programming but also that career development opportunities be opened for them as well as for the offender group.

THE WAR AGAINST COLLECTIVE VIOLENCE

In our discussion of riots, it has been suggested that collective violence tends to arise as a reaction against unmet aspirations and consists of retaliation against the symbols of perceived unresponsiveness.

This fact does not invariably imply that we must deal with collective violence by meeting the aspirations of those involved. Some past race riots, for instance, were based on the desire to retain a monopoly on neighborhoods, jobs, and living accommodations. Lynching mobs have sought to retain a social system in which other persons would remain subservient, or (in the case of religiously motivated lynchings) in which one set of beliefs would be universally enforced.

Moreover, the rhetoric of a riot sometimes disguises needs of questionable legitimacy. Some middle-class student rioters, for instance, couch a hedonistic demand for total autonomy in language deploring every evil of twentieth century existence. In other situations, the roots of collective violence are irremediable. For example, a panic may stampede persons to death, where physical safety can in fact not be assured. In such instances, action must be confined to helping people address their tragic fate more constructively, if possible.

We have suggested that at the juncture of collective violence it is no longer possible to set the clock back to the initial steps of riot history, in which citizens approach authorities with requests or demands. The situation of rioting includes various results of frustrated aspirations, such as feelings of resentment, hopelessness, helplessness, low status, and lack of identity. To dispense jobs and other material rewards is relatively fruitless at this stage, because it leaves beneficiaries in the role of passive and insignificant recipients. It thus becomes essential to promote activities that permit maximum participation, increase status, and provide meaningful life goals.

Potential participants in collective violence must be taught to see other means of achieving their objectives, in the same sense in which this lesson must be conveyed to Violent Men. Like the latter, they can be enlisted in the fight against violence, and they can be taught that nonviolent resources are available that would result in more gain and less damage to self and others. This presupposes, of course, that nonviolent means are accessible. Once it becomes true that some group can legitimately maintain that "we now know that violence pays" (the words of a college editor) the basis for such an assertion must be removed. Violence cannot be remedied when there is in fact no other way to achieve dignity and status.

One area of collective violence which requires additional exploration is the role of key rioters. Not only must we abandon the illusion that riots are created by "agitators," but we must face the more positive fact that destructive influences are exerted among riot participants by groups and individuals within their ranks. Such centers of violence-proneness can be selected for special attention and can be converted or neutralized.

I have stressed the Riot Commission's conclusion that precipitating incidents are crucial in the genesis of riots—which implies that such incidents are logical targets for prophylactic intervention. For example, increased flexibility in police handling of street encounters in hostile settings is clearly in order. We know that the answer does not lie in rapid mobility for police egress and the availability of reinforcements; at such junctures, the violence potential of the sequence has often already reached a point of no return, and only the shape of destruction can be affected. The police must learn that "backing down" or "standing up for the law" are not meaningful concepts for the assessment of strategy in the early stages of games of collective violence.

POLICE RETRAINING

The police have crucial roles to play on both sides of the War against Violence. Most obviously, they are our assault force and our first line of defense against Violent Men; less visibly, the police become involved in violence-prone games, and sometimes actively contribute to bringing these to a head. Both roles are played in relation to individual and collective violence; both contributions are matters of prime concern to society and to the police themselves.

Our research indicates that the ranks of law enforcement contain their share of Violent Men. The personalities, outlooks, and actions of these officers are similar to those of the other men in our sample. They reflect the same fears and insecurities, the same fragile, self-centered perspectives. They display the same bluster and bluff, panic and punitiveness, rancor and revenge as do our other respondents. To be sure, the destructiveness of these officers is circumscribed by social pressure and administrative rules; but it is also protected by a code of mutual support and strong *esprit de corps*. And whereas much police violence springs out of adaptations to police work rather than out of problems of infancy, the result, in practice, is almost the same.

In addition to the dangers posed by Violent Men among police, a less dramatic but more pervasive source of difficulty is that of police partnership in the games played by civilian Violent Men. We have seen that in interpersonal situations, causation is often unrelated to motivation: a fair, impartial officer can become involved in violence by unknowingly playing a part in someone else's script—and he can do so frequently and reliably. Unexamined police procedures can contribute to the officer's fate. They can do so because their prescriptions can be predicted and manipulated by persons who have a stake in police brutality.

Some prevalent beliefs about the "police problem" are unrealistic, and they can lead to misplaced programmatic efforts. The most obvious such fallacy is the premise that the "problem" consists of personality disturbances among small groups of officers, who can be fired after psychiatric screening and psychological testing. A related fallacy is the supposition that the difficulty takes the form of anti-Negro sentiment and that the solution consists of "human relations" programs, including lectures on Negro history and urban problems, dialogues with black nationalists, social psychology courses, and the like.

It is doubtful whether Violent Men among police officers could be psychiatrically diagnosed as emotionally disturbed. Theirs is not a psychological condition; it is a specialized propensity—a gift for escalating interpersonal encounters into explosive situations. This sort of conduct can be reliably isolated only by on-the-spot observations of on-the-street interactions.

Such observations are best conducted during a man's probationary period. Every recruit's patterns of social behavior could be examined to assess the degree of his violence potential and the nature of his approach to others. The critical question is, what next? If the man proves tactless, or overaggressive, or oversensitive on his maiden patrols, do we screen him out of the force? If we have no facilities for remedial training, this may be our sole option. But it is certainly not a desirable course of action. For one, there is the matter of due process. We cannot demand of a man that he display sterling conduct in an area where he has not been advised what is expected of him. Moreover, since violence-proneness consists of habits and propensities, it cannot be treated as an indictment of a man's worth. On the other hand, the willingness to modify one's conduct is obviously meritorious. And if change occurs as a result, we know that we can count on a promising officer, as well as on a mature fellow citizen.

By contrast, we must consider the fate of persons whom we are tempted to negatively assess and dismiss. It is inconceivable that such a course of action should not damage a man's self-esteem—especially when we already have evidence of compensatory conduct. And a rejected policeman could carry a sufficient chip on his shoulder to prevent his becoming a constructively engaged member of society.

Whereas the conduct of Violent Men among the police is at least partly due to dispositions brought into law enforcement from civilian life, violence-proneness in other officers is largely engendered by police organization and procedures, and by formal and informal indoctrination. Sometimes, omissions are critical. Steps or policies necessary for sound interpersonal relations may nowhere be spelled out. No one, for instance, may impress on the young officer the need to communicate to civilian spectators the import of his actions and the reasons for them. As a result, the officer may take the position that if he is asked to justify his conduct, he betrays his force unless he points to his badge in response. And he can someday provoke a riot by leaving in his wake an information vacuum in which rumors can circulate.

Ambiguity in the definition of police powers is a perpetual source of difficulty. Often, an officer discovers that he has much discretion, but he receives little guidance as to its exercise. He may be informed that he can use "reasonable" force, for instance, without being told what this means. To no one's surprise, violent incidents described in police reports often terminate in the use of "reasonable force." An analogous problem exists when officers are instructed to request identification from suspicious civilians, but are not advised as to the risks of such a request. As we have seen, much violence results from indiscriminate requests for identification and information.

Police training (both formal and informal) occurs in the shape of general principles, which are far from uniformly applicable in street situations. And verbalizations about police work, of the kind to which every new officer is subjected, are frequently misleading. Experienced officers may impress on the young recruit the need for a uniformly firm approach, or of differential approaches to pre-categorized types of civilians. Universal apprehensiveness about certain types of assignments may be communicated to the young officer, and they may induce panic in many situations.

The young officer may be brought up with myths in lieu of facts and may acquire prejudices under the guise of inside dope. Thus equipped, he may embark on self-destructive patterns of conduct that become established and cumulative.

Police structure can be improved with new definitions of criteria of conduct and with realistic preparation for life on the beat. Ultimately, such information must be communicated through directives and in-service training. The form of in-service training is important. Lectures, seminars, and other passive learning experiences, when transferred to the human relations area, are generally not very effective. In fact, they may increase bitterness and prejudice. More intensive and personally involving methods, such as sensitivity training and community-police confrontations, have more chance of impact, but their diffuseness makes them wasteful as violence-prevention techniques.

Situations that produce violence can be directly addressed, and their resolution can be worked out and demonstrated. Both idiosyncratic and prevalent errors can be subjected to analysis, dramatization, and correction. Simultaneously, successes in explosive situations can serve as positive training materials. (Creative prevention should be routinely rewarded. For instance, if an officer recruits citizens to his side in a conflict situation, or befriends someone who approaches him belligerently, or disarms a man without force, his effectiveness deserves commendation.)

Police training for violence prevention must vary with the clientele. It must be intensive, and indefinite in duration, when the objective is to redeem Violent Men. It need include only two or three sensitization sessions when its aim is to alert the average officer to violent games he will encounter on the street.

In all police training programs, the within-rank group cohesiveness of police can be turned to advantage. To accomplish this end, training can rely on peer pressure, both inside and outside the classroom. Nonviolence must become fashionable, and it must be defined as policeman-like conduct. Men who have been trained can be converted into a cadre for training others. Such emphasis is especially important for the violence-prone officer, who would feel isolated and threatened if he were singled out for individual attention. In retraining violent officers, homogeneous groups could be formed, or the men could be experimentally integrated into mixed (predominantly nonviolence-prone) groups.

In retraining officers, the procedures to be followed could take the form we have outlined for Violent Men in general. For instance, it would be possible to set up research units to deal with the problem of assaults on police officers. In such units, perenially assaulted (and hence, violence-prone) officers would be the research staff. An introductory phase of statistical research and general investigation could be followed by more intensive, clinical work, comprising counseling groups, stress situations, and various forms of simulation. At first, the contribution of the officer to violent incidents could be explored; later alternative resolutions could be worked out and rehearsed. Real-life experiments could be conducted on the street. Tapes, kinescopes, and other mechanical aids could be used, if they prove profitable. In terms of end result, such retraining efforts could produce, as important contributions to police work, case materials and other training aids, administrative guidelines, and in-depth research data.

In a sense, the problem of retraining violent officers presents fewer practical and legal problems than does the rehabilitation of other Violent Men. The structure of the police is such that job assignments are rarely questioned. The problem of skepticism and suspicion is eliminated if the task becomes personally involving and meaningful. And in the research approach, a focus on police victimization would remove much potential threat. The discovery of police contributions to violence would be made by the officers, and this discovery would lead to a natural shift in project emphasis.

There are ethical implications, to be sure, in the fact that the engineers of such a retraining program would be aware of its ultimate purpose, while the officers may only dimly suspect it. But this difficulty is inherent in any act of seduction. The redeeming quality (in all such instances) lies in the fact that aims are eventually pooled, and that free consent is ultimately achieved.

THE POLICE AND COLLECTIVE VIOLENCE

One area we know too little about is that of group violence by the police. No observer of urban tensions would dismiss the police as neutrals. Most officers delight in strong measures when dealing with rioters, and most tend to be unsympathetic to black aspirations. This latter attitude is hardly surprising, given the fact that the highest-ranking ghetto aspiration is that of relief from alleged repressive practices by the police. What most officers define as respect, most black militants regard as capitulation to illegitimate force. What blacks view as respect, the police perceive as insolence. In its extreme forms, law enforcement ideology incorporates Blue Power concepts that are fully the equivalent of the Black Power beliefs of militant Negroes. The police outlook, like that of the Negroes, is that of a minority. The police—like the Negroes—feel persecuted and abandoned; they, also, feel that they are afforded insufficient recognition. And since recognition for police-defined law and order is sparse in the Negro ghetto, the police feel offended. They react with bitterness and hate, narrowly suppressed in their daily activities, which on occasion explodes into overt violence.

During cold war periods that precede riots, police violence takes the form of harassment of ghetto militants and of retaliation against persons who show overt disrespect for police; most dramatically, the police tend to punish individuals who express their contempt physically.[11] When riots break out, police resentment takes the form of collective retaliation, frequently indiscriminate and blind. The police may thus arrest anyone within reach, and they may administer physical punishment in the process.

This observation suggests that monitoring and control procedures must be instituted during riots, to prevent the extension of riot motivation to police personnel. Officers must be clearly identified, so as to be subject to accountability for their acts. The discretion to arrest must be circumscribed, and procedures for handling suspects must be detailed. Most importantly, num-

[11] Westley, W. A. Violence and the Police. *American Journal of Sociology* (1953), 49:34-41.

erous observers, responsible to command personnel and immune to violence-proneness, must join the fighting force to insure that regulations are followed, both in letter and in spirit.

Training procedures in the pre-riot period, and retraining after the riot, must deal with the temptations of collective violence. Incidents of personalized warfare must be dealt with as the equivalents of individual violent incidents, which in essential respects is precisely what they are.

IMPLICATIONS OF OUR RESEARCH STRATEGY

We mentioned at the beginning that ours was a unique venture. We approached Violent Men for candid accounts of violence and we did so with colleagues who could penetrate their strange world with ease and familiarity. Our nonprofessional associates were persons we could rely on and whom our subjects could trust. As a result, we secured new types of data, some of which we have presented here. Our experience is susceptible to duplication, not only in research but in operational settings such as probation offices, judges' chambers, and penal institutions. Naturally, it must be made clear that adverse decisions could not follow from interview results; this framework is necessary to maintain the trust of interviewers, as well as of respondents. Another requisite for success is that the professional's premises must be shared with his nonprofessional associates.

Kinsey and his collaborators, among others, have demonstrated that information about controversial areas of human experience can be readily obtained by middle-class interviewers. We could add a footnote asserting that similar results can be secured in various contexts with appropriate personnel. This conclusion is not limited to inmates and parolees; our police researchers were able to document serious problems in situations where the average outsider would be faced with assurances that the system was perfect.

To be sure, appropriate questions must be posed. The closer we stay to actual experience, the more uncontaminated the reports we can expect. Validity is assured if each respondent knows that we are trying to view his actions from his point of view.

And the subject's own descriptions of conduct and perception can then be placed in context to arrive at more general characterizations of human personality.

The use of nonprofessional research personnel such as inmates offers new career possibilities for nonprofessionals, as well as advantages to the researcher. It has been argued that technological unemployment must be alleviated by expanding careers in the people-processing professions.[12] This imperative, as we see in the case of research, coincides with personnel needs in the field. For instance, when social scientists take increasing interest in social change, they must rely on linkage personnel to obtain meaningful information from the disadvantaged. And, clearly, penology stands in need of new approaches to persons who are currently stored in correctional institutions. Research participation can easily and cheaply serve rehabilitative goals. (The chances of recidivism among several of our associates was originally very high; instead, these persons today occupy responsible positions in the human services industry.)

Needless to say, the benefits of converting inmates into researchers are not automatic and free of risk. Like professional workers, nonprofessional participants in research must be selected with care. Unintelligent or completely illiterate persons are of limited use, as are social isolates. A cynical, exploitive, or immature outlook can create a poor prospect for programs that have the usual training resources. This is also true of rigidly held preconceptions, though to a lesser extent.

On the other hand, too close attention to selection criteria can produce a staff of quasi-professional nonprofessionals, who may be rejected by research subjects and even be considered a species of Uncle Tom. Not being trusted, they may have relatively limited useful knowledge or insight, contribute little, discover they are marginal members of the team, and develop poor motivation.

Even careful selection will not altogether eliminate these possibilities. The nonprofessional must get training that is not only directly related to research but also can provide him with incentives, support, and a meaningful self-concept. Some of this

---

[12] Pearl, A., and Riessman. *New Careers for the Poor: The Non-Professional in Human Service* (New York: Free Press, 1965) .

training may be of the sort routinely encountered in graduate schools; some may be more characteristic of social movements. The nonprofessional researcher must be, in a sense, a "convert." He must acquire a new role, a new set of values, and new models and friends while remaining in close touch with his old associates. The professional merely places others under the microscope; but the nonprofessional must convert his own life experiences into data. While the rest of us can view research as a job, the nonprofessional must see his involvement as a mission or a crusade—or he will have trouble playing the role.

A Final Word

Our view of violence is not fatalistic nor suffused with hope. It promises that Violent Men can be assessed and understood, and that they can, in time, be regenerated. And it assumes that the games played by Violent Men need not end in tragedy. By the same token, a certain amount of tragedy seems inevitable. If Violent Men come to light through violence, their classification and rehabilitation must always follow in the wake of some personal and social harm.

What of prevention? Ultimately, nonviolence presupposes opportunities shared by all and material progress matched by advances in interpersonal conduct. Our observations suggest the importance of civilized child-rearing, of education that stresses selflessness and self-confidence and that leads to positive communication. Our Violent Men, after all, are basically children who have learned to use force as a compensatory tool.

We presume that a nonviolent society has no room for agencies that profit from the exercise of destructiveness, nor for persons who direct its large-scale use. Men who press explosive buttons or who sign bloodthirsty orders are entrepreneurs of violence, and they set the stage for lone operators. The same holds for individuals who coldly plan for inconceivable contingencies, or who produce and disseminate means of destruction. When the roles exercised by such persons have been eliminated from the games societies play, we can attend to our Violent Men with a clearer conscience and a more unambiguous mandate.

Appendix

General Instructions

For each incident, one category is coded as "primary," which means that it most directly or immediately leads to the main act of violence.

Parenthetically noted are all other categories which apply to the same assailant in the same situations. (This includes all moves which lead to the violence, and all occasions for subsequent violence by same person).

Categories applicable to other assailants are separately coded.

Code

A Perseverance in—or transfer or extension of—violence
The instances denoted here are situations in which the person is engaged in assaulting others when the prospective victim arrives on the scene, and in which *the violence is simply extended to the victim* (officer),
A1 As a reaction against interference with, or interruption of, violent actions

A2   Because new victim is seen as siding with current victim

A3   Because violence is viewed at the time as appropriate behavior

An   Other or Ambiguous

B   Defense of Personal Autonomy

These are situations in which the individual appears to *react to actions by the victim which make him (the aggressor) an object of undesirable manipulation.*

B1   Violence as a reaction to touching or other bodily contact

B2   Violence as a reaction against orders or instructions

B3   Violence as a reaction against uninvited entry in home, or other trespass on self-defined area of jurisdiction

B4   Violence as reaction to being disturbed or awakened

Bn   Other

C   Protection against Concrete Danger

These are situations in which the person sees the victim as an instrument to impending doom, and reacts *in an effort to avoid or retard danger,* or to prevent being subjected to it without a fight.

C1   Violence in an effort to flee or escape arrest

    C1a   After having assaulted officer physically or verbally, and being arrested for this fact

    C1b   After being arrested or subject to arrest for violence against others

    C1c   After being arrested or subject to arrest for action not related to violence

    C1d   Without prior arrest

C2   Violence in an effort to prevent being transported or moved after being arrested

    C2a, b, c, (Same as above)

C3   Violence in an effort to avoid discovery of evidence which would lead to arrest or other unfavorable action

C4   Violence as a manifestation of displeasure with arrest

    C4a, b, c, (Same as C1 and 2)

Cn   Other

D   Defense or support of others

In these situations the person *takes the part of others* whom he views as requiring or deserving aid. The person uses violence in an effort to rescue or to increase the effectiveness of "significant others" who are objects of aggression or incursion.

D1   Violence in defense of other persons engaged in physical struggle or being physically subdued

D2   Violence in defense of others who are being—or have been—arrested

D3   Violence in defense of others who are subjected to perceived threat or danger

Dn   Other

E   Violence as an expression of contempt or disapproval

These are situations in which the victim merely serves as a negative stimulus by virtue of his identity and physical presence. Violence here serves *as a manifestation of disapproval* or to assert the person's status vis-à-vis the victim.

E1   Violence to reinforce challenge to a duel

E2   Violence following verbal threat to victim

E3   Violence following verbal abuse or expression or contempt

E4   Unannounced and spontaneous violence

En   Other

X   Unclassifiable

These situations comprise those in which there is insufficient information available for a judgment. Those which are merely ambiguous are to be coded in terms of applicable alternatives.

ILLUSTRATIVE INCIDENTS (OAKLAND, 1963 AND 1964)
Excerpts from Police Reports

Code

We responded to the apartment and were confronted with a man and woman fighting on the bed over a long barreled gun. . . We reacted by attempting to separate the combatants. . . Officer M. told the defendant to calm down and to

A1

(C2a,b)

give him the gun; Officer C. attempted to pull the gun from the defendant all the while she is struggling and holding on to the weapon, kicking, scratching and yelling profanity. Officer M. attempted to pull the defendant's hands from the weapon so Officer C. could secure it and in doing so the defendant bit Officer C. on the wrist and forearm. Once the weapon had been obtained by Officer C. who broke it open and removed a live round . . . the defendant then directed her attack upon Officer M. by kicking him in the groin area, and biting his finger (right forefinger) ; when he clutched at his hand the defendant slapped Officer M., inflicting two large scratch marks, ripped off his tie, called him a "no good mother-fucking cop," choked him and kneed him in the groin area during the ensuing struggle. . . As the defendant was being directed to the police vehicle she kicked and struggled despite efforts to calm her which required her to be carried and dragged to the police vehicle. After the defendant was removed from the police vehicle a white handled 4½″ blade steak knife was found in the front seat. . . .

A3

Susp. #1 was brought in by ambulance claiming to have been assaulted by persons unknown, susp. #1 was not visibly injured, since arriving had pushed Dr. S. and nurses around and using vile and profane language. C1P observed susp. #1, in corridor, pushing Susp. #2 around who was trying to quiet susp. #1 down. Suspect #1 was calling everybody a mother fucker, white son of a bitches, cock suckers, etc. C/P approaches Susp. #1 and told him to quiet down and asked him what was wrong. He said "Fuck You" and at that struck C/P in face with fist. . . . Wit.s' stated suspect #1 "blew up" for no apparent reason. Susp. #1 sent to ward D-1 ACH. as Poss. 5050 but, he was refused admittance as drs. stated he would not rightly classify as 5050 and that apparently he didn't like the fact that the police officers (C/P and wit. #1) were cau-

(E3)   casian and this was the reason for the assault.

R/O's called to above address by wit. (susp's wife) because she stated her husband was drunk and insulting her guests. R/O's took wit. outside to explain to her, her rights in such a matter and susp. came to door and started to call out. R/O's went in to quiet susp. and while talking

A2   to him—susp. swung at comp. and reached for R/O's neck ripping his tie off.

A/O heard a loud splash of glass hitting the pavement Wit #1 approached the A/O and said his woman, the suspect, was mad at him and he couldn't calm her down. Just then two

A3   more bottles came flying through the air and one landed just inches from the patrol car . . . As this officer started into the apartment, a drinking glass was seen to be thrown by the suspect at the A/O. This glass struck the door frame and shattered upon contact, over the A/O. A/O chased the suspect across her living room to the kitchen area and he grabbed her about the arms

(A1)   as she was reaching for another glass. Suspect began kicking and trying to free herself from the A/O's grasp. It was necessary for the A/O to subdue the suspect by placing her face down on the couch and handcuffing her arms behind her back. . . . Several months ago the A/O in-vestigated where she was the suspect in a child beating offense.

Placed subject under arrest and then with that

(Clc)
B1
(Cla)

(E2)

subject started to walk away. Sgt. C. took hold of his arm and then the subject went violent, jerking Sgt. C. around in front of him and both of them down to the street with reporting officer then attempting to hold subject. Sgt. C. had subjects right arm and both officers attempting to put handcuffs on. . . The subject was very violent and then kicked Officer B. on the left side of face and neck, throwing him backward to street behind. Additional force, club used on subject's left arm area, 1 stroke and with no results a second swing was attempted to slow subject down and his writhing, twisting, kicking, etc. Subject was struck glancing blow on left side of head. Subject was in a violent beserk condition using all the vile language at his command. . . . While at hospital on Guerney, subject again threatened to get Officer B., "I'll get you one of these days I'll get you good". . . . finally shook hands with all concerned with "I'm not such a bad guy really not such a bad guy."

B1

(C2a)
(C4a)

The reporting officer approached the suspect and since he wasn't looking tapped him on the shoulder and told him to quit blocking the exit. The suspect immediately whirled around and said "don't touch me" and shoved the officer backwards with both hands. The suspect then grabbed the officer by the tie and threw him off balance. . . The suspect was taken to the patrol wagon—fighting all the way and placed in it. The suspect got one arm free as he entered the wagon and turned to fight. Force was again used to place the suspect in the wagon.

(B2)
(Clc)

Off. C. asked susp. #1 for his name and he walked off towards the Telegraph exit. Off. C. repeated the question and susp. #1 kept walk-

ing, so Off. C. grabbed susp. # 1 right jacket
B1 sleeve and then susp. #1 spun around and
swung at Off. C.'s head. Off. C. grabbed susp.
#1 and susp. #1 grabbed and tore Officer C.'s
shirt. . . . susp. #1 was kicking, swinging his
D1 arms and using loud profanity. While Susp. #2
went to his brother's assistance using loud profane language. Susp. #2 was apprehended by
Off. B. and held bodily, however susp. #2 did
kick Wit. #2 a couple of times in the stomach.
. . . While susp. #1 was being escorted from the
(E4) dept. store he yelled profanity to the crowd
which had gathered, he yelled out "You white
mother fuckers." The crowd consisted of men,
women and children.

Comp. again identified himself as a police officer,
asked if she was O.K. and was she awake now.
Comp. assured the Officer that she was, asked
what he wanted and the Comp. then explained
the situation concerning the next door neighbor.
Defendant replied "Why that Black nigger bitch
is out to get me" and made several other remarks
concerning neighborhood problems. The defendant then directed her verbal attack on the comp.
and asked just what he wanted—to get out and
that he had no right to be in her house. With
B3 that the defendant picked up a phone lying on
the floor and struck the Comp. with it inflicting
a 2″ diameter bruise on the left cheek below the
eye and in doing so knocked Comp. to one side.
She then pushed and tore at the Comp. ripping
off his necktie in an effort to get him out the
front door and telling him he was just "an ass-
hole little boy trying to play Police Officer". . .
The Comp attempted to calm the Defendant
down, explaining he was a police officer in the
performance of duty and to exhibit some de-

(C2a) meanor and respect, all the while which the defendant insisted on directing profanities, and insults and pushing and tearing at the Officer's shirt and badge knocking off his hat and glasses. When the matter grew impossible to deal with verbally, Comp. informed the defendant she was under arrest for battery and proceeded to handcuff the Defendant after another struggle, then after great difficulty the defendant was carried, dragged and supported in every manner in an effort to place same in the patrol car . . . . was finally placed into the car by the Comp. after being kicked several times in the groin area . . . When the Wagon Officers arrived defendant was placed into the Wagon but not without a great struggle in which she kicked the four arresting officers, grabbing and tearing at the Comp. shirt and badge and in doing so bent Wit. #2's badge and inflicting several scratches on Comp's. hand (backside) .

(A3) Susps. were walking through the park drinking "Old Chateau and Greystone Wine." Susps. were with a large group of MN Teenagers. They broke off top of light pole #0180. They started throwing garbage cans in the Lake and using Loud and Boisterous Language near the concessions, Susps. entered a newly redecorated washroom and tore all the dispensers from the wall and broke everything in view. In general the place was a shambles. When Police arrived this gang split up and ran. Above two susps. . . . finally spotted hiding in bushes. Off. L. told susp. #1, "Come out." Susp. #1 started to run. When Off. L. grabbed him susp. spun around and hit Officer in forehead. Susp. was finally subdued after he put up a violent struggle.

(C1b)

Comp. observed susp. running through creek bed, and recognized susp. as one of the juveniles being in the yard at L.S.'s. Comp. called to susp., and susp. walked to within 20 feet of comp. Comp. advised susp. he was under arrest, and to come along with comp. Susp. ran into the creek bed where he was apprehended by comp. Clc (148P.C.Resis.) Susp. began kicking comp. and pulling comp.'s shirt and tie. Susp. attempted to bite comp. in the leg, then kicked comp. in the face. (243P.C.) Officer A. assisted comp. to place (C2a) susp. in patrol car, where susp. kicked and broke the glass partition over rear of the front seat.

R/O observed 2 MW 16–18 years . . . Both appeared to be unsteady on their feet and possibly drunk. R/O pulled his car alongside and while stepping out of the car said "Come here fellas." (B2) Both continued walking. R/O said louder "I said come here now hold it," whereupon the suspect ran north . . . R/O pursued suspect and caught him as he was going over the railing of a witness' back porch. As R/O grabbed suspect, Cld the suspect turned and swung at R/O with his right fist. R/O struck suspect twice with baton to subdue him and had to continue to struggle (C4a) to get suspect handcuffed.

The above named susp. was being booked for violation of parole . . . as the report was being made the susp. started running down the hall toward the exit of this division. The susp. was told to stop on several occasions but he continued to try and evade the officers. The susp. ran to the East end of the Police Building where he ran into a dead end. The susp. ran into the bathroom and Off. D. followed him. Off. M.

was stationed at the alternate exit and the susp. came out this exit and the attempt was made at this time to take the susp. into custody. The susp. at this time started fighting Off. M. and

C1c   struck him with his fist and knee. Necessary force was used to subdue the susp. at this time. Off. M. and D. restrained the susp. and handcuffed him, the susp. was still belligerent and attempted to kick both officers while being taken back to Vice Control Division.

While Officers were waiting Susp. returned and started arguing with complainant, Mrs. H. After several minutes it was determined that the Susp. was under the influence (647FPC) from the following reasons. Susp. was loud and using profanity. Susp's. speech was thick. Susp. smelled very strongly of an intoxicating beverage. Susp. was then informed that he was under arrest for 647FPC "under the influence" . . . Susp. was very uncooperative, refused to get in the back seat of the patrol car to await the arrival of the Police Wagon. Upon arrival of the Police Wagon susp. refused to get out of the police car and had to be coached. When susp. finally got out of the police

C2c   car he then refused to get in the wagon, and had to be helped in. Once in the wagon susp. suddenly turned and kicked the wagon doors open. Susp. then continued kicking at Complaint. and Wit. (Wagon Officers) Susp. kicked comp's. hat off his head. Susp. grabbed comp. by the shirt front and pulled him into the wagon. Susp. kicked comp. on the knee cap and leg. Wit. went into the wagon to aid comp., then resorted to used of baton to defend himself and comp. and subdue the susp.

Went to the suspect's residence and identified

themselves as police officers, stating that they were in possession of a search warrant for the suspect's dwelling. . . . she ran from the door toward the interior of the house yelling at the top of her voice "Joe, Joe, its the police." At this point susp. G. ran to a gun locker which con-

C3 tained 3 rifles and 1 shotgun. . . . Officers used necessary force to enter the suspect's dwelling and seized susp. G. J., who was attempting to load the 12 ga. shotgun. When officers ap-

(B3) proached susp. G. J., he as yet had not loaded the shotgun and using same as a club struck State Agent W. across the left temple with the barrel of the gun, until handcuffed was resisting violently.

A male negro holding a hunting knife in his hand had crossed Foothill Boulevard near 46th ave. While crossing the street this suspect was brandishing the knife and making swiping motions with the knife at passing cars and a bus . . . . had

(A3) broken a window out of room 106 at Freemont High and direct profane language and threats at Mr. R.B. . . . Officer B. noticed the handle of a knife protruding from the belt of the suspect's right side. When the suspect got on the sidewalk Officer B. approached him to inquire about the knife he was carrying on his person. At this time the suspect pulled out the knife, pointed it directly at the Officer and said "You mother fuck-

C3 ing cop you can't take this from me, I'll kill
(A1) you." Then the suspect started advancing toward
(E1) Officer B. and a struggle ensued involving Officer B, Officer C. and the suspect. . . . The suspect was informed that he was under arrest and he pushed and struck at both Officer C. and B. While the Officers were attempting to remove

(C2a) him from the scene to the Police Vehicle, the

suspect grabbed, hit, scratched, kicked, and bit Officer C. The suspect choked, hit, and kicked Officer B. During the struggle the knife disappeared and at this time has not been located. Further during the struggle the suspect deliberately grabbed Officer C's. watch, broke the band and threw it on the ground. The watch was later located in three parts, some of the parts are missing and the watch is not functioning. Also during the struggle Officer C's. sport coat was torn at all three pockets and apparently not repairable. Officer B. suffered damage on both arms of his rain coat. . . . The reporting officers gained control and were restraining suspect T. in the street in front of 4605 Foothill Boulevard, when Suspect H. approached from their rear and

D1 began kicking and kneeing both Officer B. and Officer C. At this time Sgt. B.M. arrived and while restraining and taking into custody Suspect H., suffered damage to the right knee of his uniform pants.

Comp. asked the suspect to accompany him outside to discuss the matter. The suspect followed comp. to the front door and stopped. Comp. told the suspect that he had been accused of bothering

C3 ing the other customer. The suspect grabbed comp.'s shirt, pulling off the flap of the left pocket. Comp. told suspect at this time that he

(C2a) was under arrest. Suspect then struck the comp. in the chest and kicked him in the shins. Comp. then struck the suspect several times with his baton knocking him to the floor and suspect then grabbed comp.'s legs and hung on.

After the driver had been asked to get out of the vehicle, officer M. attempted to drive it into the shoulder. Subject stated Officer M. couldn't move the vehicle and threatened to "Get Him

(E1) if something happened to the vehicle, if it was moved. Subject was asked to get out of the vehicle to determine his sobriety and started interfering with the sobriety tests being given by Officer T. to the driver. At this time he told Officer M. to remove his gun, and the subject would "beat the shit out of him." The subject was repeatedly told to get back into the vehicle

(B2) and he refused, stating we "couldn't tell him what to do." Officer T. took the subject by the arm and started to lead him to his vehicle. The subject jerked away again stating he couldn't

C4 tell him what to do. Subject was placed under arrest. Both officers attempted to hand-cuff the Subject, but the subject resisted. . . After the

(C2a) subject was hand-cuffed, he kicked Officer T. in the middle while he was being placed in the patrol vehicle. At the jail he again refused to walk and had to be forcibly brought into the booking room. During this time the subject kicked Officer M. in the left eye.

Def. then asked A/O "do you want to play" . . . The def. said they should go into the restroom because the police patrol the park and have arrested people there. The def. then checked the women's restroom for occupants and then went into the men's restroom. The A/O followed and upon entering saw the def. on the right with his pants zipper open and his penis sticking out. . . A/O then displayed his police star and said police. Def's. eyes widened then lunged at the A/O

D2 striking him in the face. Def. and A/O struggled and the def. broke away but was immediately confronted by a second officer and submitted to arrest.

During the discharge of duties by the COMPLAINANT's in which two male Negro suspects were being placed under custody for 484 **PC** (Shoplifting) the suspect approached and demanded that they be released, that they were with him and that they had not did anything. Suspect positioned himself in such a manner that it enabled the #1 484 **PC** suspect to escape; #2 484 suspect was placed in the patrol car during which time suspect interfered in a loud boisterous voice directing abusive language at the Complainants. . . . At this time suspect be-

C4 gan to physically attack Complainants by grabbing at Officer D.'s tie and shoving Officer C. to the side. Suspect took several swings at the Officers, striking them about the body. At this point Officer **P.** arrived and suspect was placed under arrest for assaulting a police officer. It was neces-

(C4a) sary to meet his force with physical restraint in which patrol car aerial was torn off by suspect. When he was placed up against the patrol car, he was told in no uncertain terms he was under arrest. He continued to direct his physical attack against arresting officers. When an attempt to restrain suspect became fruitless it became necessary to place handcuffs on suspect, all the time which he continued to struggle. Complainants failed to get suspect handcuffed and he was threatened with the use of the police baton. He continued his attack and it became necessary to strike the suspect several times with the baton.

D2 When he was told he was under arrest (his girl friend) kicked this officer on the left leg and yelled arrest me too. Susp. was wearing heels with sharp pointed toes. A/O suffered injury to shin of left leg—laceration and bruise.

Suspect #1 stated "I don't have to show you my license because I haven't done anything wrong,

(C3) and I think this is pretty God Damned ridiculous to go stopping people and trying to give tickets during the Christmas Season. Comp. Informed Suspect #1 that he was required by law to submit his license to a police officer on request, and failure to do so shall result in arrest. Suspect #1 then submitted license to comp. and stated "Where am I living, in some Communist

(E3) Country? You're just a snot nosed brat in a blue jacket." At this time rather than take more oral abuse from suspect, comp. returned to patrol car to write citation in peace. Comp. was only a short ways through the citation when Suspect #1 came back to comp's. patrol unit. . . . Comp. ordered suspect back to his vehicle. Suspect refused stating you don't tell me what to do you little bastard. I am going to get your badge number and fix you. Suspect #1 reached in my

E2 window and grasped my badge, and comp. stated "get your hands off of me!" Suspect #1 then stated "Oh yea." and grabbed my badge trying to rip it off and half pulling comp. out of patrol car. Comp. lifted door handle and kicked open door knocking Susp. #1 to ground. At this time wit. #1 arrived and helped Comp. put cuffs on

D2 Suspect #1. While doing this Comp. was attacked from behind by Suspect #2, who was cuffed immediately.

A/O's S. and P. were patrolling N/B on Market St. and observed 3 M/Ns (the suspect being one of them) standing on the N/E corner. . . . Suddenly the suspect yelled out, "You rotten mother fucker white cops." He shouted this several times at the A/O's. . . . Officer S. got out of the car and approached the suspect. The suspect turned and started away from the officer. The Officer told the suspect to stop and that he wanted to

E3　talk to him. As Officer S. approached, the suspect swung around and struck Officer S. on the face. As Officer S. staggered back, the def. swung his umbrella at the Officer and missed. Officer S. stepped in and grabbed the suspect by his sport coat and the suspect stepped out of the coat and started running. . . . Sgt. P. observed suspect in a bar at 16th and Market. As Officers converged on the bar and the suspect ran out the rear door.

(C1a)　The suspect fell down and as Sgt. P. and Officers W. & S. converged on him the suspect kicked out, striking Officer W. in the left knee. He slipped out of the grasp of the Officers and ran down. . . Suspect was finally stopped on 18th Street by Lieutenant H. and Officer R.O. The suspect continued to struggle and fight and Officer W. joined the Lt. and Officer and the 3 officers finally subdued the suspect and he was handcuffed. The Suspect continued to struggle, and kick and scream invectives at the Officers and was transported to Headquarters. The Suspect was put in the rear of a patrol wagon to await the arrival of reports and he again started to kicking and screaming. He kicked another prisoner and swore at him. . . .

Def. was in the bar creating a disturbance. . . . Def. had strong odor of alcoholic beverage. Eyes bloodshot, speech slurred. . . Def. placed in rear seat of patrol car and wagon called. . . . had to be transferred from K's car to R's car. A/O's opened door and def. got out and told

(E3)　A/O's that they were "fucking punks" "cocksuckers" and "assholes" and that he was going to "kick the shit" out of them. With this def.

E2　took a swing at A/O R. Necessary force used to subdue def. Def. kicked A/O K. Def. pulled both officers' ties off. Def. was handcuffed and placed

in patrol car. Def. sat there calling A/O's profane names: ex: cocksuckers, fucking punks,
(C4a) cunts, chicken shit, sons of bitches. Def. threatened A/O's several times saying if we would
take the handcuffs off he would kick our asses,
(E1) etc. When wagon officers arrived, def. said all 4
officers were fucking punks and that he would
take all 4 of us at once if we would take off the
cuffs.

INDEX